T0036283

MARY WELLS

Other Books by Peter Benjaminson

Investigative Reporting

The Story of Motown

Death in the Afternoon

Publish Without Perishing

Secret Police

The Lost Supreme

MARY WELLS

The Tumultuous Life of Motown's First Superstar

Peter Benjaminson

An A Cappella Book

Published by Chicago Review Press, Incorporated
814 North Franklin Street
Chicago, Illinois 60610
ISBN 978-1-56976-248-6

www.marywellsbook.com

Library of Congress Cataloging-in-Publication Data
Benjaminson, Peter, 1945-
Mary Wells : the tumultuous life of Motown's first superstar / Peter Benjaminson.
pages cm
Includes bibliographical references, discography, filmography, and index.
1. Wells, Mary, vocalist. 2. Singers—United States—Biography. 3. African American women singers—Biography. I. Title.

ML420.W39 B46 2012
782.421644092--dc23
[B]

2012027104

Interior design: Jonathan Hahn

Printed in the United States of America
5 4 3 2

To Mary Esther Wells, 1943–1992

and

Esther White Harrigan, 1921–1990

You quote this in the book. I don't give a damn if they think I'm crazy or what. The Lord built me like a machine, and that was to be an entertainer, a performer, a sex symbol. . . . He gave me a voice to sing, He gave me the looks, He gave me the legs.

—MARY WELLS, 1991

CONTENTS

AUTHOR'S NOTE

I LEARNED WHILE RESEARCHING this book that author and journalist Steve Bergsman had audiotaped four hours of interviews with Mary Wells between 1990 and 1992, while she was dying from cancer. He had never publicized the existence of these tapes nor had he released any of the material on them. Steve was kind enough to provide me with the tapes for use in this book. He also allowed me to interview him about his interactions with Wells during their long interview sessions. This book is also based on my own interviews with many of Wells's friends, husbands, lovers, relatives, and associates; on the transcripts from some of the interviews conducted by the producers of the TV One show *Unsung* for their August 2011 program about Mary Wells; and on my research in media archives and public records.

PREFACE

When I was a kid, if I wanted anything, I would sit on the porch and talk to the stars. And I got everything I wanted from them.

—Mary Wells, 1991

Years before Diana Ross, Mary Wells was the first Motown solo superstar, a songstress popular worldwide for her hit "My Guy." Her songs crossed the color line and reached huge white and black audiences in America and England consistently and repeatedly.

Wells hit number 45 on the *Billboard* popular music (white) chart and number 8 on the *Billboard* rhythm & blues (black) chart with her very first recorded song, which she wrote herself and sold directly to the Motown Record Company. And most of the succeeding songs she recorded for Motown did as well or better, with four of them becoming Top 10 hits. Altogether, she achieved an impressive career total of 20 Top 100 hits. She was the first artist on the Motown label to have a *Billboard* Top 10 and number 1 single, and she was the first to record an album for that label.

At the height of her career, Wells was one of the bestselling female solo singers in the world. She prepared the stage for the many female Motown vocalists who came after her, showing them what they could do and how popular they could become. As Mary

Wilson of the Supremes told the TV One program *Unsung* in 2011, Mary Wells "opened the doors for a lot of us—for me, the Supremes, and for all the other girls who have come along."

But Wells was much more than a successful singer with an alluring voice. She also displayed an irrepressible fighting spirit and a ferocious belief in her own talent. Without either of these she would never have progressed as far as she did. With them, she quickly rose to the very top of her profession.

Those same qualities, however, inspired her to leave Motown at the young age of twenty-one. And her departure gave the world its first sign that all was not sweetness and light at America's first major black-owned music company. It also meant that for the rest of her life, Wells's career proceeded in fits and starts. She spent her post-Motown days trying to fight her way back to the top. She didn't manage to do so, but she never gave up.

Whether retaining her chart-topping position in the notoriously cutthroat music business or later struggling to survive on its lower rungs, Mary's personal life remained tumultuous even by music-world standards.

She claimed early in life that she was the illegitimate child of a black father she never met. Later in life she said she had learned that her father was actually a white man. Whether or not either of these assertions was true, her mother was married to a black man Mary called her stepfather, who was often absent and to whom she never felt close. He seems to have disappeared from her life completely by the time she entered the music business in her teens. She spent most of her adult life searching for a man she could count on. But her affairs with and marital attachments to numerous men, some of whom were famous, were never able to deliver the kind of safety she appeared to be looking for.

Many of Mary's romantic and other entanglements were worthy of a daytime soap opera. In 1964 she hid in fear in a hotel bathroom in New York City as her first ex-husband shot one of her business managers in the head. Later, she married a member of a well-known music family and had three children with him, only to take the unusual step of divorcing him eleven years later to move in with his brother, with whom she had a fourth child. She also attempted suicide on two occasions.

While all this was happening, Mary was spending much of her post-Motown life on the road, where she was the acknowledged "Queen of the Oldies." She scratched out a living for years as a touring artist, managing to survive several dangerous illnesses and endure at least two spectacular auto accidents, complete with shouted prayers and flying animals in one of them. By her own account, she was kidnapped by crazed fans and driven halfway across America. She also made extensive use of illegal drugs.

Near the end of her life, Wells fought a drawn-out and courageous battle with throat cancer, in some ways the most frightening disease that could strike a singer who made her living, especially in her later years, by her voice alone, rather than from hit records and royalties. In the gutsiest performance of her life, she refused to lose hope and spent precious time during her last few months in an anti-cancer crusade that included testifying before the US Congress about the need to continue funding anti-cancer research.

Mary had her faults, but she came through magnificently when she was down on her luck and even after her luck had completely run out. As she sang with such assuredness on her very first hit, the one she wrote herself, "You're gonna want my love today." We sure do, but she is now singing elsewhere.

1

LITTLE MARY WELLS

We know that Mary Esther Wells was born in Detroit, Michigan, on May 13, 1943. Her birth certificate identified her mother as Geneva Campbell Wells, a "housewife," although she worked cleaning houses. It listed Mary's father as Arthur Wells, and identified both parents as black. But Arthur Wells is a shadowy figure.

The birth certificate said Arthur was an employee of the Fisher Body Company, which made car bodies for General Motors.

But except for his name on Mary's birth and death certificates, and Mary's claims that he was brutal to her mother, little else is known about Arthur Wells. His birth and death records can't be found. Mary always referred to him as her stepfather, never as her father. For most of her life, she told her friends that her real father was "a handsome black man" named something like George Windell or Wendell. He also cannot be found, nor can any records pertaining to his life or death.

Those who believe this account point to the real name of the man known as Shorty Wells, the third of Mary's four children: Harry James George Womack. Harry James was the name of a deceased uncle. But the name George, according to another of Shorty's uncles, Curtis Womack, was given to the child as a nod to Mary's biological father.

In 1981, however, when Mary was thirty-eight, she told several interviewers that her biological father was a white man whose family had employed her mother as a housemaid. Mary said her grandmother had recently revealed this information to her and she found it deeply disturbing. She told Sharon Davis, who was interviewing Mary for *Blues & Soul*, a UK magazine, in 1989, that after her grandmother's revelation, "I went into the bathroom and sat there for a long while all cut up because I always thought this other man was my father. . . . My father is a Sicilian, he's more famous than 'The Sicilian,' as in the movie. Some say he died in jail, some say he made a big score a couple of years ago and moved to Florida and changed his identity." As far as is known, Mary did not reveal her alleged white father's actual name.

Randy Russi, a friend of Mary's who is of Italian heritage, said Mary was so obsessed with the supposed Italian origin of her alleged white father that she wanted to talk to Russi's grandmother to see if that lady knew anything about the man. (Russi's grandparents had lived in Detroit at the same time as Mary's alleged white father.) Randy said such a meeting was never arranged.

Mary informed her bandleader during the second half of her career, Will Porter, that she was of mixed race and didn't know who her real father was. (Porter, who is considered white, speculates that he himself is of mixed race.) She'd heard that she had white relatives in either Virginia or Washington, DC, who were coming to see her in concert when she performed in the area but without saying hello.

Curtis Womack's recollection of what Mary said about her "real" father is consistent with what Wells told interviewers and slightly more detailed. Mary told him her father "was this Italian man that her mother used to work for," Curtis said. "He brought her momma home on a motorcycle one time and on the way he stopped . . . and he took her [Geneva] into a park somewhere [to have sex]."

Curtis thought the story of a white father made sense in at least one way. "You knew her daddy had to be white, Italian, or something, because Mary's tall and Mom is short and Mom looks like a real African. She was a real dark, little short woman. You would say, 'That's Mary's mother?'"

Others say they never thought Mary's father was white. Annette Helton, one of the original Vandellas, while calling Mary a "lighter complected black woman," said Mary "never appeared to be mixed." Helton spent time on the road with Mary along with numerous other black female performers who routinely borrowed makeup and cosmetic tools from each other. She said that if Mary had appeared to be racially mixed, the matter would have come up in conversation. Sally Womack, whom Mary lived with for a year, also said that Mary's skin did not indicate any white parenthood. And photos of Mary don't help settle the matter.

Curtis said that the closest he and Wells came to meeting her alleged white father was in the 1970s when they met in Las Vegas with people who allegedly knew him. The father was said to be working for a casino there. These people gave Mary presents, and she and a man who said he was Mary's father talked on the telephone. But Mary and that man never actually met.

Because no one knows when this alleged father left Michigan or when he moved to Nevada—assuming that he even existed—tracing him is impossible.

Adding poignancy to these accounts was that they were told in the context of a city with a long history of racial tension. At the time of Mary's birth, Detroit was a majority white city with a substantial black minority. And, only a few weeks after she was born, murderous riots broke out between black and white Detroiters.

In 1943, Detroit was overcrowded with war workers. Hundreds of thousands of people, both black and white, mostly from the South, had immigrated to the city during World War II to help staff its booming war production industries. On Sunday, June 20, 1943, a hot and humid day, more than one hundred thousand people jammed onto Belle Isle, an island in the middle of the Detroit River.

Interracial brawls soon broke out. A rumor spread that white sailors had thrown a black woman and her baby off the Belle Isle Bridge. Black rioters began smashing the windows of white-owned stores in black districts. On the next day, white rioters, taking their revenge, pulled black commuters off buses and trolleys and out of cars on Woodward Avenue, the city's main street, and beat them senseless. By the third day, federal troops and the Detroit Police Department had finally restored order. Thirty-four people had been killed, twenty-five black and nine white. Seventeen of those twenty-five black people, and none of the white ones, had been killed by police. Hundreds of people were injured and eighteen hundred were arrested. It was the worst riot in the United States since the Tulsa race riot of 1921. A commission led by an army general later concluded that the police had overreacted in many instances.

Neither Mary nor any of her relatives were caught in this maelstrom, the first of two major racial conflagrations that scarred Detroit during the twentieth century (the second occurred in 1967 and forty-three people were killed). Considering that history, it's amazing that in 1959 Detroit spawned the Motown Record Company, which aimed at selling the same music to both black and white listeners, and that Motown, with Mary's help, succeeded.

Even though her family was unscathed by the 1943 riot, Mary wasn't particularly lucky in her upbringing. The first area she lived in was an African American neighborhood on Detroit's East Side called Black Bottom. (The name referred to the area's dark soil; the neighborhood had been home to various ethnic groups before becoming black in the twentieth century.) Wells told one interviewer that she was too young to remember this community in any detail but called it "the bottom of poverty." When Mary lived there it was a poor black residential neighborhood consisting mostly of wood-frame houses. Immediately to its north was the lively black entertainment district known as Paradise Valley, but Mary was too young to patronize it. (Both Black Bottom and Paradise Valley were demolished in the 1960s, and the area now hosts successful mixed-income housing developments.)

Mary's family soon moved to an area on Detroit's West Side now called the Cass Corridor. The new neighborhood was a working-class residential area of brick and wood-frame houses, many occupied by two families, interspersed with a number of small brick apartment buildings. It wasn't ritzy, but it wasn't as poor as Black Bottom.

In the 1920s and '30s, the area, which wasn't far from General Motors headquarters in Detroit's New Center neighborhood, boasted a car dealers' row. In the '50s, when Mary was still living there with her family, a furniture store, a florist supply company, an International Order of Odd Fellows (IOOF) Hall, and a vending machine company all operated near Mary's house. A public swimming pool, the Louis Stone Pool, operated by the Detroit Department of Parks and Recreation, was less than a block from Mary's address, although she never mentioned swimming there. (The pool has since been closed and is covered with graffiti.)

Mary lived with her stepfather and mother and two older brothers, Thomas and Fletcher, in one half of a two-family brick-veneered house at 4439 Fourth Avenue. Another family lived next to them in the house's other half. A structure that might have been a garage stood in the backyard. (Mary's house and some houses nearby have since been replaced by a low-rise apartment project. Others were demolished for the construction of the north-south John C. Lodge freeway during the 1950s.)

Mary attended and graduated from the neighborhood's grade school, Jefferson Junior High School, and Northwestern High School. She sang in the chorus in both junior high and high school.

Although Arthur Wells was often absent from the family home, Mary said that when he was present he often verbally and physically abused his wife. Mary told Curtis Womack that she never knew, especially on weekends, when her stepfather would start abusing her mother. When she was a little girl, she'd jump on Arthur's back in futile attempts to stop his aggression. Although Arthur "was the sweetest guy when he wasn't drinking," she hated him. His alleged abuse of her mother made her particularly sensitive throughout her life to the threat or actuality of such treatment.

Maye James-Holler (born Maye Hampton), Mary's best friend when both were teenagers, described Mary's mom as a "sweet lady, a limited sort of a fun lady." But Maye also called her a woman "who liked her drinks a lot." Several other friends of Wells said the same. In any case, Mrs. Wells worked as a domestic during the day and was home only in the evening. Mary "started being the mother and taking care of her own mother as soon as she could," Maye said.

Claudette Robinson of the Miracles described the young Mary as "poor but hard working," and in fact, by age twelve, Mary was helping her mother with her work as a house cleaner. "Day work, they called it, and it was damn cold on hallway linoleum," Mary told an interviewer. "Misery is Detroit linoleum in January, with a half-froze bucket of Spic and Span." According to Wells, her mother didn't have much choice of occupation. "Until Motown came to Detroit, there were three big careers for a black girl—babies, factories, or day work. Period."

Mary loved her mother dearly and, later in life, expressed deep sympathy for Ginny's hard life as a cleaning woman. "When it's just the two of you," she told Gerri Hirshey, who quoted her in her book *Nowhere to Run*, "a kid can see something going out of her mama's face, you know. Like a dress you can wash but so many times and it ain't going to size up so smart on the hanger. We were just two women alone, helping each other out . . . but we were always clean and neat, and we had *something*." When Mary started making money from singing, she bought diamonds and minks for her mother before she bought them for herself. "I wanted to do something to help her because I had seen a lot of her youth fading away from not being able to enjoy life."

Mary also battled two serious illnesses in her childhood. Beginning at age three, she was bedridden for two years with spinal meningitis, a disease that left her temporarily paralyzed, partially deaf, and temporarily blind in one eye. According to one of her friends, it could have been worse: for a while Mary was not expected to live. But the doctors gave her a new medication, which saved her life. Her mother tried to cheer her up in the hospital by decorating her room with balloons, but when Mary recovered she had to learn to walk all over again. For the rest of her life, she bore a tiny scar on her forehead from falling out of a hospital bed when the nurses weren't watching her. And her vision in one eye was permanently damaged.

Then, at age ten, she almost died of tuberculosis. (She had another bout with TB in 1965, when she was twenty-two.) She spent so much time in hospitals and with doctors that her early ambition was to become a nurse, a doctor, or a scientist.

Geneva Wells returned Mary's trust and loyalty as best she could. Her attempt to cheer up her daughter in the hospital was characteristic: Mrs. Wells gave Mary the maximum support she could throughout her life, eventually living with Mary and helping to care for Mary's children.

Mary's uncle Clem, a preacher at the New Beulah Baptist Church, also supported her, both spiritually and morally. "He gave her life structure," Maye James-Holler said. Mary remembered happily attending Uncle Clem's church with her family and singing there from age three on. Mary also said church helped her mother: "She always stood better when she came out of there on Sunday." For a while, Mary even lived with her uncle and his wife. Her grandfather, who helped raise her, offered additional emotional sustenance. "Her grandfather and her uncle gave her moral and religious training," Maye said.

As a teenager, Mary also depended a great deal on her friendship with Maye. "Oprah and her friend Gayle King? That was me and Mary," Maye said. "Mary even had the exact same laugh as Oprah."

Despite this support, Mary never remembered her youth as happy. "My generation grew up pretty fast and alone," she told one interviewer. "They basically kind of grew themselves up."

Wells loved science in school, and she also played the clarinet and sang in the school choir. She dressed like her friends did, often wearing loafers, white bobby socks, a pleated skirt, and a pink sweater. But she was two years behind her fellow students due to her years in the hospital, and she once complained to her mother that other girls said bad things about her behind her back. Her mother replied, "If they're talking about you, it means you're going to be something in life."

The question was what that something would be. Mary wanted to be a scientist but knew that her parents couldn't afford to send her to college. And her grades were too poor to hope for a scholarship. "My mother fought with my stepfather, and there was a lot of confusion," she said. "I was very sensitive and it made me nervous, and my grades went down to a *C* average."

Mary enjoyed singing and remembered being enchanted by the movie musicals of the time she saw at local theaters, movies such as *Seven Brides for Seven Brothers, Funny Face,* and *Gigi*. "Wow, they [the singers and dancers] were having so much fun and making money," she told Steve Bergsman in 1991. "It looked like an easy living . . . almost like being in heaven."

Wells had discovered her goal in life. "I knew I could sing and I loved to perform, so I figured I could go this way," she said. "All the entertainers looked so glamorous and wonderful, so I started writing songs" in imitation of the popular songs she heard on the radio.

Informal bands and groups were springing up everywhere in Detroit those days, partly because the public schools offered an extensive program of music education. Also, as Motown vocalist Claudette Robinson pointed out to *Unsung*, "We didn't have computers. We didn't have phones. . . . For entertainment, you played kick the can when you were very young and perhaps board games. . . . And one of the ways of making entertainment was to make music." Robinson's failure to even mention television is characteristic of people born in the early 1940s. TV didn't become a regular feature in most American households until the 1950s, when the behavior patterns of people born earlier in the previous decade had already been established.

Mary sang as much as she could, performing pop songs of the day solo and in groups, some of them all-male except for her. "They didn't want me in there, but I was persistent," Mary said.

Robert Bateman, a member of the all-male Motown group the Satintones, remembers that when he and the group were performing, "Mary . . . approached me out of nowhere and said, 'Why don't you guys get a girl in your group?'" Bateman put her off because some of the other group members "were just interested in getting into her pants," and he thought her membership would disrupt group solidarity. But he told her that he was considering her request and to keep asking.

At this moment, when Mary the sixteen-year-old high school student started pushing her way into groups that didn't necessarily want her, her youth was over. After she had spent her short childhood in loyal and serious support of her mother and in battles for her own health, she turned her fierce energy to loyal and serious devotion to her career.

Mary's talent and ambition soon led her to her first and only female boss: Detroit vocalist and music biz entrepreneur Johnnie Mae Matthews, later known as "the Godmother of Detroit Soul." As a vocalist, Matthews sang with a group called the Five Dapps, who recorded a single, "Do Wop A Do," on Detroit's Brax record label; as a solo performer, she ended up releasing more than twenty-five singles on various labels.

She founded her own record label, Northern Records, in Detroit in 1958. One of many business people at the time who had noticed Detroit's immense reservoir of musical talent and were trying to make a buck off it, Matthews had also signed up a group called Popcorn and the Mohawks and then another called the Distants, later known as Otis Williams and the Distants, which in addition to Williams included some of the other young men who later became the Temptations.

Although Mary had high hopes when she first signed a contract with Matthews, she was disappointed. Matthews never paid much attention to her, or to Popcorn and the Mohawks, but instead concentrated on the Distants, recording their first two songs, "Come On" and "Alright," soon after they arrived. As Williams told Mark Ribowsky for his book *Ain't Too Proud to Beg: The Troubled Lives and Enduring Soul of the Temptations*, "Johnnie Mae immediately put us out front." Mary quit soon after.

The Distants were pleased that their songs had been recorded and that, as a result, they had performance dates in the Detroit area, but they were disappointed to receive no royalties whatsoever. (Matthews paid for their studio sessions, their suits, and their meals, but her contract allowed her to deduct all their expenses from their royalties.) When Williams confronted Matthews about this, she threatened to fire the current Distants and reconstitute the group, whose name she owned, with five new vocalists. In response, the Distants quit.

But Mary did have some fun during her time with Matthews: an affair with Otis Williams. In his book, *Temptations*, Williams wrote that he and Wells carried on a secret relationship in one of Matthews's offices while both worked for her. Somewhat less demurely, Williams later told Ribowsky, "Mary and I had a little thing going there; we'd get together behind closed doors and do the horizontal mambo."

After Mary left Matthews and Williams, she started dating Wilson Pickett, the future singing great, and the two told each other they were going to be major stars. (Pickett, already further along this road than Mary, was singing with the gospel group the Violinaires, which toured with various gospel stars.) Pickett said he liked Mary's singing, but he, like Williams, appreciated other things about her as well.

"I can see Mary as a young girl," Pickett told Gerri Hirshey. "There she is, leaning against the brick wall in Detroit, those big eyes, a short, tight mohair skirt. Oooh, she had a *walk*."

Mary liked Pickett, but her real heartthrob was successful Detroit vocalist Jackie Wilson, although she didn't know him. "She had a terrible crush on him," her friend Joyce Moore (born Joyce McRae) said. So Wells decided that since she was having difficulty launching a singing career, she'd hook her wagon to Jackie Wilson's star by writing a song that he would sing.

2

TWENTY-TWO TAKES

Pop music is music for lonely people made by other lonely people.

—RECORD PRODUCER KIM FOWLEY

HAVING BEEN BROUGHT UP RELIGIOUS, the teenage Mary was used to talking to God. So, she later related, "I went into my closet, my secret closet" and asked God to help her write a song for Jackie Wilson. The song "Bye Bye Baby" entered her mind, and she wrote it down. "Mary was a very mystical woman and a spiritual little soul," Curtis Womack said years later.

Looking for a way to get the song to Wilson, she remembered that Robert Bateman of the Satintones had told her to keep asking for membership in his singing group. She also realized she was friendly with a girl Bateman wanted to date, so she offered to introduce Bateman to the girl if he would arrange for Mary to sing the song for Motown Record Company president Berry Gordy Jr. She knew that Wilson recorded for the established Brunswick Record Company, not the struggling young Motown, but Gordy had written several pop hit singles for Wilson, including "To Be Loved" (which eventually became the title of Gordy's autobiography), "That's Why (I Love You So)," "I'll Be Satisfied," and, in 1958, "Lonely Teardrops," which not only hit number 1 on the *Billboard* rhythm & blues chart but rose to number 7 on the *Billboard* pop chart as well. She wanted Gordy to pass her song to Wilson.

Mary didn't realize that due to a change of executives at Brunswick and a dispute over royalties, Gordy no longer worked with either Wilson or his record company. Instead, he was searching for a female solo artist who could become a star of his new company. If any songs she brought to Gordy were going to be recorded, the Motown Record Corporation would record them.

After memorizing her song, Mary sang it for Bateman. He said he liked it and that he'd arrange to let her sing it for Gordy. Her opportunity finally came when, directed by Bateman, she caught up with Gordy at the 20 Grand, Detroit's hottest nightclub.

Gordy, busy directing a performance by vocalist Marv Johnson on one side of the club and on his way to direct the Miracles on the other side, literally walked away when the teenage Mary started talking, saying he was too busy to listen to her sales pitch. Mary followed him down the hallway almost in lock step, begging for an appointment so she could present him with the song she had written. Finally, annoyed, Gordy turned around and told her to "sing it right now." Mary immediately sang "Bye Bye Baby," a capella, on the spot.

Several people have described Mary as "shy and winsome," which is the way she often acted. But her actions in this case were anything but shy, and they are revealing. Throughout her life, she went straight toward any goal she wanted and did not stop until she had achieved it or had run out of time on earth. "She stood for all the courage and perseverance that any female should need to enter into show business and have a place in it," said vocalist Martha Reeves, who knew Mary at Motown and often performed with her later in life. What Gordy saw was a young doe-eyed black girl from the Detroit ghetto, who, author J. Randy Taraborrelli noted, favored tight gowns that fanned out at the knees. Her enormous eyes and the Lauren Hutton–like gap between her two front teeth enchanted Gordy and would enchant many others. At seventeen, Mary was physically an adult and an attractive one.

The voice Gordy heard one critic later described as "a unique, contrasting blend of intimacy and assertion, a softness and a forcefulness all rolled into one." Wells also knew how to present a song as a result of her high school musical training: "I belted it out," she told Bergsman.

Mary impressed Gordy so much—he later called her "a soulful sounding chick"—that he told her to show up at Motown the next day. When she arrived, with her mother accompanying her, Gordy told Mary she would record her song herself. Wells was so excited she whooped loudly and jumped around the office. "I just had wanted to be in the record business. I didn't think I could ever be an artist," she said later. Gordy signed her as a Motown recording artist that day, July 8, 1960. The legal age for signing contracts in Michigan was eighteen and Mary was seventeen, so her mother was required to cosign the contract.

Signing a record company contract was a real coup. "There were so many singers out there, but not many of them had record deals," Mary Wilson of the Supremes told *Unsung*. However, the Motown contracts Mary Wells and her contemporaries signed were heavily loaded in the company's favor. Motown vocalist Brenda Holloway told *Unsung* that a common failing among Motown recruits was that "We didn't read the small print." All they knew was that they needed money and "You put a record out, you get money. We didn't know how much, but that was our motive."

The company Mary had just joined would soon become legendary, and its name would eventually become a synonym for much of the popular music produced by black Americans, whether they recorded for Motown Records or not. But when Mary joined it, it was in its early stages. Gordy, one of eight children of an African

American couple who had migrated from Georgia to Detroit with business on their minds, had founded Tamla Records, Motown's predecessor, just eighteen months earlier.

Although his father worked energetically in the grocery, printing, and plastering businesses and his mother worked in insurance, Gordy didn't respond to their efforts to lure him into the business world. Instead he played the tunes of the day on the family's basement piano. Sometimes he sang in talent shows. Unfortunately for his hopes, no one found his playing or his singing all that overwhelming.

Trying to chart his own path in the world, the teenage Gordy surprised everyone by becoming a boxer. He was only five feet six inches tall, but by working out constantly at the gym he added enough muscle to his thin frame to move from flyweight through bantamweight to featherweight (126 pounds). Confident in his own abilities, he dropped out of high school and fought as a pro for two years but finally realized there was no future for him in the boxing game. His problem was that he wanted to be rich, and while heavyweight champions in the United States often become rich, lightweight contenders do not.

At loose ends, Gordy was drafted by the US Army and sent to Korea, where he spent part of the time as a driver for an army clergyman. He was discharged unharmed after two years. (While in the service, he performed in army talent shows.)

On returning to Michigan, he combined his early musical interests with his family's business acumen by opening a jazz record store in Detroit. He enjoyed jazz tremendously, but not enough other people did, apparently, because his store went bankrupt two years later. This was a turning point. Gordy swore to himself that from then on he would market only musical products consumers liked.

Meanwhile, although economic necessity forced him to take a job as an auto worker on the Ford Lincoln-Mercury assembly line, he continued dabbling in the music business by writing tunes for Jackie Wilson, whom he'd met at the gym. Gordy's work in an auto factory—with its emphasis on mass-producing similar models using many identical parts, giving the product a high polish and gloss, and rigorously controlling the quality of the finished items, all resulting in a profitable outcome—also may have given him some ideas about how to run a music business.

Gordy was a spectacular success as Wilson's songwriter, but he wanted wealth instead of chump change, and in his estimation, chump change was all songwriting would ever bring him. To remind himself of this, he framed and hung on his wall a check he had received from a record company for one of the hit records he had written. It was for $3.19.

Gordy decided to try another approach. While hanging around the numerous musical venues in the Motor City and talking with other patrons, he learned there were many aspiring singers in Detroit who would be willing to pay someone to record them and then to get the record played on local radio stations and purchased by an established music firm. He soon became a small-time record producer, selling the master recordings he made to various record companies.

This activity, although more profitable than composing, still didn't make the money Gordy was hoping for, and money was constantly on his mind. The title of one of the early hit songs he wrote, "Money (That's What I Want)," stated this with refreshing directness. According to one of his associates at the time, while Gordy was researching the record business, "He'd poke his nose into one sector of the business, take a sniff and ask, 'Is this where the money is?' Then he'd go to the next sector, sniff, and ask, 'Is this where the money is?'"

By 1959, Gordy had found his answer. Fortunes were being made by companies that not only produced and recorded tunes, as he did, but also pressed them into for-sale copies for distribution across the country. Having convinced most of his family members of his prospects, Gordy persuaded them to lend him $800 through the family's financial cooperative. With this capital he founded the Motown Record Company. Where the other capital that Gordy must have received came from remains a mystery. Even in Detroit in 1959, $800 was not enough to set up such a business.

What isn't a mystery was Motown's aim, which was to sell black music to both white and black listeners and make a fortune by doing so.

Gordy and his small staff, which included many of his relatives, moved into a couple of shabby two-story houses on West Grand Boulevard in the New Center area of Detroit. (He eventually acquired seven such houses before breaking down and renting an actual office building.) He may have been attracted to the neighborhood, which wasn't far from where Mary lived, because a short distance away was the headquarters of General Motors, at the time the world's largest corporation, and Gordy was nothing if not ambitious. His first step was to convert some of the rooms, including a bathroom, into recording studios. The Motown Museum occupies two of those houses today.

Gordy knew his capital wouldn't last long and that two-thirds of all newly established businesses in the United States went belly-up in two years or less. So he decided that the only way Motown could be a success was to produce nothing but hits. This was a bold goal, since only one in five records produced in that era entered the Top 100. But he didn't stop there. He announced that for a Motown record to qualify as a hit in his estimation, it had to make the Top 10 on the popular or pop music chart, where all sorts of records competed, rather than on the rhythm & blues chart, where black records jostled each other. This bordered on lunacy, but Gordy, who has often been compared to Napoleon Bonaparte in both stature and determination, was absolutely dedicated to this goal. He made the policy official by hanging a gigantic sign on one of the houses. "Hitsville, USA," it read.

Gordy believed that lyrics were the key to capturing the attention of record buyers and making his records into hits. He rejected dream images or poetry for the songs his company released: what he wanted were stories, and stories written in the present tense, to capture the attention of busy listeners. Not "My girl broke up with me" but "My girl is breaking up with me." He also made certain that the sounds his records produced would come through clearly on the car radios and portable radios of the time. With the General Motors buildings looming nearby, he came to feel more strongly than the other record producers in Detroit that the car radio was where hits were made.

Even after becoming the president of a record company, Gordy continued to profit from his songwriting talent. His knowledge of the craft allowed him to order changes in a song, sometimes minor ones, that would make it a hit rather than an also-ran. And he wasn't shy about expressing his opinion. When Smokey Robinson showed him notebooks in which he had composed one hundred songs, Gordy, after reviewing them, told Robinson that none of them were worth recording. As time went on, Gordy pressed and distributed very few of the songs that his producers had recorded. By restricting his output and by concentrating on what he considered hit material, Gordy was soon working his way toward what would become, with significant help from Mary Wells, a stunning accomplishment: during Motown's peak years, one in every three records the company released was a hit.

Curtis Womack later said that Gordy's virtually instant decision to hire Mary showed that Gordy "had the sight," and indeed, Gordy had an amazing ability to pick successful recording artists out of nowhere. Martha Reeves insisted, however, that Mary's musical talent was "easily recognized. When she approached Gordy she was a writer, a singer, and a performer already, although her dream was just being a writer."

The story of how Mary sang her way to signing with Gordy, although true, acquired legendary status as the way a Detroit teenager with no professional experience but plenty of guts broke through to the big time. Her fans referred to the incident throughout her life. Her mother occasionally teased Mary by saying, with a smile, "Sister [Mary] didn't write 'Bye Bye Baby,' I did, and I took it to Berry Gordy because she was such a poor critter." "Critter," which she pronounced "cree-a-tar," was her pet name for Mary.

Mary often talked about the incident on stage, especially after performing her megahit, "My Guy." "'Bye Bye Baby' was how I got where I am," she'd say, "because there were a lot of girl singers I liked that were better than me." But, she'd add, hers was the voice that reached millions of people, and that was because God had given her that song, her first. She'd then perform it to close the show, although sometimes she'd add a verse from the song "Shout" as a dynamic coda to her act.

Although thrilled that her song had been selected for recording and doubly thrilled that she had been selected as the vocalist to perform it, Mary was also excited because she thought she'd be recorded on the locally famed Tamla label, on which Gordy had released "Shop Around," a number 2 pop chart hit for the Miracles. "Wow, I'll be on Tamla," she thought. But Gordy told her he wanted to release her song on the new and relatively unknown Motown label, which had taken its name from the company that owned it.

"I felt terrible about that," Mary said. "In Detroit, Tamla was the company. I had no idea the whole world wasn't receiving Tamla. So when I found out I wasn't going to be on Tamla, I said, 'Wow, I get all the bad breaks.'"

Motown and Tamla were the two main labels for the records produced and pressed by the Motown Record Corporation. (The name "Tamla" was Gordy's homage to one of his favorite actresses,

Debbie Reynolds, star of the movie *Tammy and the Bachelor*. He didn't call his label Tammy because he feared legal action from the movie's producers and from Tammy Records in Ohio, which also released records on the Tammy label.) Gordy later created many others, including Gordy, Hitsville, Miracle, Mowest, Prodigal, Rare Earth, Soul, and VIP. Disc jockeys preferred to play records with as many different label names as possible, even if all the labels were owned by only one company, because it made the payola many of them were accepting less obvious to regulators and to the public. (Payola is the record industry term for illegal under-the-table payments to DJs in return for radio play.) Motown exploited the DJs' desire with a vengeance by outproducing most other record companies in the number of different labels it slapped on its discs.

Not that she had any choice, but by going along with Gordy and making her debut on Motown, Mary became one of the first few artists recorded on what would become the most famous label in black music history. After three hits by Mary on the Motown label, Gordy transferred many of his other promising artists, including the Supremes, from Tamla to Motown.

Mary recorded "Bye Bye Baby" as a raw, gospel, bluesy R&B "shouter" in the tradition of vocalist Etta James. Reviewers noted that while Mary's voice in subsequent songs was smooth and alluring, her voice on "Bye Bye Baby" could be described as a "gutsy gospel growl" and that she sang the song with the gravelly voice of the most fervent of singers. Mary said that was because Gordy required her to sing the song twenty-two times during one recording session. She didn't like repeating the song so many times in a row, and her gravelly growl wasn't the only indication of that exasperation: she ended the song with three banshee-like wails, a performance she never repeated on any other record.

Part of the success of "Bye Bye Baby" was the underlying seriousness with which Mary sang it. This was the real Mary. She could certainly tell jokes and have a good time, go out and dance, and later in life get drunk and play pranks, but she spent most of her life from sixteen on as a striver. In "Bye Bye Baby," one of the only two songs that Mary wrote unassisted at Motown, she's telling a man who walked out on her that she won't take him back, that she doesn't need him anymore, and that she's moving on. The real Mary would be disappointed many times during her life, but she would always move on, under her own power, in an attempt to do better, sometimes in an attempt to do much better, either romantically or professionally.

The twenty-two repetitions of "Bye Bye Baby" were necessary, Mary said, because at the time Motown had only a one-track recording system. On such a system, the background singers, the backup band, and the vocalist had to record simultaneously. Often, if the lead singer, a background singer, or a musician made a mistake, the whole taping was ruined, and everyone had to go back and start again. (Mary didn't mention it, but having to go as high as twenty-two takes might also have been a result of her inexperience, as well as the inexperience of some of the other performers and engineers working for the young company.)

Mary also recorded the song "Please Forgive Me," which Gordy wrote and which was placed on the B-side.

Released in December 1960, "Bye Bye Baby" reached number 8 on the *Billboard* R&B chart, number 45 on the *Billboard* pop chart, and number 41 on the *Cash Box* pop chart soon thereafter. It stayed on the *Cash Box* Top 100 chart for four months.

"'Bye Bye Baby' was the beginning of my good times, the beginning of my dream," Mary told an interviewer. With the success of this record, Mary became the Motown Record Company's first successful female solo singer.

"Bye Bye Baby" was the first and last song she ever wrote for Motown. Neither Wells nor Gordy ever said why she never wrote additional songs for the company, but while Motown already had writers capable of writing hit songs, it had no other successful female soloists. Gordy apparently decided that Mary's voice and appearance were far more potentially lucrative for the company than her songwriting skills.

Many record company owners added their names as cowriters to records they didn't compose or even help compose in order to pocket some of the songwriting royalties they hoped the record would produce. Gordy often listed himself as the cowriter of individual Motown records, but he truly did participate in the writing and composing of many of them, although sometimes only in the sense that adding a key musical phrase or making a small change in the melody could be considered cowriting.

In the case of "Bye Bye Baby," Gordy let Mary keep all the writing credit, although he later claimed he had made substantial changes to the song. As her longtime friend Randy Russi put it, Gordy, filled with gratitude that he had found the right female solo artist for his company, "was straight up and did Mary right" in this instance. Martha Reeves noted that with moves like this, on top of signing Mary to Motown in the first place, Gordy "became a father figure to her" and thus a very important person in Mary's life.

Mary's success startled Detroit. "You heard 'Bye Bye Baby' at least six or seven times a day on [Detroit area radio stations] WCHB, CKLW, and WXYZ," Reeves told Susan Whitall, the author of *Women of Motown*. (Reeves was in the process of joining Motown herself.) Tony Russi, Randy Russi's brother and a fan of Mary's, remembers hearing the song in 1961 on the radio in Florida, where he lived, and marveling at "this new record by this seventeen-year-old girl." His mother bought it for him for sixty-seven cents in a discount record store.

Mary was thrilled by the success of "Bye Bye Baby." But her new renown didn't yet interfere with her ability to live a normal life in public. Maye James-Holler, who as Maye Hampton became Mary's best friend during this time, remembers the days soon after "Bye Bye Baby" when the two of them were still able to act like other Detroit teenage girls of that era. Sock hops were held every Wednesday, Friday, and Sunday at the Greystone Ballroom, and Maye and Mary went to several of them. Admission was twenty-five cents. DJs would emcee these events and bring along artists whose records they were playing. The artists would sing along or lip-sync while the DJs played their records and the kids danced.

At one of these events, Maye and Mary danced enthusiastically with various boys for hours, then realized they needed someone with a car to drive them home. They got in a car with a couple of guys going their way who took them to an apartment where a party was just winding down. The boys disappeared for more than an hour while Maye and Mary stayed at the party, talking and laughing with others but wondering where the guys had gone. When the boys returned, the two girls noticed that the guys' hands were greasy and that they smelled strongly of fried chicken. "They didn't want to buy us food, so they ate without us," Maye said. Maye and Mary found this enormously funny and laughed about it for hours, and years, afterward.

Mary may have been hungry for fried chicken that night, but she wasn't hungry for drugs or alcohol. "When we met," Maye said, "I drank Scotch, and she didn't drink anything." Others confirmed that Mary would go to parties as a young star and drink nothing. She wouldn't drink in private, either.

Maye and Mary did try marijuana, though, on one occasion. "We smoked it while we sat on the couch watching TV and went crazy," Maye remembered, "laughing at every single thing the newsman said. We were eating so much our stomachs were hurting. It was funny and scary." It got so scary, in fact, that they flushed the remaining weed down the toilet.

Even then, however, Mary smoked two packs of cigarettes a day. While describing her early days at Motown, Wells once remarked,

"We were kids trying to act like adults. I'd smoke a cigarette and try to fit in."

Mary continued to smoke two packs a day until the last two years of her life. Steven Cohen, her manager in later years, remembered that during meetings with Mary "the room would fill with smoke, and smoke would pour out the door when we opened it." Friendly Womack Jr., her future brother-in-law, remembered, "I used to tell her she was a singer and shouldn't be smoking, but she'd laugh and smoke cigarette after cigarette."

Besides accompanying Mary everywhere, Maye also improved Mary's appearance, she said, by teaching herself how to do hair and then dyeing Mary's when Wells decided she'd look better with a different hair color. (Blonde and red became Mary's favorite hair colors in lieu of black later in her career, although she achieved the blonde look more often with a wig than a dye job. During the late 1960s and early '70s, she wore her hair naturally to express sympathy with the black pride movement.) Maye also began applying Mary's makeup for her. And Maye was especially proud when Esther Gordy Edwards, Gordy's sister and a Motown executive, told Maye that "ever since you've been working with Mary, she looks so nice."

Mary not only looked nice, but she was also doing nice things for Motown. Her next record, which was a bigger hit, made Motown's executives confident they were pointing her in the right direction. The song, an up-tempo doo-wop tune written by Motown songwriter William "Mickey" Stevenson that used extra strings, was called "I Don't Want to Take a Chance." Mary sang it smoothly, strongly, and melodically. The strain and hoarseness that were so evident in "Bye Bye Baby" were gone. Backed with "I'm So Sorry," it was released in mid-1961 and not only rose to number 9 on the *Billboard* R&B chart but reached number 33 on the *Billboard* pop chart, moving Mary's career nearer the top.

The success of this record astounded Mary even more than that of her first one. With the charting of "I Don't Want to Take a Chance," she had become the first female soloist on the Motown label to reach the *Billboard* Top 40.

Wells had had no idea she would rise this fast. She soon decided, she said, that she should assume a "more sexy" name to go with her stardom, "like Camille, or Brandy, or something more sophisticated, like Michelle Wells." When Wells suggested this, Gordy, very aware of the value of the name of a singer who had recorded two hits in a row and seemed likely to record more, started laughing hysterically. "You want to change your name?" he said between laughs. "The answer is no. We're billing you as Mary Wells and you're going to stay Mary Wells."

3

ON STAGE WITH MOTOWN

As soon as he could, Gordy started sending Mary out to appear at theaters and clubs, first in Detroit and later all over the country. She would continue to perform on stage for paying audiences for most of the rest of her life.

She immediately encountered racial segregation. Motown promoter Al Abrams, who is white, took Mary to perform at the Detroit Yacht Club in 1961. Accompanying Abrams was a former Motown employee, Judy Berger. The club manager took one look at Mary and told Abrams and Berger she wouldn't be allowed to perform. When they asked why not, he said, "because she's wearing a pants suit." Berger, who was wearing a dress and was Mary's size, said, "Hey, no problem. I'll change clothes with her."

The manager then said, "No, there's more. She's black and she can't perform here." Dismayed, Abrams and Berger first protested, to no avail, and then told the DJ who was the master of ceremonies at the show, Dave Shafer of Storer Broadcasting, what was happening. Shafer said if Mary couldn't go on, he wouldn't either, and left with the Motown contingent. Yacht Club executives protested Shafer's departure to his bosses but were told he had acted correctly. The club eventually amended its policy. Such a change was inevitable. As Abrams put it, “The General Motors, the Chrysler kids all wanted to see and hear Mary.”

At the beginning of her career, Mary’s performances certainly were energetic. “She danced back and forth on stage while singing,” Martha Reeves said. “She was very animated, a delight to watch, and my idol.” Emulating the male performers of the time, such as Jackie Wilson and Chubby Checker, Wells did a lot of current dances while she sang, including the monkey, the hully gully, the mashed potato, and the pony. “I danced like mad,” Mary said.

Soon after Wells started performing, she was dancing the pony so enthusiastically on one Cleveland stage that one of her breasts jumped out of her dress. She nonchalantly tucked it back in, but by then many of the boys in the audience had rushed down front, hoping it would happen again. Frankie Lymon and the Teenagers were also performing on the show, but Mary’s accident helped her to dominate it. Curtis Womack wasn’t there, but he definitely heard about the incident. “Mary’s was the first ‘wardrobe malfunction,’” he said, referring to singer Janet Jackson’s similar “accident” four decades later.

In her later years, Mary gained some weight and cut back on the hoofing, often restricting herself to swaying from side to side as she sang her hit tunes. All her life, though, Wells “had her own style and a sassy, sexy voice,” Carolyn Gill-Street of the Velvelettes said. “We admired her ability to do what she did and do it so well.”

Wells “always got the audience involved,” Reeves noted. Mary learned how to warm them up by bantering before she began singing and often encouraged them to sing and dance along with her on her most well-known songs. As part of the encouragement, she would hold the microphone out toward the crowd and yell “par-tay, par-tay” several times.

“Not only was it a popular thing to do, she loved to hear the audience sing and found joy in it,” Reeves said. Photographs of

Mary performing show her holding the microphone out to the crowd and eagerly awaiting their response. Guitarist Cornelius Grant later insisted, "Mary never got a negative reaction from the audience."

But Wells, who later described her youthful self as a "ghetto girl," had to work her way up to her energetic performing peak. In the beginning, she said, she prepared for her early performances by "learning how to dress." She dressed like a teenager at first but then managed to procure some adult performing duds from a local dressmaker who made entertainers' clothes.

Very soon, she became the first female Motown vocalist to wear the long, elegant dresses that became the standard for the company's female performers. She also attempted to distinguish herself visually from the other female Motown vocalists, as well as emulate Etta James, by wearing bouffant-style blonde wigs.

At the beginning, Mary had to struggle to overcome her inexperience on the professional stage. Her nervousness didn't help. "The first time I went on stage, I almost had a heart attack," she said. Choreographer Cholly Atkins's stage preparation course, later part of Motown's Artist Development Department, had not yet been formed. Maxine Powell's class in charm and demeanor was the entire department at the time. Although court papers indicate that Atkins gave Wells a couple of lessons in onstage movement at the very end of her Motown career, Wells insisted that the company never helped her with her performance skills. She said it was she who later hired Atkins on a private basis after she left Motown to help her spruce up her post-Motown performances.

At an early engagement at the Apollo Theater on 125th Street in New York City, a legendary venue, Mary told a startled audience that she hoped she "wouldn't make a boo-boo," then sang "Bye Bye Baby" out of key all the way through. Adding insult to injury, a law enforcement officer, his suspicions aroused by her poor performance, came backstage to make sure she was over seventeen, the legal age for performers at the time. Motown executives had to return to the Apollo the $300 the theater had paid for Wells's appearance.

Claudette Robinson, the only woman in the Miracles, said that Mary's Apollo experience was hardly unusual. At the day's first show, Claudette remembered, "Guys were sitting all along the front row, and their whole attitude was 'OK, show me what you can do.' Entertainers were always scared they weren't going to make it." Audiences at the Apollo were opinionated and vocal, and by booing and jeering could cause management to remove acts from the stage in mid-performance.

When Robinson's group, the Miracles, did their song at the Apollo, Robinson said, their nervousness distracted from their performance, but "somehow they took pity on us. We were truly, truly blessed that [the Apollo audience and management] let us slide through." Even so, she said, the promoters told Gordy they wanted him to return the money they had paid him for the Miracles. He refused. In any case, Robinson said, "After the first day, we got better."

The Apollo was rough in other ways. Robinson and Martha Reeves said performers had to do as many as six shows per day when playing at the theater. Adding to the stress was that, although the shows started at noon and did not end until 1:00 AM, the artists were not allowed to leave the building between performances. That left them stuck for thirteen hours in a theater Reeves called "raggedy, dingy, and dark." She noted that dinner during their stay at the Apollo consisted of hot dogs warmed on the light bulbs, followed by sardines and popcorn, and topped off with tap water.

Gordy often sent the young Mary on tour with his already established groups. The Miracles would go to California, playing at clubs such as Basin Street West in San Francisco, Whisky a Go Go on Sunset Boulevard in Los Angeles, and still other clubs in San Diego and take Mary with them as their opening act.

Pete Moore of the Miracles called Mary's voice "a very strong and powerful voice for a female and a very expressive voice." He insisted that Mary had "the strongest voice of all the female artists at Motown, even stronger than Tammi Terrell's" and noted that most of Motown's female vocalists "were softer singers like Diana Ross, and the Marvelettes."

Moore went on to call Wells "very, very talented and bubbly and a very nice girl that everyone liked. She got along with everybody, had an outgoing personality, and was widely admired for her singing ability."

But the nonstop touring she did for Motown caused some strain. She and her companions were hundreds of miles from home, living on a bus or in a series of cheap hotels, trying hard to remember where they were, and performing while disoriented and anxious. They often sought relief.

Later in life, Mary said that when she and Levi Stubbs, the lead singer of the Four Tops, were young performers, they drank Robitussin cough medicine topped off with liquor as an antidote to life on the road. On one occasion, Mary remembered, she overdid this a bit and felt like crawling out on stage when it was her time to perform.

For a short time, while back in Detroit between tours, she ingested diet pills and liquor to get high. The resulting panic attacks were intense, and Mary decided enough was enough. Throughout the rest of her early career, she abstained from both drinking and drugging. "She wanted a girl's drink every now and then, but that's all," Maye James-Holler said.

In any case, something other than drugs, liquor, and music was soon occupying her mind. She had acquired a boyfriend, Herman Griffin, who conducted her backup band while she sang. Pete Moore liked him too. "He did splits while conducting the band and a whole dance routine. He was really entertaining. The audience liked to look at him as much as at her," Moore said.

4

HERMAN GRIFFIN

MARY ALSO LIKED LOOKING at Herman Griffin. She appreciated the skill with which he helped her during her early appearances and his expertise in directing her backup band.

Wells liked competent, attractive men who were nice to her. But she also thought Griffin might provide her with the love she needed and desired, a love no one in her family was giving her. "I wish my mother would call just one time and only ask how I'm doing personally," Mary told Maye James-Holler. Her family members "just ask me for money."

"Mary was always looking for love," Maye said. "She was just looking for someone to love her for herself, but she got mixed up with sharp boys."

Even though she was often away from her family after she signed with Motown and rented her own apartment, Wells, still a teenager, remained in her family's orbit during her early days with the company. Her mother visited Motown every payday to collect Mary's check and did the best she could to oversee Mary's career. Mary's apartment was near her mother's house. She was constantly in contact with her mother about business and money, but she often fought with her. "I was trying to get away, run away from that," she said. She began her escape effort by dating Griffin in 1960, soon after she had arrived at Motown.

Griffin had cut a notch into music history in 1958 when Berry Gordy, who had not yet founded Motown, wrote and produced Griffin's song "I Need You." It was the first song to be published by Gordy's Jobete music publishing company. (Gordy had named the company after his three children, Hazel *Jo*y, *Be*rry IV, and *Te*rry.) Gordy and the woman who would become his second wife, Raynoma Liles, dubbed themselves the Rayber Voices and sang background for Griffin while he sang lead. The disc itself was released on the HOB label, the initials of the House of Beauty hair salon Liles frequented.

Wells may not have heard the song, which wasn't played on the radio much, but she was impressed by his third record, "True Love (That's Love)" backed with "It's You," because it was released (in 1960) on Tamla Records. But what most impressed Wells about Griffin was his onstage performance. "Backflips, somersaults, and splits were as much a part of his act as his bluesy tenor," one reviewer wrote. Club audiences were amazed at Griffin's acrobatic versatility. His records went nowhere, however.

Later on, dressed in a striped mohair suit, Griffin often conducted the band while Wells performed and did his dance routine behind her simultaneously. He even did backflips during the big windups of some of Wells's songs. This disconcerted some viewers and pleased others.

In her taped interview with Steve Bergsman, Mary said she saw Herman "as a big nightclub singer who had the fancy car and the great clothes and the finesse of an artist." She even scouted out his family home. "I went over to his father's house. He had a pretty nice home and was a real nice man. I thought it would be a great family to be a part of."

Griffin certainly knew how to attract attention. Author and record producer Randy McNutt, in his book *Guitar Towns,* describes Griffin as a short, wiry man, who, despite his diminutive size, spoke in a surprisingly deep voice, probably because he smoked so much. McNutt said Griffin punctuated every other sentence with the word *dig*, as in "You dig, my man?"

Once, McNutt said, "Griffin arrived at a recording session with two women draped in fur boas carrying a portable TV and a bottle of gin. When I asked what the TV was for, he replied, 'Dig, my man, the World Series is on tonight!'"

McNutt said Griffin looked ten years older than his twenty-four years, and Katherine Anderson Schaffner, a former Marvelette, while describing Griffin as a "nice guy," said that he looked too old for Mary and acted like he was much older. (He was only five years older than Mary.) But Schaffner may have been unfamiliar with his stage acrobatics.

In any case, Griffin had another sort of appeal in Wells's eyes. Motown had sent him on the road with her as her valet, driver, and protector. As Curtis Womack said years later, "Mary tended to get attached to someone who was taking care of her like that."

She did get attached, and she married Griffin on June 23, 1961, when she was eighteen. Under Michigan law, she had to get permission from her mother before marrying and did so. She failed to ask for permission from Motown, however, and Gordy was not pleased. When Gordy had sent Griffin to travel with Mary, he had told Griffin, "Don't you even think of getting into that" (having sex with Mary). So when Wells and Griffin turned up at Motown married, Gordy and his executives were furious. They put Griffin on the hot seat, accusing him of marrying Mary so he could lock himself onto a rising star. Griffin kept saying, "No, no, no, it was Mary, it was Mary. She wanted to get married. It was all her, not me" until they finally let him out from under the swinging light.

The marriage was rocky from the start, Wells said, because "I was still a kid" and Griffin spent three evenings a week out of the house. He told her he had a friend in the record business who knew the industry well and that he spent those nights learning the business at the friend's house. This bothered Wells. "I didn't like being alone. . . . I was used to being in a house with a big family," she said. That his excuse for not being home sounded extremely fishy also bothered her.

Annette Helton of the Vandellas said Griffin "always appeared kind of mean, kind of stern." He didn't treat Mary nicely and always spoke to her "in a snappy sort of way."

Soon Mary and Herman started arguing. Wells said the arguments were "nothing physical, except when I got ready to leave one day and he tried to close the door to keep me from going out and my finger got caught in the door and started bleeding. From that incident on, we never got along together."

About eight months after they were married, the real trouble began. Wells and Griffin were invited to a party that all their recording business friends were attending. Wells didn't go, but Griffin did, and her friends told her later that Griffin had had sex with a prostitute at the party. "I got really really hurt, sad, and enraged, because it was embarrassing to me, in front of all my friends," Mary said. Making it doubly hurtful was that the young Wells felt that she "didn't know anything about sex or lovemaking" at the time. She confronted Griffin, who denied it ever happened, but too many of Wells's friends had told her it actually had occurred for her to believe him.

Griffin tried to keep the marriage going but was unable to soothe his young bride. "I couldn't make love anymore," Wells said. "I was still a kid and would lose nights saying 'Leave me alone.' I was really hurt and would yell at him and cry a lot and be upset." Everything was completely gone. "Herman kept trying to make up with my heart but I could never get back to him, and I thank God for the records I had at the time." She replaced Griffin as her bandleader with another Motown staff musician, and her records required her to spend lots of time out of town touring.

Meanwhile, Griffin was regretting his extramarital fling. After she broke with him emotionally and then left on tour, Wells said, "I think he realized how much he loved me." But she wouldn't go back to him after she returned from the road. "I couldn't stay there with him and he wouldn't leave, so I left. I went back to my mother's." Her friends told her he "was losing his mind" because she left him, but she said, "I just couldn't go back to him because I was too hurting." She never lived with Griffin again and soon filed for divorce.

On May 22, 1963, Wayne County Circuit Court Judge James Montante granted Mary the divorce she wanted. Wells had sought an amount described in legal language as "larger than $10,000" from Griffin that she said she had entrusted to his safekeeping. The judge awarded her instead a six-unit apartment building at 5116 West Chicago Boulevard in Detroit that was known as the Griff-Wells Apartments, which the couple had been buying and which Mary soon appointed her mother to manage. (Mary and Herman had been living in one of the apartments. The building is still operating as an apartment house and is now known as the Gibbs Apartments, after its present owner.) Montante gave Griffin the couple's $10,000 automobile, a 1963 Cadillac, and ordered Wells to pay Griffin $1,000 for helping to develop her singing career. She had just turned twenty.

In later years, Mary was always charitable when talking about Griffin. When she saw him again during the 1970s, she remarked, "Oh that poor man. All they put him through." In 1991, she told Bergsman that Griffin didn't do very well at Motown "because they were so wrapped up in my career, they neglected his." A less generous person might have remarked on what Herman had put *her* through, but she never did.

In spite of the divorce, Mary still thought Herman had the ability to help her rise in the music business and continued to rely on him for professional advice. As Maye James-Holler put it, "Mary believed in Herman. She thought he cared about her career."

As an essentially fatherless young woman only just out of her teens, it was natural that Mary would rely on Griffin, even after she had divorced him. And she wasn't the only one who saw Herman as someone who could fill that role. "When you look at people, especially kids, you think this person could be a president, this one could be an executive, this one a teacher," said Claudette Robinson. "When I looked at Herman, I thought to myself, This person has the ability to start his own business."

Robinson also noted, however, that "it's difficult for a husband or wife [or a recent husband and wife] to run the other's business. They're too close and they lose the professionalism along the way."

5

AMBUSHED BY THE GIRL GROUPS

In September 1961, Gordy put out a third Mary Wells record, the blues-style ballad "Strange Love" backed with "Come to Me," written and produced by Mickey Stevenson, and it fell flat, not appearing on any chart. (Despite its failure, Motown vocalist Martha Reeves later told people that "Strange Love" was her favorite song by Mary. She was impressed in part by Mary's almost operatic tones on parts of the song.)

In November, Motown also put out Mary's first album. Titled *Bye Bye Baby, I Don't Want to Take a Chance*, it consists mostly of gospel-like and bluesy tunes previously popularized by Marv Johnson and Barrett Strong. Mary was excited to see the album go on sale, but it didn't make the *Billboard* album chart.

The major reason for these failures was that the music business was changing: Mary's competition had become much more formidable. When she was recording her first single, her competitors both inside and outside of Motown had been a mixed bag of white and black men and women, some singing as soloists and some in groups, all performing in various styles. In late 1960, however, Mary, Motown, and everyone else in the record business suddenly found themselves up against—or working with—a new phenomenon: the girl groups.

The Shirelles, an all-female, all-black non-Motown group, released "Will You Love Me Tomorrow," which rose to number 2 on the R&B chart and number 1 on the pop charts in late 1960 and early 1961. Their sound was so much in demand that their record company, Scepter Records, re-released an earlier tune of theirs, "Dedicated to the One I Love," which soon joined "Will You Love Me Tomorrow" in the Top 10. Having two songs in the Top 10 simultaneously was rare for any artist or group.

Girls and women have been singing in groups since the dawn of time, and the Andrews Sisters and McGuire Sisters were very popular in the United States in the 1940s and 1950s. But after the spectacular rise of the Shirelles, every record producer in America suddenly wanted one, two, or three girl groups. If he couldn't recruit any, he formed his own. Phil Spector worked with the Crystals, the Blossoms, and the Ronnettes. Jerry Leiber and Mike Stoller created the Dixie Cups, the Shangri-Las, and the Exciters. Many other girl groups sprang up to join them, including the Angels, the Bunnies, the Chiffons, the Chantels, the Cookies, the Jelly Beans, the Pixies Three, the Revlons, the Royalettes, and the Toys. Some of the new girl groups were formed by producers who broke up one group and recombined some or all of the members into other groups with different names.

A number of the groups, including the Shirelles, the Blossoms, the Dixie Cups, and the Exciters, consisted entirely of black women, while some were mixed and others consisted entirely of white women. This either wasn't clear or didn't matter to fans of the earliest groups, who were familiar with them mostly through radio or record play.

In comparison to these new arrivals, Mary was a soloist and sang more like the mature, bluesy soul singers who had preceded her. The girl groups didn't do blues. They sang innocent, vulnerable adolescent lyrics, as in "Chapel of Love" by the Dixie Cups and

"Leader of the Pack" by the Shangri-Las, over a high-production, harmony-heavy vocal and instrumental background best exemplified by Spector's "Wall of Sound."

Mary and Gordy reacted to the craze, although Motown never grafted the intensity of the Wall of Sound or its imitators onto Motown songs. Mary's next single, "The One Who Really Loves You" backed with "I'm Gonna Stay," issued in February 1962, was a spectacular success. It rose to number 2 on the *Billboard* R&B chart, number 4 on the *Cash Box* pop chart, and number 8 on the *Billboard* pop chart.

Vastly different from Mary's previous gutsy, gospel-type recordings, "The One Who Really Loves You" sounds like a girl group tune in both tempo and tone. Although the all-male Lovetones back Mary on this song, they do a good job of adding a girl group sound to Mary's dulcet tones, which sound more innocent and yearning than on her previous discs. Mary marveled at the record's success. "I didn't think 'The One Who Really Loves You' was going to be a Top 10 hit, because I was so used to people giving me records where I belted out songs," she said.

Starting with this production, Gordy and Wells changed Mary's style so effectively in response to the girl group phenomenon that pop music writer Alan Betrock would include Mary, a soloist, in his book *Girl Groups: The Story of a Sound*, the first book ever written on this subject. Motown also continued moving forward with the Marvelettes, the Vandellas, the Supremes, and other groups and ended up capturing a large share of the girl group market. The new style Mary was helping to pioneer at Motown became the basis of what came to be known as the Motown sound, essentially a black idiom stripped of the heavier parts of its soul and lightened with the air of innocence. Mary was among the first vocalists through whom Gordy found his way to that sound, which made the company a major player in the music industry for years to come.

As former Motown songwriter Brian Holland put it when discussing the girl groups, Gordy always thought that "the songs that were popular at the time were the better songs to have" and record. In other words, when the girl group sound flooded the market, there was only one way for Motown, under Gordy, to go. Infantry officers traditionally have been counseled to lead their troops "toward the sound of the guns," and that's exactly what Gordy did.

Author Tony Turner has theorized that Wells's rise was aided by her ability to reproduce the girl group sound as a soloist with low-profile, temporary backup. Certainly her solo status helped her to stand out, but also, as he noted, Mary didn't have to deal with "all the pettiness that can afflict . . . vocalists on the way up or the way down." In other words, Mary didn't have to go through the drama of dealing with other permanent group members as they competed with each other and jockeyed for position.

6

SMOKEY ROBINSON

SHOCKED AT THE FAILURE of Mary's third record, "Strange Love," Gordy had appointed songwriter Smokey Robinson to replace Mickey Stevenson. It was Robinson who wrote and produced "The One Who Really Loves You."

Gordy obviously had made the right choice. As Brenda Holloway put it, Mary "didn't come into the fullness and ripeness of her artistry until she started working with Smokey." The songs Mary sang under Smokey's direction were the classics she will always be remembered for. They were also among the best songs Motown ever produced. Will Porter, Mary's future bandleader, noted that as late as 2011, these songs, unlike many others from the 1960s, "don't sound dated. Classic stuff doesn't sound dated."

This is less true of the songs later written for Mary by Motown's premier songwriting team of Edward Holland, his brother Brian Holland, and Lamont Dozier, known jointly as Holland-Dozier-Holland, or H-D-H. Their best songs were written for the Supremes, not for Mary.

While Gordy and Stevenson had encouraged Wells to belt out her first three songs in a low-down blues and gospel style, Robinson, partly in reaction to the girl group phenomenon, recognized Mary's true artistic asset: the girlish, sensuous, and vulnerable quality of her voice. Stevenson noted years later that when Smokey was producing Mary's songs, Mary "had an innocent sound, almost a childlike innocence. It wasn't a great voice, but it was such an innocent voice, you were drawn into her sincerity. She had not been tainted."

Adding to the appeal of Mary's music, and setting her apart from most girl groups at the time, Robinson wrote sometimes sensuous, sometimes double entendre lyrics for her. As a result, in contrast to the deluge of more playful and adolescent-sounding girl group records flooding the market, Mary's records, despite her innocent voice, sounded as though they were made by a knowing, worldly veteran of love. Listening to them, "You would think she was a much older person," Mary Wilson of the Supremes told *Unsung*.

Robinson also changed Mary's sound by adding attractive guitar chords to the mix. And he encouraged her to sing in a higher register, with a sincere pop style in which only a touch of suffering and sadness could be heard. She followed his directions, then added her own smooth, knowing coyness, like a layer of delicious frosting, right on top.

Underlying the entire structure was a calypso beat. Robinson, a big fan of vocalist Harry Belafonte's calypso tunes, purposefully added this beat, which he called "an island-flavored bongo bop," to almost all the songs he wrote for Mary.

In fact, from that time forward, "Mary became my pet project," Robinson said. He "liked writing for her voice and experimenting with her sound." He told an interviewer that Mary "was a completely devoted artist. I'd teach her these songs at the piano, and as I went over the phrasing patterns, she paid strict attention." He added that "she was always excited about the songs."

But Robinson also allowed her some freedom as a singer, Mary told Steve Bergsman. "He would play and sing it, and then I would record the melody . . . in my head. I would get as close as I could to singing the basic melody; then I would emphasize certain points on certain phrases to make the picture of the song." Wells said that although Robinson "wanted me to put more of myself into each song," she sought feedback from him on "whether I was singing it closer to his dream, the way he wanted it." Robinson would respond with advice aimed at particular passages, like, "Sing it like it really hurts you, Mary."

Mary insisted that "once I got into a song and put my life into it, what's natural would come out of me." Sometimes that happened on an extended basis. When she was recording "The One Who Really Loves You," Wells was singing over a prerecorded background track that kept running after she ran out of scripted words. A natural trouper, she just started ad-libbing, and the words stayed in the song.

Maye James-Holler said the word among Motown producers was that it was simple to work with Mary. "She would hear a song one time, and then she could record it. They didn't have to take the time to tell her 'hit this note and this note.' She'd just go in there and Smokey would sit there, singing it, just laying down the chords, and she would learn it right away."

Robinson told one interviewer that Mary "would stay in the studio forever, never complaining or resisting a single suggestion." Another Motown insider described Mary in the studio as "pliant."

Motown lyricist Eddie Holland said that as far as working with producers went, Mary never had "an attitude because she had the biggest hits or because she was the star, even though she did have tremendous success at Motown." That quality made her different from other 1960s stars, Holland said in 2011, and "much different than stars now, who go for playing a lot of head games."

Wells's next song, "You Beat Me to the Punch," sounds very much like "The One Who Really Loves You," but on this tune, bongos and vibes aid Mary's haunting vocal. Critic David Ritz noted that "You Beat Me to the Punch," in which a boy and girl meet and then break up, "goes from ecstasy to agony in two minutes and forty seconds." It definitely adheres to Gordy's belief that pop songs should have definite story lines.

Others enjoyed "You Beat Me to the Punch" because it showed that in courtship, the best-laid plans are often trumped. In the song, the woman makes her plans to get together with the man, but he moves faster than she does and brings them together. In the end, however, she discovers he's a playboy and beats him to the punch by breaking up with him before he can break up with her.

Brenda Holloway noted that the *punch* reference is in tune with the era's boxing craze, which involved the rising fame of such big-name fighters as Muhammad Ali and Sonny Liston. Holloway told *Unsung* that she was at the fights while she was pregnant and was jumping up and down with enthusiasm, even though people were telling her, "Sit down. You're going to have a baby." She responded, "I don't care."

Released in August 1962, "You Beat Me to the Punch" became a number 1 *Billboard* R&B hit and reached number 9 on both the *Billboard* and *Cash Box* pop charts. With this record, Mary, whose tunes were now consistently played on white radio stations, became a major crossover star.

The song inspired an answer song, "You Threw a Lucky Punch," recorded by Gene Chandler. And "You Beat Me to the Punch" received a Grammy nomination for best rock 'n' roll recording of the year. Although the song didn't win the award, it was the first tune by a Motown vocalist or musician ever nominated.

(Also nominated for best rock 'n' roll record that year were "Alley Cat" by Bent Fabric, which won the award, "Big Girls Don't Cry" by the Four Seasons, "Breaking Up Is Hard to Do" by Neil Sedaka, "Twistin' the Night Away" by Sam Cooke, and "Up on the Roof" by the Drifters. It was a memorable year for pop music.)

"You Beat Me to the Punch" is backed with "Old Love (Let's Try It Again)," an early effort by Holland-Dozier-Holland. While not as striking in its storytelling as "You Beat Me to the Punch," "Old Love" attractively emphasizes the conga beat and bongo drums even more strongly than its A-side companion.

A definite chemistry had arisen between Mary and Smokey, who were, after all, an attractive young couple spending hours alone in a studio. And of course Smokey, who was married, was writing the songs that were moving Mary from star to superstar.

Bergsman asked Mary about any attempts by Robinson to get personal when they were working together. She claimed that he did make some low-key moves but that nothing ever happened. "You know how guys might try to touch you, in a playful way . . . and I'd say, 'Hey, Smokey, wait a minute.' . . . I wouldn't let him go so far because of Claudette [Claudette Robinson, his wife] and because I was just so career-inclined in those days.

"We weren't personal," she added. "Our relationship was music-wise, even if he might have wanted it more. And maybe to a certain extent I might have wanted it more at the time. But because I went through so many changes as a kid with my stepfather and seeing . . . my mom and him, I think I was frightened of a relationship and scared that it was going to get torn apart. So rather than make it personal, I built a friendship, which to me is more important, because friendship is always there." (Mary seems to have glossed over her relationship with Herman Griffin when she said this.)

She told another interviewer that she and Smokey were "similar in mannerisms" and "like cousins who lived down the block from each other."

Although their closeness remained professional, Robinson and Wells pushed the boundaries of record-biz acceptability in 1962 when Wells recorded the then–semi-scandalous song "Two Lovers." In this tune, she projects no shame, but plenty of vulnerability, over loving two men at the same time. She manages the amazing feat of sounding innocent and scandalous simultaneously while appearing to admit to conduct that even today would be somewhat shocking.

In terms of its lyrics, however, the song is a trick, because the end of the song reveals that the two lovers are really the two personalities of one man. In those innocent days, this trick flabbergasted many people, even professional songwriters. After he listened carefully to the song, Motown lyricist Eddie Holland told *Unsung* that he said to himself, "Man, Smokey tricked me on that one."

One secret to the song's longevity, aside from its catchy tune and trick ending, was that even after hearing it for the first time, many of Mary's male fans probably disregarded the ending and concentrated on the theme. Dennis Bowles, son of Motown musician Thomas "Dr. Beans" Bowles, wrote in his book *Dr. Beans Bowles*, "When Dad played 'Two Lovers' . . . I used to fantasize, in a kid's way, of myself being the other lover." He wasn't alone.

Such male interpretations aside, plenty of other people found the song realistic, and intriguing, solely from a psychological standpoint. In fact, Robinson said his motivation for writing the song was that his wife, Claudette, had the power to make him feel "very sad" or "very happy" with just one word or action.

"Two Lovers," released in October 1962 and backed with "Operator," was Mary's second consecutive number 1 *Billboard* R&B hit, and it hit number 7 on the *Billboard* pop chart and number 10 on the *Cash Box* pop chart. In fact, 1962 was her annus mirabilis: in that one year, three of her records had risen into *Billboard*'s and *Cash Box*'s pop charts' Top 10, a rare achievement. "Two Lovers" remained a hit in 1963, when *Billboard* voted it number 81 among the Top 100 songs of that year.

During 1962, Motown also released Mary's second album, *The One Who Really Loves You*, which, like her first album, failed to hit the *Billboard* album chart.

However, in 1963, Mary's third album, *Two Lovers and Other Great Hits*, rose to number 49 on the *Billboard* album chart. Illustrating the ups and downs of the album business, in the same year, Motown released Mary's fourth album, *Recorded Live on Stage*, and it failed to chart. But albums were more profitable for record companies than the singles those companies released, so it's likely that Motown made a profit on most of Mary's albums anyway.

7

THE MOTOWN REVUES

You're on the road, the great American road!

—Voiceover from an auto company documentary

Racial discrimination and money were major problems for Motown in 1962. Prejudice permeated the big talent agencies that arranged group performance tours for both white and black artists, and high touring costs prevented Gordy from sending each of his acts on individual road tours. But Gordy hit upon a solution. Since it cost less to send all his acts together on tour at once, he launched them as the "Motortown Revue" or "Motown Revue." This not only saved money but also helped get gigs. With so much ticket money involved, the talent agents' greed overcame their racism.

The departure of the first Motown Revue from Motown headquarters in 1962 was hardly promising. The artists, many of them very young, were nervous about leaving their families for the first time. They rubbed their hands together in an effort to keep warm while they waited to board their decrepit-looking buses. Many of them carried bag lunches their parents had packed for them.

But the departing musicians had the advantages as well as the appearance of youth: they demonstrated what can only be called school spirit. In her book about women in rock, Gerri Hirshey describes the group as looking like a pep squad for an inner-city high school, with every student in the "graduating class" beaming his or her best "most likely to" smile.

The size of the group may have compensated for any fear the artists felt. Forty-five performers participated on the tour, traveling together for thirty days on one bus and a few trailing cars. On the earliest of these tours, Mary rode the bus with the Supremes (who were not yet stars), the Contours, and the Marvelettes. On the later tours, however, after she had become Motown's biggest star, she'd ride in one of the cars. (The cars were used not only for the big stars but for carrying the musicians' instruments as well.) Whatever the mode of transportation, one participant noted, "You forget what day it is; you forget where you are. You had to write it down."

The ramshackle nature of the tours is made clear by the fact that on several occasions, the performers' luggage fell off the top of the bus. "You'd have to get off at the next exit and go back around and try to find it," Claudette Robinson told *Unsung*, all the while hoping their suitcases hadn't broken open and scattered their garments over several lanes of dangerous highway. More seriously, auto accidents killed or injured several performers and handlers over the years.

Wells's relationships with her fellow performers on these trips ranged from the sublime to the burlesque. Brenda Holloway called Mary "very quiet and reserved." Stevie Wonder would sit next to Wells on the bus while she told him what the sky, the stars, and the clouds looked like. She would tell him, "You probably see things that are much more beautiful than what I can see." Mary later said, "We were always uplifted by the remarkable way Stevie handled himself."

On the other hand, when Wonder, then thirteen, was in a different mood, Wells said, "I'd have to be careful not to be alone with him, because his hands were all over me." Knowing he also liked the somewhat shorter Wanda Young of the Marvelettes, Wells would tell him to "go over to Wanda. She's more your size." But soon Martha Reeves and the Vandellas started taking motherly care of little Stevie.

Other problems also surfaced. Backstage areas at most theaters weren't luxurious: Martha Reeves told *Vanity Fair*, "We played some places that had horse stables in the back with straw on the floor, places where you had to build a fire in the wastebasket to keep warm." Wells also was troubled by the miniscule spending money Motown provided her. She said she occasionally made dinner on the road out of little jars of pigs' feet she bought at 7-Eleven stores.

Moreover, Mary and her colleagues had great difficulty finding anywhere decent to stay at night. Especially in the South, hotels that would accept black customers were hard to find, meaning that the performers would spend only half their nights on any tour at a hotel. They would spend the rest of them sleeping on the bus, leading to many cranky people and much body odor. The audiences were mostly unaware of either, since the stage usually separated them from the entertainers and the entertainers didn't act out inappropriate feelings on stage.

Under such conditions, it was natural that some of the artists, including Diana Ross of the Supremes and Wells, fought with each other on the bus. Ross's favorite trick was to put her feet up on the back of Wells's bus seat to await Wells's standard response, which was to turn around, slap Ross's feet, and tell her to put them down. Often this led to further words. On at least one other occasion, Wells urged Ross to wear a girdle, "'cause you jiggle so much." This led to more words. When the two teenagers calmed down though, Ross would visit Wells's room and ask her for advice on makeup and men.

Wells attempted at least one good deed on an early Motown tour, and also managed to get involved in two somewhat farcical incidents. The good deed involved Claudette Robinson, who, although pregnant, had taken Smokey's place in the Miracles on one of the tours. She did this so the group would continue to have an income from touring while Smokey returned to Detroit to fight a bad case of Hong Kong flu. Not many people spotted the substitution, because few had seen either of the Robinsons in performance. Claudette's soprano also sounded a lot like Smokey's, especially when she was singing Smokey's parts, so fans would encourage Claudette by yelling "Go, Smokey!"

On the nights the performers stayed in hotels, Claudette and Wells often were roommates, and Wells soon became aware that Claudette was bleeding to an extent that threatened her pregnancy. Knowing that Claudette had had several miscarriages and aware of the couple's desire to have a child, Wells called Smokey from Atlanta and told him what was happening.

Smokey immediately called Claudette and tried to convince her to come home, but she refused, saying the fans wouldn't accept a three-person Miracles group. (Besides Smokey, Miracle Pete Moore was missing because he was in the army at the time.)

There were other pressures on Claudette. Each day, Gordy's sister, Motown executive Esther Edwards, kept asking Claudette, "Can you make it one more day?' Claudette said.

When she did return to Detroit, around Christmastime, Claudette was down to eighty-nine pounds, despite being three months pregnant. The expectant couple was devastated when, in Claudette's fifth month, she miscarried. Nevertheless, Smokey remained forever grateful to Wells for her timely warning, as did Claudette.

On another occasion during this tour, a disturbed woman attacked Motown vocalist Kim Weston, thinking that Weston was Wells. The woman, whose motive for attacking Wells was unclear, managed to pull Weston's wig off before being subdued.

The most serious incident during this tour occurred just after the revue had finished playing a tense concert in Birmingham,

Alabama. Although the show was an integrated one, a rarity in the South in those days, there were rumors of trouble in the crowd during the concert, and a Motown musician was challenged by a security guard after using the only men's restroom, which the guard apparently considered whites-only. At the end of the concert, the entire group was slowly boarding the bus when several loud sounds were heard. One of the musicians said someone was throwing rocks at the bus and another cried out that they weren't rocks, they were bullets.

At just this moment, Wells told Steve Bergsman, she was carrying several bags onto the bus when the person in front of her tripped, causing Mary to fall on top of her. As all the performers tried to get on the bus at once, pressing against the downed Wells, she tried to struggle free of her bags and the other downed woman. Wells said she took a while to disengage herself and rise, causing emotions to rise high at the bus entranceway. Later the rumor floated around that Wells had "refused to get up," which she denied. "You know how [panicked] people start pushing you? That's what happened. It was horrible," she said. The driver later found bullet holes in the bus, but no one had been hurt.

In another published version of this episode, Martha Reeves fell on the floor of the bus and claimed she'd been shot. Almost every single person anywhere in the vicinity of the incident has insisted on a different account of what actually transpired during those few moments.

The episode was frightening and may have permanently altered Mary's view of the world. She had been surprised on this tour by the difficulty of finding hotels, and her dismay was deepened by other aspects of southern behavior that were clearly segregationist. She had lived in a poor, mostly black neighborhood in Detroit, but separation of the races in Detroit was not endorsed by law, so she had never encountered things like the segregated water fountains in New Orleans City Hall. "They had a drinking fountain there that said 'White Fountain' and another that said 'Negro Fountain,'" Wells said, "and that was a government building! I didn't bother to look at the sign and started drinking. People started looking at me and I thought, Oh, they know who I am, I'm Mary Wells, and then people said, 'Girl, look at the sign,' and I looked up at the sign, and I was so hurt. Me in my little Motown star bubble, then everything kind of crashes." She also couldn't help but notice the continued presence of segregated restrooms, with the white restrooms inside the building and the black ones outside, in back.

Moreover, although it took her some time to realize it because she was usually blinded by the lights, many southern concert halls required white fans to stay on the ground floor and black fans to sit in the balcony. After realizing this, Wells said, "I tried to give both audiences my attention, and it was hard . . . some of them were down here, and some of them were up there, and I was trying to communicate with both of them."

Wells called the Motown Revue tour her "higher education," but Gordy was already very aware of southern attitudes toward black people. He refrained from displaying pictures of Wells, the Marvelettes, or other black entertainers on their early album covers so southern record stores would not refuse to stock them.

Wells was discouraged by all of this, but whenever she walked out on stage she'd get more applause than any other performer. And no wonder. She was the only solo Motown star of the time. The names of Wells, the Miracles, and the Marvelettes dominated the tour's ads. Her prominence, and the applause it engendered, coupled with her talent, encouraged her to perform whatever the difficulties. Even when she wasn't feeling well, "She'd drag herself on stage anyway and do a first-rate show," Maye James-Holler recalled.

Even after Mary's popularity grew and she began touring by herself, her routine remained physically taxing. During one 1962 tour, she did most of her sleeping in the back seat of her car while being driven from one appearance to the other.

"I would arrive at a dance when it started, wouldn't leave until it ended, and travel all night and the next day to my next engagement," she told the *Detroit News*. The tour lasted for two months. When she returned to Detroit, she spent six days recovering in a hospital, causing her to miss two scheduled gigs.

The quality of Mary's backup bands varied considerably through her performing life but went through at least three stages. Her earliest backup band, the same group that accompanied all the other Motown acts at their first performance at the Apollo, "chicka-boomed along with wedding hall mediocrity," one critic remarked. Those that backed her during the rest of her Motown career were composed of the first-rate, high-class professionals who made many of Motown's recorded tunes so memorable. Later in life, however, Wells's lack of money restricted her to hiring less-talented musicians and vocalists.

As famous as she became, Mary remained a "laid-back regular person" all of her life, according to Maye. A big exception to Mary's generally relaxed nature, however, was her relationships with the groups that backed her. Even when she was performing with first-rate bands, she would berate them backstage if they hadn't been up to what she considered par. "I was supposed to listen to the band while she performed and tell her if I'd heard anyone make a mistake," Maye said. If Maye reported a mistake to Mary, Wells "would bring the band backstage and give them what for."

Prodded by her perfectionism, Wells's musicians were almost too responsive on one occasion. Led by her bass player and conductor, Joe Swift, they moved so quickly in support of Mary at one performance that Swift inadvertently contributed a famous spoken-word line to a non–Mary Wells record. It happened in a Chicago theater in 1963, when Little Stevie Wonder had just finished performing "Fingertips—Part 2" and had left the stage. Mary and her musicians were waiting to go on.

As Stevie walked off the stage, Swift and Mary's band moved immediately into position on it. But the crowd was loudly demanding an encore, and Stevie's conductor, Clarence Paul, also offstage by now, pushed Stevie back on. Stevie was unaware his musicians were gone; he was, of course, blind. So he reacted by immediately starting a reprise of "Fingertips," and the band had no choice but to go along. Swift, unprepared for a performer and a song that were totally different from what he had expected, shouted, "What key, Little Stevie, what key?" Nevertheless, Stevie and the band's reprise was so magnificently done that Motown, which was recording the show, decided to issue this performance as the finished record, including Swift's shouted query. Their judgment was correct: the record, Stevie's first to hit any chart, became his first number 1 *Billboard* pop and R&B hit.

On another occasion while she was at Motown, Mary's perfectionism about backup musicians manifested itself in outright rudeness. At a Brooklyn, New York, club, the Temptations asked Cornelius Grant to play guitar for them when that group, before it had made any of its own records into hits, was backing Wells. Grant said he saw pencil marks all over the group's sheet music, or chart, for "Two Lovers" and "You Beat Me to the Punch," and asked his fellow musicians, "Do you really play it like it is on the paper? Let me watch you do it the first time. I don't want to embarrass you or myself." During the first show, Grant saw that the musicians did indeed play it differently than the chart indicated. He then played well on the second show, but before he did so, Wells berated him because conductor Swift had told her Grant had held back. "She never gave me a chance to explain," Grant said. "She said I was holding out for more money and told me to go out there and play or be fired. Her attitude was, 'You work for me. I don't have to be nice or anything. I don't have to deal with you.'" Grant was forgiving about the incident, saying that at the time, Wells was "young and inexperienced about being a star. There's no manual, you know."

Somewhat less charitably, Grant remembers a later instance when he and road manager Joe Schaffner were driving Mary, in her Cadillac, from Virginia to New York City. "Mary was very highly sexual," Grant said. "She had us stop in DC at this hotel, where there was a guy she was dating. We had to drive and park in the hotel while she went upstairs and had her little sexcapade." Grant said he and Schaffner had to wait in the car for one and a half to two hours before Mary returned. "Joe had had to do all the driving, and he was tired. If she knew she was going to be a while, she should have let us take a break and eat breakfast. But we were just her limo drivers."

Mary also had no problem protecting what she considered her turf from her fellow performers. Motown producer Robert Bateman remembers that in Motown's early days, he produced a record featuring vocalist Gladys Horton and Mary was furious at him because, she said, "You made *her* [Horton] sound like *me*!"

Most people who worked with Mary at Motown, however, saw Wells, in Martha Reeves's words, as "very warm, compassionate, and caring." Mary and other Motown artists on tour "were hoping people liked us. We weren't waiting for someone to honor us. We were flattered to be on stage and in awe of show business."

After overcoming some initial timidity on stage and becoming a Motown star, Mary looked like an empress when performing. She would sweep on stage "coiffed in the long blonde wigs and sequined sheaths her fans expected of Motown's first diva," Susan Whitall wrote. She had long black bouffant wigs and bright blonde ponytail wigs as well. And off stage she was "very sweet to the people," Maye James-Holler said. "When they wanted to come backstage, and she'd be so tired, she let them come in anyway, autograph the photos of her that they brought her, and let them take pictures."

One particularly dedicated fan, Tony Russi, was only eleven years old when he first met Mary. His parents had taken him and his brother, Randy, to the Miami Zoo and were on the way back when he saw the Motortown Revue bus in the parking lot of Miami's Sir John's Hotel. The two boys begged their mother to let them visit the entertainers. Their mother was apprehensive about this, so Tony called the hotel first and was put through to Wells, who was rooming with Martha Reeves. Wells told the boys to come on up, invited them in, and had a pleasant conversation with them. "The other members of the Revue all came to Mary's room to see who these little white kids were," Tony Russi remembered. "That was the first time I had met black people, other than the maids of some of my friends." The Motown magic was working.

Newspaper reporters flocked to interview Wells as well, and for this reason Motown hired a speech coach to help Wells talk to interviewers. As Mary put it, "I really had to learn how to communicate with people that I didn't know." The coach, a high school English teacher, encouraged Wells to stop saying uh and stop pausing unnecessarily between sentences so interviews could be done more quickly and professionally.

8

DAVID RUFFIN AND HOLLAND-DOZIER-HOLLAND

I'm going to be very honest with you. Each guy that I was with I believed I loved him very deeply. Each one. That's why I'm scared of any relationship now. Because I'm getting older and I cannot deal with it.

—Mary Wells, 1991

On the first Motortown Revue tour, Wells spent a lot of time talking to David Ruffin, who would soon be named the new lead singer for the Temptations. Rumors flew about an alleged affair between the two.

Wells later insisted that although Ruffin lavished consoling words on her about her problems with Herman Griffin as they rolled across America in the crowded Motortown Revue bus, nothing happened between them because she was still married to Griffin. Even though the other artists would get together in the hotel lobby after the show to socialize, and often to pair off, she reverted to her default mode when unattached and off stage: she skipped the socializing and stayed alone in her room.

After divorcing Griffin, however, Wells lightened up and engaged in an affair with Ruffin that lasted for about six months, she said. "He fell in love with me and wanted to marry me, but I was so much into my career." That didn't prevent her from fuming over Ruffin's lady-killing prowess. "David was a good-looking guy and he still is a fine-looking guy," she said in early 1991, shortly before Ruffin's death. "The girls would be hanging all over him. I would be backstage watching him, and I would get jealous. Then he would get jealous when I went out there. So I said this is not going to make it. This is just totally ridiculous." She soon broke up with Ruffin.

Mary was somewhat perturbed when she returned to Motown from the tour to learn that the last two records she had produced under Smokey Robinson's direction, "Laughing Boy" backed with the bluesy "Two Wrongs Don't Make a Right" and "Your Old Stand By" backed with "What Love Has Joined Together," were not doing as well as her previous three records.

On "Laughing Boy," which opens with a dramatic instrumental flourish before Mary enticingly enters, she is accompanied by the female background singers the Andantes, who sing "ha-ha-ha-ha-ha" choruses behind her, and by the male background singers the Lovetones. Released in February 1963, the song rose to number 6 on the *Billboard* R&B chart but could not push past number 15 on the *Billboard* pop chart or number 27 on the *Cash Box* pop chart. (the B-side tune "Two Wrongs Don't Make A Right" managed only to reach number 100 on the *Billboard* pop chart.)

"Your Old Stand By," cowritten by Smokey Robinson and Janie Bradford and released in spring 1963, peaked at number 8 on the *Billboard* R&B chart and could hit only number 40 on the *Billboard* pop chart and number 48 on the *Cash Box* pop chart. (Its B-side, "What Love Has Joined Together," failed to chart.) Wells's previous three tunes had hit number 1 or 2 on the R&B chart and numbers 7 and 9 on the pop chart. She wanted to climb dramatically to the top, not bounce gradually downward toward oblivion.

So, in line with Motown's system of rotating artists among different songwriters and producers until a new magic combination was found, Mary was allowed to do a second song with H-D-H.

Working with H-D-H was different than working with Robinson. "They were more precise; they were more like a computer," Mary said. "Eddie Holland wanted everything right on the *T*."

While Robinson would merely play and sing his songs for Mary prior to the recording session, H-D-H, according to Mary and the Holland brothers, would record the instrumental tracks for the song on tape, sometimes before the song even had a title, and give the tape to Mary two weeks in advance of the recording session so she could play and replay it at her convenience and become completely familiar with the music. Then Eddie Holland, after writing the lyrics, would go over them with her, with the tape playing in the background, before the recording session. "If I took one-and-one-half hours just before the recording session to work with the artist on the song," he said, "it would be fresh in their minds." Noting that he used this procedure with all artists assigned to him at Motown, Holland said it was necessary. "Our songs had a little more complicated rhythm and lyric flow. I wanted to make sure the artist understood the song and captured the nuances and feelings written into it."

Mary said that although "Brian Holland could play piano and sing too," he usually stayed relatively quiet during these sessions. "He was the brains of the operation and worked the hardest. [Brian] would go without sleep for two or three days to work on songs while other guys would be out in the streets playing around." Although Brian Holland demurred, saying "We all worked equally hard" and "The other guys didn't play around," Eddie Holland joined Mary in praising his brother's perfectionism. "Brian did the arrangements in his head with the musicians," Eddie said, "and he was very particular about how the rhythm sounded, how the guitar sounded, and truly meticulous." At that time Brian was the lead producer on the team, and he, Eddie, was just trying to learn how to write songs.

Eddie said that sometimes, when he proposed a lyric line, Brian would tell him that it was getting in the way of the guitar rhythm. "I'd say, 'What rhythm?' And he'd say, 'The rhythm I have in my head.'" On other occasions, when Brian would be working out the song on the piano, Eddie would make a singing suggestion, and Brian would say, "No, I've got another instrument filling up that spot."

Naturally, the two of them would have disputes. Sometimes, Eddie said, "Brian would be concentrating so heavily on the rhythm and I'd say, 'You can't do that at that point,' and he'd say, 'That's how I want it.'" Or, Eddie would tell Brian that at one particular point in the song, "You've only given me three lines, and that's not enough for me to finish this thought." At that point, Brian would interrogate him, saying, "You can't finish that thought in those three lines?" and often refused to give Eddie more space.

Mary said that the third member of the team, Lamont Dozier, who also wrote many of the lyrics, was "a genius who didn't even have to work hard to be a genius." Dozier "just naturally rambled off stories and lyrics like this [she snapped her fingers] and they'd be fantastic. He'd also keep everybody laughing." Eddie Holland agreed with Mary's characterization of Dozier, although he noted that "Berry Gordy felt that Brian was the only genius among the three of us." Dozier "loved to ad-lib and sing songs off the top of his head. He rattled things off quickly."

Eddie insisted, though, that while Dozier wrote "from the head," he himself wrote "from the heart." When writing lyrics, "form and rhyming were not sufficient." In contrast with Dozier, Eddie said, he believed in making sure that the lyrics connected with the listener emotionally.

To Bergsman, Mary noted that it was Gordy, firmly at the head of the Motown machine, who made the ultimate decision as to which songs would be released. "H-D-H would write songs and come to me after they had recorded them. I would put my voice on them and put my technique into them. Then we would take them into Berry. . . . If, say, I recorded twenty-two songs, he would pick maybe ten or twelve . . . or maybe he would say, 'Go in and record some more stuff.'" Or he would direct other producers to write some tunes for her.

Gordy hedged his bet with Mary's next record by releasing it with H-D-H's "You Lost the Sweetest Boy" on one side and Robinson's "What's Easy for Two Is So Hard for One" on the other. "Mr. Gordy said it was the best thing to do," Brian Holland noted of the somewhat unusual single. Eddie Holland said that "it's more interesting for record buyers if you mix it up a little bit" this way.

Released in August 1963, Mary's upbeat, bouncy rendition of "You Lost the Sweetest Boy," the H-D-H tune, reversed her decline by scoring number 22 on both the *Billboard* and *Cash Box* pop charts (eighteen and twenty-six places on the respective charts above "Your Old Stand By"), although it reached only number 10 on the *Billboard* R&B chart.

Robinson's song, the equally bouncy "What's Easy for Two Is So Hard for One," enhanced by lively hand claps alternating in rhythm, did almost as well on the charts, scoring number 29 on the *Billboard* pop chart and number 8 on the *Billboard* R&B chart.

This double play arrested Mary's plunge on the charts and demonstrated that Robinson's inability to inspire Mary's fans had been only temporary. More important, especially for her morale and Motown's, the record gave Mary her first double-sided hit, an industry rarity.

Another aspect of Mary's association with H-D-H soon developed: Brian Holland became Mary's lover, according to Mary. (Brian Holland would not comment on any relationship they may or may not have had but noted, "Mary liked me as a person more than the others.")

Although he had started out as a Motown vocalist, like Mary's ex-husband Herman Griffin, Brian's voice had not been heard on records since the first tune he sang tanked and he moved to songwriting. When Mary told Steve Bergsman about Brian's performance as a songwriter, she had referred to Brian as "quiet," "stern," and a "nerd." But, characteristically for Mary, her interest in him was piqued when he started acting as her protector. During recording sessions, when his fellow songwriters would make cutting remarks about mistakes she made, he would glare at them until they were silenced, endearing himself to Wells. (Brian Holland said he does not remember doing this, but "it could have been true.")

Wells now saw Holland, who was already married, not only as a great songwriter who would soon make it to the top, but as "a real nice guy, very deep mentally, very educated." She said she was impressed that he had earned good grades at school and that he had been struggling to write hit songs since before she had sung her first composition for Gordy. She said she tried to inspire Holland by working really hard on the songs he gave her.

She also realized he needed a lot of encouragement, and she gave it to him. "He'd come over for dinner sometimes. We'd have dinner together, and then he'd start writing these great songs, really great songs," she said. Mary said Brian wrote the song "You're a Wonderful One" about her. Brian Holland denied this. "I don't think that's true. It's not about anyone in particular," he said, calling the timing of the song "coincidental." Released in February 1964, the tune soon became a hit for Marvin Gaye.

According to Mary, Holland proposed to her, and, as an additional demonstration of his love, organized her twenty-first birthday celebration at Motown. Holland said he wasn't in charge of the party, although it's possible that his sister, Carol Holland, was. He also said he never proposed to Mary. "I was always married." Asked why Mary would say something like this, he said, "You can't tell what's going on in a woman's head."

Mary said that although she was tempted to accept Holland's alleged proposal, her background rose up to oppose her desires. Particularly during this part of her life, Wells said, the influence of her religious upbringing was strong. Although "I really loved him," the fact that Holland was married persuaded her to ease off on the relationship.

In the process of doing that, Mary had a brief affair with a man named Benny Mullins. It may have been her only romance with someone who was not in the music business. Mullins owned a barber shop on Detroit's Twelfth Street, the main drag of the black community, which catered to theatrical figures. "All the big shots went there," Maye James-Holler said and described Mullins, who was single, as "the cutest thing . . . quite good looking." After dating for two or three months, Mary and Benny became engaged and went so far as to leak their wedding plans to *Jet* magazine. The Rev. C. L. Franklin, father of singer Aretha Franklin, was going to preside at the July 31, 1965, ceremony at the New Bethel Baptist Church in Detroit. Then something happened. "He did something," Maye remembered. "He had too many women and something popped up, like another girlfriend." Wells, uninterested in taking on another faithless husband, canceled the wedding plans.

Later in her career, gossip columnists would link her romantically with Beatle Paul McCartney, baseball superstar Willie Mays, and vocalist Marvin Gaye. She denied ever having any of these alleged liaisons. Mays, in also denying any romance with Wells, said, “I never met the kid” and added, “I hope she doesn’t get into trouble because of the rumor.”

In truth, Mary was anything but a snob in her choice of boyfriends and husbands. She wanted someone who would take care of her, his social or industry status be damned.

Meanwhile, her already high status at her company was about to go even higher as she rose to her Motown peak.

9

"MY GUY"

A record is your footprint in time, and these artists have left some magnificent ones. That's a piece of a guy or girl's life, and that's their best effort. That's their best effort.

—Ewart Abner, former president of Motown Record Company

As a result of the hits Smokey Robinson and, to a lesser extent, H-D-H wrote and produced for her, Mary had become a Motown goddess: its premier female vocalist, a position she would hold without challenge from 1962 to 1964.

Her fans, many of them young, reacted with frenzy to Mary's new fame. "We would literally have to hide her, to get her from the car to where she was performing, because the children would tear her apart," Motown singer Mabel John told Susan Whitall.

Brenda Holloway said that at Mary's apogee in the early 1960s, everybody at Motown thought, "She's an untouchable, because she's the one with all the hits. We were wannabees. We were trying to be her. Everything she touched . . . turned to gold. She was Miss Motown."

The Andantes and the Lovetones, who had provided background singing for "You Beat Me to the Punch" and "Laughing Boy," were, respectively, a veteran Motown backup group and a respectable but not famous group of three male jazz singers who were friends of Mary's older brothers. By contrast, singing backup for Mary on "You Lost the Sweetest Boy" were members of the Temptations and the Supremes, soon to be two of the nation's hottest groups. This was not a one-shot deal: the members of the Supremes went on to do the background singing on other Wells tunes. And on one occasion, the Temptations were sent from a club in Brooklyn, where they were performing solo, over to the Apollo in Manhattan to provide backup for one of Mary's performances.

(Mary also recorded three songs with the Four Tops: "Can't Get Out of This Mood," "I Remember You," and "I've Grown Accustomed to His Face." These songs were likely the products of the Tops' first recording sessions at Motown. As of this writing, Universal was planning to release these previously unreleased tracks.)

Robinson and Wells, sensing they were on the roll of their lives, marshaled their best talents for a maximum effort. Robinson wrote the music and lyrics for Mary's next song, which he called "My Guy." A rare upbeat and jaunty song about love and loyalty, its tune is light and catchy and its lyrics memorable. It's hard to write more classic rock lyrics than these:

> Nothing you can say
> Can tear me away
> From my guy.
> Nothing you could do
> 'Cause I'm stuck like glue
> To my guy.
> I'm sticking to my guy
> Like a stamp to a letter
> Like birds of a feather
> We stick together.

I'm telling you from the start,
I can't be torn apart from my guy.

The remaining lyrics contain Robinson touches best described as "where polite language meets the street," including such lines as "You best be believing / I won't be deceiving / my guy." (Similarly, on the song "What Love Has Joined Together," Mary sings lyrics cowritten by Robinson stating, "What love has joined together, can nobody take it apart.")

Analyzing the appeal of the song, Eddie Holland told *Unsung*, "You know how women think . . . especially when they're young . . . there's nothing you can tell those young girls about their boyfriend."

Mary's delivery in "My Guy" was sweet and jaunty, sophisticated and assured, and decidedly feminine. Author David Ritz, referring to both the lyrics and to Mary's style, memorably called the song "a fluttering study in fidelity."

Aiding the tune's success was that while it was black music, it was far from raw soul. It was directly aimed at pop radio stations and pop record sales. This song, which became the template for most of the other Motown classics of the 1960s, was built on a strong melody, a noticeable beat, and accessibility for all. The beat, a Motown trademark, was much stronger than those on the rhythm tracks used by white singers during these years. And the fact that Mary's rendition of this song—like Diana Ross's delivery of later Motown hits—was feminine, soft, sweet, and romantic, added immensely to its appeal.

Gordy's dream for Motown, after all, had been to produce not the sound of black America, but, in his words, "the sound of young America." In "My Guy," he certainly succeeded. "This song was the epitome of the Motown Sound," Mary Wilson said.

Over the years, the tune and lyrics of "My Guy" have come to be a symbol of what critics praised as the "spellbinding simplicity" of early Motown. "My Guy" also was boosted into semi-immortality by something the Motown house band added to it at the beginning and a twist that Mary inserted at the end.

On the day of its recording, according to the book *Standing in the Shadows of Motown* by "Dr. Licks" (Allan Slutsky), the Motown studio musicians had been working all day. With only a half hour left in the session, they had become bogged down in the intro section. As time and patience ran out, trombonist George Bohanon turned to studio bandleader and keyboardist Earl Van Dyke and pointed out that the melody from the song "Canadian Sunset" fit right over the chord changes of the "My Guy" intro. Van Dyke not only took Bohanon up on his implied suggestion, but added the left hand from Eddie Haywood's "Begin the Beguine." (The "Canadian Sunset" beginning is easily recognizable in "My Guy" after someone points it out; otherwise, it just sounds like an unusual intro to a great recording.)

"We were doing anything to get the hell out of that studio," Van Dyke said. "We knew that the producers didn't know nothin' 'bout no 'Canadian Sunset' or 'Begin the Beguine.' We figured the song would wind up in the trash can anyway." Van Dyke was usually right with such predictions. This time he was way wrong.

Now came Mary's part. As soon as Robinson had played the song on the piano for Mary, she told herself, "I love this song. I hope it's a Top 10. It's a completely beautiful melody." She decided she loved it so much that she "had to put something real cute on the end. And I thought about Mae West."

Supported by the Andantes, Wells recorded the ending the way Mae would have sung it were she trying to entice a lover upstairs. She adopted a sexy musical stutter. "I was really joking," Mary said. But the producers said, "Keep it going, keep it going." She did:

> There's not a man-n t-day [Mary stutters]
> Who could take me away

From my guy.
(Tell me more!) [from the Andantes]
There's not a man-n t-day, [she stutters again]
Who could take me away,
From my guy.

The stuttering aside, Holloway insisted that Mary's voice, especially in this song, "had something in it that no one has been able to come up with. . . . It's like Bette Davis. There's not another Bette Davis. There's not another Marvin Gaye, and there never will be another Mary Wells."

"My Guy" is backed with "Oh Little Boy (What Did You Do to Me?)," one of the few Motown songs that actually begins with the word "shoo-bop." It also is one of the few to sound like the performance of a Renaissance chorus.

Released March 13, 1964, "My Guy" rose to number 1 on the *Billboard* and *Cash Box* pop charts, Wells's first time at the very top of either of those charts. (*Billboard* did not publish an R&B chart from November 30, 1963, to January 23, 1965.) It remained among the Top 40 hits on the *Billboard* pop chart for thirteen weeks. *Billboard* ranked it as number 17 among the Top 100 Songs of 1964. Among the top one thousand most popular single records released from 1955 through 1996, *Billboard* ranked it number 437. (In 1999, the curatorial staff of the Rock and Roll Hall of Fame, in conjunction with a group of rock critics and historians, voted it into the hall's permanent exhibit of "The Songs that Shaped Rock and Roll.") Not only did it become Mary's signature song, but it also made her the nation's most popular singer.

In April 1964, Motown issued Mary's sixth album, *Mary Wells Greatest Hits*, in an effort to capitalize on "My Guy." The effort was a success. Loaded with popular Wells tunes, including "My Guy," "The One Who Really Loves You," and "You Beat Me to the Punch," the album rose to number 18 on the *Billboard* album chart, a high-water mark for Wells.

In May 1964, the company issued Mary's seventh album, *Mary Wells Sings My Guy*. It was successful, but probably because it was the second album in succession on which "My Guy" had appeared, it rose only to number 111 on the *Billboard* album chart.

Nevertheless, "My Guy" caught on so fast with white fans that Curtis Womack, who later became Mary's long-term lover, was briefly troubled. As a musician trying to cross the racial barrier, Womack remembers thinking, "This song ain't like 'Bye Bye Baby,' and it ain't like 'You Beat Me to the Punch.' It sounded just like something [white vocalist] Patti Page or one of them ladies would be singing, and I thought it wasn't going to go with black people like it did. But it *did*. It went with everybody."

"My Guy" has remained stuck in the minds of millions over the years, even more so than other pop hits. Barney Ales, Motown's vice president and director of sales, was quoted in 1992 as saying that there's "no one age thirty through age fifty who doesn't know the words to 'My Guy.'" For once, he was exaggerating only slightly.

"My Guy" remains a favorite backup tune in Hollywood movies and TV commercials to this day. It also remains the music to which thousands of people continue to fall in love. In 2010, one music business expert said that not twenty-four hours go by without "My Guy" being played on some radio station somewhere in the world.

The *Indianapolis Post-Tribune* noted without exaggeration in 1989 that the song had become part of American culture. "It doesn't die," Wells said.

10

"THE GIRL WHO BEAT THE BEATLES"

There're two more t-things
That I n-need to s-say about "My Guy."

The success of "My Guy" had other pleasant consequences for Wells. After the song was released, she was paired with Marvin Gaye, becoming the first of several female Motown vocalists to serve as his duet partner. Motown execs paired the two not only because her voice blended well with his, but because of her sexy persona, which they hoped would increase Marvin's personal appeal. They also thought that linking the struggling Gaye to a star like Wells would boost his career. They were right on both counts.

The first Wells-Gaye duet was "Once Upon a Time," in which two lovers tell each other how happy they are to have found each other but nevertheless sound wistful and melancholy. The second, "What's the Matter with You Baby," also is somewhat wistful, being simultaneously playful and accusatory. Listeners apparently appreciated the relative emotional complexity of both songs, and the record carrying them, released in April 1964, became a two-sided hit. "Once Upon a Time" rose to number 19 on the *Billboard* pop chart and number 27 on the *Cash Box* pop chart. "What's the Matter with You Baby" rose to number 17 on the *Billboard* pop chart, and number 25 on the *Cash Box* pop chart. On the UK pop chart, "Once Upon a Time" rose to number 50.

The album on which "Once Upon a Time" first appears, *Together*, was Mary's fifth and was issued the same month the single of "Once Upon a Time" and her sixth album, *Mary Wells Greatest Hits*, was issued. The album pulsates with romantic love and youthful enthusiasm and peaked at number 42 on the *Billboard* album chart.

Although Gaye recorded subsequent duets with Kim Weston, Diana Ross, and Tammi Terrell, Wells's soothing tones were a perfect match for Gaye's. Even after Mary had left Motown and Gaye had reached his sex symbol status that culminated in the 1980s with his "Sexual Healing" tour, he often sang Mary's "Two Lovers" as part of his performance. (Wells and Gaye also recorded four additional duets at Motown—"Back in My Arms," "In Case You Need Love," "Let's Talk It Over," and "Oh Lover"—that Universal Music is considering releasing.)

Gaye and Wells seemed made for each other. "Marvin really was a gentleman," Mary said, "a shy, soft-spoken person. He was insecure, but his voice was like heaven. He was kind and gentle and a man you could trust. He would do anything for you, I mean, *to perfection*. He was the ideal man for anybody." Wells's opinion of Gaye was the universal female view at Motown. "All the girls at Motown were in love with Marvin Gaye," Mary Wilson said. "I mean, if we were on tour, everyone would want to sit right next to Marvin Gaye." Although Wells and Gaye became great partners musically and great friends personally, their relationship remained platonic.

Mary had helped Gaye, but she competed with the Beatles. In doing so, she became the first American female vocalist ever to beat the Beatles, even briefly, when a wave of what came to be called Beatlemania was sweeping the country.

In early 1964, the Beatles monopolized the number 1 *Billboard* pop chart position for an astounding fourteen consecutive weeks. Then, in May, Louis Armstrong took the top position away from them for one week with "Hello, Dolly." Mary's "My Guy" knocked "Hello, Dolly" out of the number 1 spot the next week and held it for two weeks, before the Beatles retook number 1 with "Love Me Do."

Motown PR man Al Abrams immediately issued a Motown press release proclaiming Mary "The Girl Who Beat the Beatles."

With "My Guy," Mary also managed a counter-invasion by making the song a hit in Britain, where it rose to number 5 on the UK chart. British record enthusiasts voted her top female artist in the international section of *Melody Maker*'s Readers' Poll for 1964 and top female R&B singer in a *Record Mirror* poll. In a tribute to the song's British staying power, when it was released again in England eight years later, it rose to number 14. As this successful rerelease indicated, the record had begun a Motown boom in Britain that lasted for years. Author Nelson George pointed out to interviewers for *Unsung* that the craze extended into the 1980s, as British R&B artists such as Paul Young, Culture Club, and Bananarama either covered Motown songs or recorded songs that sounded like Motown songs. To this day, George said, echoes of "My Guy" can still be heard in British pop music.

The Beatles themselves were heavily influenced by Motown's music. Smitten by Mary and her singing, they recorded three Motown songs on their second UK album, *Meet the Beatles*. Former Motown songwriter Mickey Gentile told *Unsung* he was surprised while talking with Beatle Paul McCartney to realize that "Paul knew everything about Motown. He knew all the producers. All the songs. I said, 'Gee, here is this Beatle telling me they know more about me than I know about myself.'"

But Mary's influence on the Beatles went deeper than that. Keeping the sound of Mary's songs in mind, George believes that she might well have inspired the production of many early "sweet and optimistic" Beatles songs, especially those sung in falsetto. "Not that many white singers at the time were doing falsetto."

In May 1964, however, Mary was surprised when the Beatles expressed no animosity about being forcibly vacated from their accustomed top spot, even if only temporarily. "They never did mind it," she said. "Those boys were real sweet."

Before the Beatles returned to England from their 1964 American tour, John Lennon went to see one of Mary's performances. For years afterward, he called Mary the group's favorite American singer and its "sweetheart." A British journalist quipped that Mary "had the highest-paid publicists in the world."

The Beatles invited Wells to join them as one of their opening acts during their fall 1964 UK tour, making her the first Motown act ever to perform in the United Kingdom. This astounded her colleagues at Motown, some of whom still saw themselves as struggling artists working for a small Detroit record company. When Wells actually opened for the Beatles, Mary Wilson told *Unsung*, "We were all kind of like 'whoooa!'"

Wells appeared as one of seven opening acts on the tour, which consisted of fifty-four shows at twenty-seven venues in England, Scotland, and Northern Ireland in thirty-three days—beginning October 9 and ending November 10. The other opening acts—The Rustiks, Michael Haslam, Bob Bain, the Remo Four, Tommy Quickly, and Sounds Incorporated (who also backed Mary when she sang on the tour)—were all British.

David Bell, who lived in Derbyshire, remembers seeing Mary perform during this tour, when he was seventeen. Bell said that he angered his girlfriend, who was sitting on his lap throughout the performance, because "I took no notice of her, instead focusing all my attention on the beautiful lady on stage. . . . Mary was the first black person I had ever seen in my life, and I was mesmerized by her beauty and exotic appearance."

According to Martin Creasy's book, *Beatlemania! The Real Story of The Beatles UK Tours 1963–1965*, Tony Newman, the Sounds Incorporated drummer, told an interviewer that he and his bandmates enjoyed performing with Mary, adding that they "were all shocked at how black she was. Of course, she was equally surprised at how small and white we were."

Mary also was surprised at British politeness. She marveled to one reporter that British audiences "dig the music, but they don't interrupt the singer until after he is finished singing."

The Beatles, especially Lennon, treated Mary like a goddess. He explained years later that before the Beatles had become famous they'd "been hearing funky black music all our lives [on imported records] while people across Britain and in Europe had never heard of it." Lennon said that on first hearing those records, brought over to England by seamen landing in the port of Liverpool, his home city, he had thought to himself, "Why can't I sing like that?"

Maye James-Holler, who accompanied Mary on the tour, told *Unsung* that on another occasion while they were touring, McCartney sang a high "Wooooo!" in imitation of the Isley Brothers, and asked Maye if he had "a colored folk's soul."

Lennon and the other Beatles remained reverent toward Mary after meeting her. Mary said all four Beatles would visit her in her dressing room before every show to talk to her and look at her. "They'd come in and say hello and sit down and talk for a while." Lennon would tell her jokes that were "mostly like parables. You have to be pretty smart to catch on to the way he jokes." One night McCartney asked her, "Why don't you wear some bangs, like the way we've got our hair fixed? Let me comb it for you," and proceeded to do so. George Harrison, whom she called the most intense of the four, would just sit back and observe, saying nothing. Sometimes one of them would ask her if she was satisfied with the food she ate in England or if she wanted something different to eat. The young men would only consent to leave when she'd say, "Look, I've got to get dressed to go on stage." And every night of the tour, when she would go on stage, all four "would stand backstage and watch me perform."

Newman said he remembered McCartney listening backstage to the bass licks when Mary performed "My Guy." "You have to remember these were unheard-of grooves at the time," Newman said.

Understandably, although she was only one of the opening acts rather than the featured performer, Mary felt like the star of the tour. The feeling stayed with her: she returned to England to tour several times over the next twenty-four years.

11

TROUBLE AT THE TOP

Money was not the main thing. The most important thing was all these people were just loving us.

—Mary Wilson of the Supremes

The one evil that hits all entertainers is the big head and (can't nobody tell you shit) you think you did it all alone. You don't need the team anymore. It takes more ingredients than simply being a singer or having a song to be successful.

—Dennis Bowles in *Dr. Beans Bowles*

Mary was now a stratospheric success. She was far and away Motown's biggest star. Various members of the Supremes, who spent much of their time hanging around Motown's lobby waiting for unpaid or low-paid jobs as hand-clappers or background singers, remember seeing Wells and her entourage sweep majestically past them. Author Tony Turner noted the loftiness of Mary's stature at the time. "She was the top star in that period at Motown. She didn't compete with the other groups. She was removed from that. She had the hits. She was *Mary Wells*."

To her contemporaries, Wells never lost her regal standing. Brenda Holloway, looking back at Motown from the perspective of

2011, said, "Kim Weston had the body, Claudette Robinson was the lady, and Diana Ross had the face and eyes" but added without hesitation that "Mary Wells was the queen."

In 1964, Mary's fame attracted the most flattering of attentions: imitation. An undisguised answer song to "My Guy," "Your Guy," was recorded that year by Bobby Wells (no relation). Another song also released in 1964 was "My Girl," written by Smokey Robinson and sung by the Temptations. In 1965, "My Girl" became a number 1 *Billboard* R&B and number 1 *Billboard* pop chart hit. Also in 1965, the nation's top DJs, polled by *Billboard*, voted Wells the nation's top R&B songstress.

Even filmmakers took notice. Michael Roemer's 1964 independently produced movie *Nothing But a Man* features her hit tunes "Bye Bye Baby" and "You Beat Me to the Punch" on its soundtrack along with tunes by Martha and the Vandellas, the Miracles, and Little Stevie Wonder. On screen, black actor Ivan Dixon and black vocalist and actress Abbey Lincoln acted out the story of a southern black man who refused to bow to bigotry. (Dixon and Lincoln enact a pretend fistfight in the film while "You Beat Me to the Punch" plays on the soundtrack.) The movie was allegedly Malcolm X Shabazz's favorite film.

Ironically, Mary's success also received an indirect nod in the form of alleged bootlegging in 1964, by none other than Raynoma Liles, also known as Mrs. Berry Gordy.

Although by 1962 the Gordys were estranged, Berry had sent Raynoma to New York City to run a Motown creative outpost there. Due either to romantic or business-related tensions between Berry and Raynoma, or more likely a mixture of both, Berry refused to budget the additional money Raynoma believed she needed to make the New York outpost thrive.

Enraged by this decision, Raynoma hit upon another way to obtain the funds she needed. She decided to use Motown's pressing plant to print an extra five thousand copies of "My Guy" and sell them directly to New York City record stores and distributors, bypassing the required royalty and other payments and keeping the money for her own office's budget.

According to Raynoma's account of this incident in her book *Berry, Me, and Motown*, she told herself over and over that as executive vice president and co-owner of Motown, she had a perfect right to take such action for the good of the company. Motown's reaction was somewhat different: company executives back in Detroit called the FBI, which arrested Raynoma on federal charges of interstate record bootlegging. After she had spent a night in jail, Motown offered to drop the charges against her if she accepted a divorce agreement and monetary settlement dictated by Berry and gave up all interest in and control over the Motown Company. Raynoma agreed.

All this was just a sideshow, however, compared to the much bigger problems Mary's superstardom began to cause for Motown, and, ultimately and most tragically, for Mary herself.

At age twenty-one, a mere five years after Motown had plucked her from obscurity, Wells had come to consider herself hard-done by the company that had lifted her from poverty to the top of the music world. Considering that her first song for Motown was a hit, and that in four years she had risen from number 41 to number 1 on the pop charts, it's not surprising she felt this way. Mary saw herself not only as the Girl Who Beat the Beatles, but the Woman Who Made Motown a Success.

As Wells told Steve Bergsman the details of her Motown career, a theme kept recurring: how unappreciated she was considering how many contributions she had made to Motown, even as an inexperienced vocalist, contributions that were never acknowledged and for which she was never compensated. "I don't think I ever got the recognition I should have gotten," Wells said of her first recorded song, "Bye Bye Baby."

Aside from reaping enormous financial rewards from her voice, Motown profited from her creative ideas, Mary said. "Motown was basically following moves that I would make" in other areas. "When I'd go into the office . . . Berry would want to talk to me and get some more ideas from me about different things." For instance, she gave Gordy "ideas for different bass lines" when he was recording "Bye Bye Baby," and it was her idea that Motown go into filmmaking.

When Bergsman quoted from a publication about the giant publicity effort Motown was putting behind her career, Mary responded, "It looks like they were doing a lot, but you're talking about in spaces [spurts], not done right behind each other. . . . You talk about maybe doing the Dick Clark show, then about five months later you do a magazine article, one magazine article, and that might be in just Denver.

"People didn't have a lot to read about me in the earlier days," she continued. "Motown didn't have too much money, so they didn't put out a lot of publicity on me." Indeed, news clips are sparse from the early days of Wells's career. This may be partly because white-owned and white-staffed newspapers in those pre–civil rights days weren't particularly interested in writing about black music, at least not before Motown had succeeded in making such music a mainstream concern. But it also was Motown's fault. Company insiders say the young company failed to concentrate on and professionalize its public relations operation until the spring of 1964.

As soon as that decision was made, the company began issuing a blizzard of press releases and soon scored a major coup by arranging for Wells to be a guest on *The Steve Allen Show* on May 29, 1964.

Ironically, Wells's appearance was a telling indicator of the company's previous PR deficiencies in that it indicated how little the company's acts were known outside pop music audiences at the time. While Mary was talking with Allen during the interview portion of the show, she was asked to name some of Motown's other artists. When she mentioned Little Stevie Wonder, the audience roared with laughter. When she mentioned Smokey Robinson and the Miracles, the people laughed again. They very likely had never heard of these acts and thought the names were funny. Mary kept her cool and merely remarked to Allen and the audience that they would be hearing from these groups later on.

When Mary complained to Bergsman about lacking "recognition," however, she mostly talked about cold, hard cash. "What shows success is money, what you can profit or make off what your trade or occupation is. I wasn't getting the money that I should have. . . . I was being used."

She went on to say, "I had made the company so much money you just don't realize it, because this is a part of history that has never been talked about. They used to call me the girl with the golden goose . . . everything I touched turned to money, without Motown putting any money behind me." Eddie Holland agreed. Mary "was the girl selling the company. I mean really establishing, making this company," he told *Unsung*.

When Bergsman questioned Wells about her contracts with Motown, she called her state of mind at the time she signed them "insanity" and denounced the contracts themselves as unfair.

Mary's ire arose partly from the fact that under her recording contract with Motown, she earned only 3 percent of 90 percent of the suggested retail price of each copy of each of her records sold, less all taxes and packaging costs. These were similar to the terms of many recording contracts at the time. Under the same contract, she, not Motown, also paid for hiring background musicians and for studio time. These were major expenses at Motown, partly because Gordy often insisted on very long in-studio recording sessions to get the sound of a record just right. The twenty-two takes Wells and her accompanying musicians recorded of "Bye Bye Baby" is just one example of this. To be sure, Gordy probably improved the record's quality, and thus its sales, with such perfectionism, but all the expenses, including the fees for the studio musicians, who were paid by the hour, were charged to Mary, not to Gordy or Motown.

In fact, she paid for all expenses related to her recording career out of her royalties—another standard feature of recording contracts. It also was common for recording artists to earn less than they thought they should, or, in fact, very little from the records they produced. But Mary's contracts angered her. "When the real royalties started coming in [minus the deductions Motown took], they said it took so much to record that I didn't get any royalties," she said.

Mary also disliked her Motown management contract. Under Paragraph 13 of that document, for instance, "all moneys that the manager [Gordy] may have to lay out for promotional purposes for the Artist [Wells], such as: publicity, uniforms, musical arrangements, all travel and out-of-town hotel expenses, long-distance telephone expenses of both the Artist and the Manager, and all other necessary expenses are accepted by the Artist as a loan to the Artist from the Manager, and shall be paid back to the Manager by the Artist from the Artist's earnings." In other words, Wells also paid all of her own publicity, touring, and travel expenses, including the cost of Gordy calling back to Motown to find out what was happening.

Mary also was incensed by the percentage that other people at Motown took as the real or alleged writers or cowriters of her songs. And there was another big bone of contention—she specifically accused Motown of underreporting the number of her records that had been sold, thus supposedly paying her even less than she would have earned after expenses.

When Mary would tell Motown executives she thought she deserved more money for a particular hit record, she said, they would tell her that her record only sold five hundred thousand copies. That, she said, was "totally ridiculous. Here, you [could be] talking about a Top 10 pop record and a Top 10 R&B record, and then you're [possibly] talking about the B-side being a Top 15 pop record and a number 1 R&B record. And you're saying that this is all it did?" There's no evidence that Mary ever attempted to have her Motown royalties audited, but even if she had, an accurate audit might have been impossible, since Motown divided each year's sales into two periods and allowed its artists to audit the figures for only one of those periods each year.

When Motown executives told Wells that this was truly the number of records sold, she thought they were lying. "It made me feel very inferior and made me feel like I was being used and abused," she said. The result of her stay at Motown, Mary asserted, "was that I owed the company money for being its major female star."

Backing up the company's contention that Wells was not cheated out of royalties by underreporting of her record sales, depositions in a suit Mary brought against the company when she was trying to leave show that Motown executives testified under oath that "You Beat Me to the Punch," sold 422,573 copies. They also said that "Bye Bye Baby" sold 142,553 copies, "I Don't Want to Take a Chance" 53,347 copies, "Laughing Boy" 120,869 copies, and "You Lost the Sweetest Boy" 371,488 copies. "My Guy," the Motown executives added, had sold 603,750 copies as of June 30, 1964. The executives said these figures sometimes compared unfavorably with the number of records sold by other Motown stars.

These figures seem low. For instance, Esther Gordy Edwards later testified, also under oath, that "My Guy" sold two hundred thousand copies in England alone. Some analysts of Motown's sales figures believe that its executives, knowing its artists were due a percentage on all sales, foreign and domestic, usually mentioned only domestic sales when asked about royalties.

The "My Guy" sales figures were undoubtedly low because they were compiled only two months after the record had hit number one. Many copies were likely sold in America, England, and other countries after that date. But because Motown didn't join the Recording Industry Association of America, which verifies record company sales figures, until 1980, the disputes over the royalties Motown paid Mary and all its other vocalists in the 1960s and 1970s may never be laid to rest completely.

Motown stood out from other record companies in another important way. At most firms, each artist dealt with his or her record company through an outside, independent manager and an outside, independent attorney, both of whom the artist paid directly. But Gordy hired and paid the attorneys who allegedly represented Mary's interests. And the manager of most of Motown's artists, including Mary, was Gordy, the majority stockholder, owner, president, and chairman of the board of Motown. Mary paid him 25 percent of her gross income for his managerial services.

When Mary finally hired her own attorneys in the process of trying to leave Motown, they argued that because of his enormous personal stake in his company's fortunes, Gordy had a major conflict of interest over the expenses assigned to Mary and how much of her time should be used supporting other Motown acts or the company's general goals. What happened if Mary's interests were sometimes different than Motown's? Gordy's argument was that Motown was a united company, operating in the interests of all of its executives and employees at all times.

The unusual nature of Motown's grip on its artists was illustrated in 1986, when the music industry trade press criticized MCA Records for purchasing an artist management firm that represented two of its own artists, Jimmy Buffet and New Edition. The criticism occurred although Buffet and New Edition constituted only a small percentage of MCA's large roster.

Mary also complained that despite her repeated requests, Motown refused to give her a copy of her contract with the company after she had signed it. Raynoma Gordy added substance to this complaint by writing in her autobiography that one day Wells approached her at Motown headquarters in Detroit and asked her for a copy of her contract, insisting she had a right to see it. Mrs. Gordy said she replied, "Wait a minute. It's a standard contract, and it's just a formality. What are you talking about, rights? We're not here to steal your money. You'll always be taken care of. Don't even worry about it." She said she did not give Wells a copy of her contract.

Ironically, and possibly fueling the singer's emotions, Motown tried to calm Mary the same way that some white-owned record companies handled their black artists. "They'd give me a new car and expect me to be grateful," Wells said. Motown executives also made much of the fact that they had given her a "$500 mink stole" for her twenty-first birthday in 1964.

To Wells, it seemed especially unfair that while her own career at Motown had started with a hit record, Motown had supported the Supremes until that group, for years called the "no-hit" Supremes, finally made the big time with their tenth record, "Where Did Our Love Go?" Mary was convinced that the money that nurtured the Supremes was money she had earned, and that that she should have been able to keep it. As Joyce Moore put it, "If you make a million dollars off a person, at least put some of that money back into that person."

By this time Mary was a long way from her first months in the recording industry when, according to vocalist Aretha Franklin, "she was as naïve as the rest of us." The two women were about the same age and began their careers at about the same time, although at different record companies. "We knew we wanted success, and that's about all we knew," Franklin said. "Contracts? Royalties? We didn't have a clue." Obviously, Mary felt she had learned a lot about the music business since her early days as a performer.

But she wasn't earning very much. Motown executives later testified under oath that in 1963, probably Wells's biggest-earning year at the company, her income before taxes consisted of $17,754 in record royalties and $63,267 for personal appearances, bringing her total income before taxes to $81,021. Other people who knew Mary provided numbers fairly close to Motown's. Pete Moore of the Miracles said that when Mary was not yet a star and was opening for his group at California nightclubs in the early 1960s, she was making $1,200 to $1,500 per week, which would be between $62,400 and $78,000 annually. Friendly Womack Jr., who later became one of Wells's brothers-in-law, said that while Mary was a Motown star she was being paid $1,500 per week in cash, or $78,000 a year.

Her income was paltry compared to her equivalents in the music business. For instance, in 1963, when Wells puts four of her tunes in the Top 40, Jackie Wilson, who scored only three Top 40 hits that year, was paid $231,862. Additionally, Wilson had earned $300,000 annually in both 1961 and 1962 while Wells was paid far less. Comparisons with Mary's other near equivalents indicate they all earned larger amounts in earlier years than she earned in 1963, with Dinah Washington earning $100,000 in 1949 and Sam Cooke $250,000 in 1958.

In defending Mary's contracts and earnings and those of almost all other Motown artists, which were similar to Mary's, Berry Gordy argued that no other record company developed its artists through an in-house training program to the extent that Motown did. He also noted that few other record companies kept their artists under contract if they didn't make hits year after year.

Unfortunately for Gordy's argument, while these defenses apply to many Motown artists, they do not apply in Mary's case. Motown gave her very little training, and she started recording hit records from her first day as a Motown artist.

Gordy's best argument over the years has been that if he had never existed, most of the artists who owe their fame to Motown would most likely never have become stars. There were other record companies attempting to harvest Detroit's abundant musical talent at the time, but no one can know what success they might have had in Motown's absence.

In the end, to the dismay of most people who cared about her, Mary concluded that she needed to leave Motown and go out on her own as a recording artist. In hindsight, she was wrong. At the time, the only person inside or outside of Motown who is known to have agreed with her was Herman Griffin, her ex-husband, who doubtless saw himself making big money as the manager of an independent superstar.

Eddie Holland told *Unsung* that "Herman was the key" to Mary's leaving, and his brother Brian called Herman the Svengali behind Mary's departure. Brenda Holloway also attributed Wells's determination to leave Motown to Herman's guidance.

Holloway expressed astonishment at Mary's lifelong tendency to be unduly influenced not only by Griffin but by the opinions of her other lovers, husbands, and boyfriends. According to Holloway, "Women are easily led when they don't have a father in their life."

On a more basic level, Holloway noted, "Mary wasn't a thinker, she was just an artist. And although she was developed as an artist, she wasn't developed as a person." She and Mary were "young and uneducated. We didn't read the *Wall Street Journal* and then sit down and talk about it."

Everyone else, whether Mary consulted them or not, said they opposed the move.

Mary's mother argued that Mary should stay at Motown on the rather self-serving grounds that "these are the people who made you, and if I call and say I need something, I don't have to worry." Smokey Robinson also tried to convince Mary not to leave. The hit songs he had written for her, and the hit songs he was likely to write for her in the future, were the main reasons many Motown people thought she should stay with the company.

Esther Gordy Edwards said Wells would have done better by staying at Motown. "I think she would have been a super superstar if she had stayed." Motown songwriter Mickey Gentile was even more blunt. If Mary had stayed at Motown, he told *Unsung*, "she would have been Diana Ross."

Maye James-Holler said that when Mary kept telling her "she was beat out of money by Motown," and had to leave, "I told her, 'Why don't you get a lawyer and renegotiate your Motown contracts?'" In retrospect, that was exactly what Wells should have done. She was the company's major solo star and its only female solo star. There were no replacements on the horizon. She had Motown by the throat and could have squeezed it for almost any amount she wanted.

In fact, Mary told Steve Bergsman that after she began formal negotiations in 1964 to leave Motown, Gordy offered her 50 percent of the company if she would stay. "And I turned it down," she said, "because I was very hurt. I felt like, why should we have to go through all these changes, mental changes, pain changes, in order for him to do something towards me that was right? So I said to him, 'Forget 50 percent. I just want out. I can't deal with it any longer.'"

She earlier had told the same story to her friends, who were aghast to hear that she had not considered the offer of half of a rising record company. If she was telling the truth, it would have meant not only that she could practically have written her own contract, but also that all artists who became successful at the company, including Diana Ross, whether she had anything to do with them or not, would have poured money into half-owner Wells's pocket, just as they were pouring it into Gordy's.

Trying years later to defend her decision to abandon Motown, Mary told Russi she had believed that because she had made such a big fuss about wanting to leave, the company would have found a way to punish her, possibly by "not releasing stuff [records she had recorded]." That probably wouldn't have happened. Although Motown had delayed some of Wells's releases during her years with the company, that was a result of Gordy's insistence on releasing only material he considered hit quality, rather than any desire to chastise Wells. In any case, refusing to release Wells records for other reasons would have cost Gordy much more money than it would have cost Wells.

At times, Wells blamed Gordy and other Motown executives for not telling her more about the music business and the ways that staying with Motown would have benefited her. But with the head of steam she had built up against them, the young Wells might not have listened.

She noted at one point that she was only twenty-one at the time, and "I left Motown because I wanted to see what I could do on my own. It was just like anybody else leaving home for the first time."

Eventually, however, Mary came to regret her decision. Holloway told an interviewer years later that Mary had come to believe that leaving Motown was "the worst mistake she ever made."

Wells's change of heart occurred after she got to know firsthand how tough it was for her to survive without Motown. In an interview in the 1980s, she said, "If I had been more on top of knowing more about the inside of the business, I probably wouldn't have left. I wouldn't have been as sensitive and as emotional about the situation." In 1983, she bluntly told a reporter for the *Michigan Chronicle*, "I should have stayed at Motown."

12

FIGHTING MOTOWN FOR HER FREEDOM

BB: What about pressure on Motown artists to leave for other labels? You had to deal with that almost from the start, didn't you?

Gordy: The artists were being approached all the time by different people but those approaches fell on totally deaf ears for many years. I remember Smokey coming to me after a few hits with the Miracles. He said that a lady came to him from Scepter Records and offered him a million dollars to come with them.

BB: I guess that was (Scepter President) Florence Greenberg. How did Smokey respond?

Gordy: Smokey was insulted. He said, "How could she think I would [leave], what did she think of me?" I told Smokey, "You'll have a lot of that." Other times, artists might mention various situations where they were approached in subtle ways, but there was never a problem until about 1964. Then Mary Wells left.

—Berry Gordy in *Billboard*, November 5, 1994

On May 13, 1964, when "My Guy" was riding high in the *Billboard* Top 40, Motown threw Wells a fabulous twenty-first birthday party attended by all the Motown big shots. The highlight of the party came when Gordy presented Wells, the company's biggest star, with a mink stole.

Just one week before the party, Wells had recorded the ironically titled tune "When I'm Gone" in Motown's studio. No one of any prominence at the company knew that its top solo vocalist, her ego ballooning as a result of her international superstardom and her resentment growing at what she saw as underpayment and under-appreciation, had decided to leave.

Sometime after the party Mickey Stevenson told Gordy he'd heard that Griffin was telling Wells, and others, that she was being treated badly at Motown. Gordy immediately telephoned Wells and asked her to meet with him in his office. She asked Gordy to come to her home, Apt. 401 at 3320 West Chicago Boulevard, and he dutifully went over there. (The building has since been demolished.) After some small talk, Gordy asked Wells if she was unhappy about anything.

He had a lot at stake. The three-year contract Mary had signed in July 1960 already had been unilaterally extended by Gordy, as was his right under its terms, for another three years. But under Michigan law, because Mary had been a minor when she signed the original contract, she had the right to disaffirm it when she turned 21.

According to Gordy's autobiography, *To Be Loved,* after he asked his question, Wells looked at him as if she felt sorry for him. Understandably, he thought this was a bad sign. Then she told him she wanted him to talk to her lawyer, a New York attorney named Lewis Harris, who would visit him at his office the next day. Gordy thought this was an even worse sign.

Wells's account of the meeting, as told to Steve Bergsman, is that Gordy came to her apartment "and talked to me about why I didn't want to come back to the company." She said she told him, "I enjoy singing, but I could go to church and sing for free."

The atmosphere became highly emotional, according to Wells. Gordy "practically got on his knees" and begged her not to leave. "What I had done was turn the pain loose, and I threw it back on him," she said. "And the pain must have been really agony for him. . . . When you're young, you don't realize these things. . . . I probably wouldn't have left if I knew he was in that much pain."

Gordy probably *was* in pain as he left Mary's apartment, but all he told her on his way out, he wrote, was, "Think about staying with the company."

Attorney Harris duly arrived at Gordy's office the next day, June 17, and told him that Wells, now twenty-one for more than one month, wanted to disaffirm her contract with Motown. When Gordy asked him why, Harris said Wells could get a better deal with another company.

In his book, Gordy says that he then told Harris, "There's more value here than meets the eye, and money is only part of it. Let me show you the whole picture." He then took Harris on a tour of Motown's writers' and producers' rooms, the studio, the management operation, the promotion and sales departments, and the artist development (training) department.

"Even before the tour was over, Harris was full of praise," Gordy wrote. "'Mr. Gordy,' he said, 'I've never seen a company that does so much for any artist.' He was convinced there was no place in the world for Mary but Motown and assured me he was going to tell her just that."

Whether Harris knew that everything he saw was supported in part by revenues from Mary's records or realized just how big her contributions were, isn't known. Gordy hasn't said whether he explained such details to Harris. Harris said later that he thought Mary's contract had expired. He might never have seen it, as Wells has claimed she didn't have a copy at the time.

In any case, Gordy presented Harris with a brand-new contract for Wells to sign. Its terms are unknown. Harris said he would tell Wells that Motown was the best place for her and that she ought to sign the new contract and stay with the company.

Gordy's offer, and her attorney's endorsement of it, were far from what Wells was expecting. She fired Harris immediately and hired a Detroit lawyer, Herbert Eiges. Eiges came out of his corner fighting. His first move was to present Gordy on July 12 with notification from Wells, this time in writing, that she was disaffirming her Motown contract.

Gordy was quoted as being "surprised and hurt" when he learned that Wells was "apparently receptive" to offers from other record companies. "We loved her," he told author David Ritz. "Everyone at the company had a great relationship with Mary."

Eiges filed suit in Wayne County Circuit Court on September 4, 1964, demanding Wells be freed from her Motown contract because she'd been under twenty-one when she'd signed it and now wished to exercise her right to extricate herself. The legal arguments in the resulting court case revolved around somewhat narrow issues.

One was whether Wells had given up her right to leave at that point by continuing to work for Motown for a few weeks past her twenty-first birthday. That tack had worked for another recording company on at least one previous occasion. After Bob Dylan's first album for Columbia Records had gone nowhere following its release in 1962, Dylan had claimed that because he was a minor when he signed his contract with Columbia, he could disaffirm it at age twenty-one. The company argued successfully in that case that the singer had used its studios six or seven times since turning twenty-one, thus affirming the contract.

Court pleadings in Mary's case also dealt with the question of whether the $300,000 Motown said it had invested in training and promoting Wells would be unfairly lost by the company if she were allowed to leave.

Apparently, Wayne County Circuit Court Judge John Wise thought that Motown's positions on both arguments were weak. On October 5, 1964, exactly thirty-one days after the case had been filed, and while Wells was touring with the Beatles in England, he ruled Wells's Motown contract null and void as of that date.

What looked like a complete victory for Wells, however, was actually a great deal less than that. As a result of a general settlement approved by the court, Wells gave up the right to rerecord any of her Motown songs for other companies for five years. And Twentieth Century Fox Records, which turned out to have been negotiating with Wells since July 1964, agreed to pay a percentage of Wells's Twentieth Century royalties to Motown for three years (the time remaining on Wells's renewed Motown contract had it not been declared void).

Most seriously, Wells gave up all future royalties on the records she already had made for Motown in return for a payment of $30,000 from that company. Wells said she regretted this part of the settlement for the rest of her life.

The deal made sense at the time, because Motown executives stopped promoting a song as soon as they thought it had completely exhausted its sales potential, and royalties accordingly dropped off. No one could foresee that an enormous wave of nostalgia for songs by Wells and other Motown stars would develop in future years.

This meant that within Wells's lifetime, advertising agencies, big corporations, Muzak, and Hollywood could and would, endlessly and legally, recycle many of her Motown tunes without paying Wells a dime for the privilege. In contrast, Mary Wilson of the Supremes, who did not sign away her royalties when she left Motown, told one author that years after departing she was earning $80,000 a year in royalties from her hits for that company.

But Motown, too, was hurt by Wells's successful battle to leave. As a young, struggling company, it wasn't exactly rolling in money, and it was a pipsqueak compared to the giant music corporations that could, financially speaking, eat it alive. Mary Wells was its major star. If the big boys like Twentieth Century Fox could watch complacently while Motown nurtured youthful black musicians and then tempt them away with huge bundles of cash, Motown's future looked bleak as anything other than a black feeder to the majors.

"Some people thought, 'Well, that's it for Motown,'" author Nelson George told *Unsung*.

Gordy took immediate action. Neither his long business relationship with Mary, nor the fact that he no longer had to pay her royalties on songs that she already had recorded for him, prevented him from putting into deep storage the tapes of her unreleased songs. He then rerecorded some of those songs with other soloists and groups, the standout example being the Supremes.

Although the Supremes hadn't had any Top 10 hits yet, Motown seemed to see the group's future success on the horizon. It had used that somewhat eerie foreknowledge to reassure the record industry that even with Wells, Motown's big star, on the way out, the Supremes would pick up her baton. In a press release Motown sent to *Billboard* and other publications during Mary's attempt to depart, Barney Ales, Motown's vice president and sales director, said he "would like to alert the industry to a group of young ladies called the Supremes," who "will have the next number 1 record in the U.S., 'Where Did Our Love Go?' on Motown."

The odds were against Ales's brash prediction. The Supremes had already recorded one single for Lupine Records as the Primettes and eight additional singles as the Supremes for Motown. Each record had carried two songs, and none of those eighteen tunes had come closer to the top than number 23 on the *Billboard* pop chart.

The group's most recent song, "Run, Run, Run," backed with "I'm Giving You Your Freedom," had made it only to number 94 on the *Cash Box* pop chart. Many record companies would have told the Supremes to take a hike long before 1964. However, in July 1964, not long after Ales's press release, "Where Did Our Love Go?" hit the big time, rocketing to number 1 on the *Billboard* R&B chart, the *Billboard* pop chart, and the *Cash Box* pop chart. It held that position on all three charts for two weeks.

Mary and Maye James-Holler were driving together when they heard the Supremes on the radio giving their all to that tune, which they believed had been earmarked for Mary. Maye said, "Diane is singing your song!" Mary's reaction was "That's OK. That's Berry's song," which in legal terms it was. But in emotional terms? "Mary's a Taurus," Maye said later. "She's just laid back."

As time passed, Motown continued to punish Mary for her abandonment of the company that had nurtured her professionally. At the time of the contract dispute, Motown had been planning an international and upscale offensive, with Mary becoming the first Motown act to tour the United Kingdom as well as the first Motown performer to appear at New York City's chic Copacabana nightclub. Because Mary's lawsuit seeking release from her Motown contract was still in court when the UK tour arrangements were completed, she started the tour October 9 and completed it thirty-three days later, even though the decision releasing her from her contract had been handed down October 5. But the UK tour was her final act even semi-related to her Motown employment. Motown gave the Copa gig to the Supremes.

Motown did not issue Mary's version of "When I'm Gone," which she had recorded just before telling Gordy she was through, until 1966, although the company did have Brenda Holloway rerecord a version that was released in 1965. "When I'm Gone" is a haunting, sensual tune in any context and obviously had Top 40 potential;

Holloway's version reached number 25 on the *Billboard* pop chart. It's easy to see, though, why Motown waited so long to issue Mary's version, which went nowhere when the company finally released it. If Motown had released it in 1964 or 1965, many listeners, well aware that Mary had recently ruptured her business relationship with Gordy, might have giggled knowingly at lyrics such as "We're happy in the public eye / They think you're such a wonderful guy / But they don't know how much you can lie."

Motown gave other tunes that Mary already had recorded to others for rerecording. The company also gave to other vocalists an unknown number of unrecorded songs that had been written with Mary in mind. Eventually, the company allowed other Motown soloists and groups to rerecord songs by Mary that it had previously released.

Gordy also insisted that all Motown contracts signed by artists when they were under twenty-one be renegotiated and re-signed so that no one else could ever do to him what Mary had done. This tactic resulted in several artists staying at Motown longer than they wanted to, at least in retrospect. Martha Reeves, for instance, found herself committed to a new Motown contract that required her to do two years on top of the eight she had originally signed up for in 1962.

Despite all of Gordy's moves, however, Motown still had a huge problem. As Mary put it, Motown "had to find somebody to take my place" as a solo artist. Although the Supremes took over as the company's big hit-makers, the spot of top female Motown soloist remained unfilled for years.

Motown eventually saved itself through the creativity of its songwriters and producers and the willingness of its vocalists to work extremely hard for what was often less than they could have earned elsewhere.

First, Motown vocalist Chris Clark, a six-foot, white, blue-eyed, platinum blonde whose admirers complimented her by calling her "the white Negress," attempted to replace Wells in the affections of her fans. But although Mary called Clark "the best singer at Motown after I left," Clark had nothing on Wells in the hits department. Her one hit, "Love's Gone Bad," which made it to number 41 on the *Billboard* R&B chart in 1966, rose only to number 105 on the *Billboard* pop chart. Clark eventually rounded off her Motown career by cowriting the screenplay for Motown's first movie, *Lady Sings the Blues*, which stars Diana Ross.

The company was more successful with Kim Weston. Her most popular single, "Take Me In Your Arms (Rock Me a Little While)," released in 1965, rose to number 4 on the *Billboard* R&B chart and to number 50 on the *Billboard* pop chart, and her duet with Marvin Gaye, "It Takes Two," released in 1966, rose to number 4 on the R&B chart and number 14 on the pop chart. She then declined rapidly on both the R&B and pop charts.

Motown did slightly better when it attempted to slip Brenda Holloway into Mary's star slot. Holloway had practically cast herself as a second Mary Wells by singing along to "My Guy" at a DJ convention in a successful attempt to capture Gordy's interest. Not only did Motown hire her, the Beatles chose her as one of the opening acts for their 1965 American tour, a spot Mary had filled on their 1964 UK tour.

Holloway had shown herself to be serious competition for Wells at Motown even before Mary left the company, when Holloway's tune "Every Little Bit Hurts," rose to number 13 on the *Billboard* R&B chart and number 13 on the *Billboard* pop chart in mid-1964. She rose higher on the R&B chart (to number 12) and hit number 25 on the pop chart when she rerecorded Mary's tune "When I'm Gone" in 1965 but declined thereafter.

Eventually, Diana Ross solved Gordy's casting problem in a big way. After years of captivating the public as lead vocalist for the Supremes, she separated from that group in 1970 and replaced

Mary as the company's superstar female soloist, a position she kept until she left Motown in 1981.

Mary certainly noticed Motown's attempts to create a successor after she left, and she was generous in her evaluation of the other soloists' talents. When Chris Clark rerecorded the Wells tune "Whisper You Love Me Boy," in 1968, Mary called it "a slap in the face because it was so much better than mine."

Although the Supremes had saved Motown from a devastating post-Mary decline, relations between Mary and her first employer remained tense for many years.

In 1983, Motown produced a television special titled, *Motown 25: Yesterday, Today, and Forever*, and invited Mary to appear on it.

Although some would say it was amazing that Wells was invited at all, she was of course the entertainer who had given the Motown label its first number one hit and the one who had held the company together economically while the Supremes were struggling to gain traction. Mary performed gamely for the broadcast, singing one verse of "My Guy" while sporting a bulky blonde wig and wearing a blue gown that was attractive but appeared to be made of a substance resembling Bubble Wrap. It more or less disguised the fact that she was pregnant with twins.

Many of Mary's friends and supporters considered it a gross insult that she was given only thirty seconds of stage time in a segment of the show that was meant to honor individual DJs and TV personalities as much as individual vocalists. If so, the insult was followed by injury when Mary later miscarried the twins. She didn't blame it on the performance, however, noting that both her mother and grandmother had miscarried sets of twins.

In any case, Michael Jackson outshone Mary and every other artist on the show by introducing his moonwalk during his appearance. And the after-the-show argument over Mary's treatment was overshadowed by gossip about the behavior of insecure superstar

Diana Ross during the taping of the show. During one performance, apparently believing that her former singing companion Mary Wilson was going to upstage her, Ross shoved the microphone away from Wilson's mouth and pushed Wilson herself toward the back of the stage to prevent the anticipated atrocity. This incident, although not broadcast, was much talked about.

As the number of Motown "returnees" at the 1983 show indicated, Gordy had been unable to prevent an exodus from his company. Included among the departed were Barrett Strong (whose recording of "Money, (That's What I Want)" was essentially Gordy's and Wells's business credo, set to music), Brenda Holloway, Kim Weston, the Isley Brothers, Gladys Knight and the Pips, David Ruffin, Jimmy Ruffin, Eddie Kendricks, Diana Ross, and others. Gordy admitted later, "I would not always pay what it would take for them to stay. That might have been a mistake."

He didn't consider this a devastating financial miscalculation, however, and from his perspective, it may not have been. When Gordy sold Motown to MCA Incorporated and some outside investors for $61 million in 1988, he was beyond pleased. "From eight hundred dollars to $61 million, I had done it. I had won the poker hand," he exults in his autobiography.

As she left Motown in 1964, Mary also thought she had won.

13

AN EXPLOSIVE CONFRONTATION

Untune that string, and hark what discord follows.
—*Troilus and Cressida*, by William Shakespeare

In early 1964, months before she walked out of Motown, Wells had begun discussing a move to a larger and richer record company—one that would pay her more. In the process, she and Herman Griffin decided they needed a third person on their team.

Their gaze settled on another hard driver in the competitive Detroit recording industry: Robert West. This six-foot-one music producer and entrepreneur had big plans, a hard-boiled personality, extensive record industry experience, and a history of competing against Motown. Unfortunately, he also had an out-of-control temper, as well as a handgun he always carried and didn't hesitate to draw and point at others at the least provocation.

Despite West's rough edges, Griffin and Wells were impressed that he had sold several hit records to New York companies, including the Falcons' "You're So Fine" to United Artists and Bettye LaVette's "My Man, He's a Lovin' Man" to Atlantic.

"West had worked with Atlantic and had been to New York," LaVette noted. By contrast, she said, most of the people in the record business in Detroit "had never talked to anyone from New York before. So if you had that, it gave you kind of a leg up."

West also had plenty of incentive to try to show up Berry Gordy, a fact that no doubt appealed to Mary and Griffin. An early pioneer in the field of black crossover music, West had been embarrassed by Gordy's ability to woo away his best performers as well as by Gordy's superior business skills.

In the late 1950s, West had begun to produce recordings by black artists that would appeal to both white and black listeners. He hired Marv Johnson as the vocalist for one of these attempts, but the song failed to chart. Johnson promptly separated from West and rose to number 9 on the *Billboard* pop chart on the United Artists label in 1960 by recording "I Love the Way You Love," which was cowritten by Gordy.

West then released "Where's the Joy, Nature Boy?" sung by so-so vocalist Brian Holland, which also failed to succeed as an R&B or pop song. Holland thanked West politely, then signed on at Motown.

Something obviously was not working, but the energetic West tried again, releasing a record by Little Joe and the Moroccos featuring vocalist Joe Harris. That record didn't do well either. Harris eventually became a member of the successful Motown act the Undisputed Truth.

Finally, in 1959, West had his first significant success as a record producer. After his recording of "You're So Fine" became a Detroit-area hit, West decided to gain national distribution by licensing the master recording of the tune to United Artists. As a result, the song reached number 2 on the *Billboard* R&B chart and number 17 on the *Billboard* pop chart.

Yet West failed to take the next logical step and fell even further behind Gordy as far as making real money was concerned. Gordy, angered by the low royalties he was receiving for hit songs that he wrote and then licensed to other companies for manufacturing and distribution, began to expand Motown's in-house capacity in order to keep a bigger share of a song's profits. He developed the ability to press his own records and then began to distribute them nationally instead of licensing them to other record firms. West did none of these things. Either he didn't realize that he needed to, or he lacked the money or connections to make the effort.

Nevertheless, West persevered. He thought he heard something in the sound produced by Florence Ballard, Diana Ross, and Mary Wilson, who then called themselves the Primettes, and recorded the very first song this group committed to vinyl, "Tears of Sorrow." But by the time West released this record, the Primettes had migrated to Motown and become the Supremes, a name Berry Gordy by then owned through his contract with the group. West was forced to release "Tears" as a Primettes record and it flopped, failing to hit the R&B or pop charts. The Supremes went on to become the world's most successful female vocal group and a moneymaking machine for Motown, not for West. By 1964, when West was only fifty-two, it looked like his career was tanking.

At that moment, Griffin and Wells were not only plotting to put Wells's career partly in West's hands but also trying to convince other talented people to escape Motown's grip and join them.

Wells herself started with a direct, solo approach. She called Brian Holland and asked him to write songs for her that she would then record with another company. According to court documents filed in connection with Mary's suit for freedom from Motown, Holland refused, pointing out that he had an exclusive contract with that company.

Then Griffin joined Wells in making the same pitch to Motown producer Mickey Stevenson, asking him to produce records by Wells for companies that might include MGM, ABC Paramount, and United Artists. Stevenson said he told Wells and Griffin he couldn't do that because of his Motown contract. Griffin and Wells then suggested, according to Stevenson, that he secretly produce some Wells records that the couple would then take to other companies. He refused.

At around the same time, Stevenson said, he was approached by record business entrepreneur Clarence Avant, who claimed to represent MGM Records. Avant told Stevenson MGM was interested in acquiring Mary's services but only if it could hire a Motown producer to go along with her. Avant also said that if Stevenson and Wells moved to MGM as a team, he could assure Stevenson an annual income of $60,000 to $70,000 a year, a commanding figure in 1964. Stevenson refused that request as well. (Years later, Avant became president of Motown Records.)

West called Clarence Pauling, a Motown producer and songwriter, soon thereafter and offered Pauling 10 percent of Wells's gross earnings if Pauling would produce records by her for a company other than Motown. Pauling said he refused.

The emphasis on finding a producer for Wells stemmed from Wells's and Griffin's belief that the right person doing this job could make songs recorded by even superstar singers much more attractive. However, the effort hadn't worked. West and Griffin decided to sign Wells with a New York City company and worry about the issue later.

So in July 1964, West and Griffin flew from Detroit to New York to negotiate on Wells's behalf with Twentieth Century Fox Records and other interested parties. Wells, along with her personal manager and best friend, twenty-three-year-old Maye James-Holler, was already there. Then at the height of her popularity, Wells had just finished a weeklong engagement at Freedomland U.S.A., in the Bronx. (Having opened in 1960, the history-themed park, although proclaimed the East Coast equivalent of California's Disneyland, was built over a swampy area and plagued by mosquitoes. It went bankrupt and was demolished shortly after Wells's engagement there ended.)

After arriving in New York City, West and Griffin moved into a suite on the seventh floor of Manhattan's Savoy Plaza Hotel. Wells and Maye James-Holler were staying in a similar suite on the fifth floor. At about 11 PM on July 23, Maye was in the suite she was sharing with Wells. "Mary had jumped in the shower and had gone to bed," Maye said. "I was so tired I just wanted to lie down," but first she had to prepare some papers for the next day. Griffin and West had been out but had returned to their room a few moments before. Griffin, nattily dressed in his customary suit and tie, went down to the room occupied by the two women, knocked on the door, and told Maye, who was working at the desk in the living room, that he had to tell Mary something. He went into the bedroom, talked to Mary for a minute, and then returned to the living room.

Maye, who could overhear the conversation between Griffin and Mary, said Griffin was "talking crazy about West." Both Griffin and West had been drinking before Griffin came down to visit Wells. "They always drank," Maye said. "Herman drank more than West, but he was a fun guy. If he got sloppy drunk, he'd dance. West was more like a business guy. Even when he was drunk, he was always serious."

Griffin was still in the women's suite when West knocked on the door and Maye admitted him. While the two men talked in the living room, Maye walked through the bedroom she shared with Wells to use the adjoining bathroom. When she came out of the bathroom, she could hear West and Griffin starting to shout at each other. "They were talking crazy," Maye said. "Then they started arguing. Mary was in the living room telling them to calm down."

When the men didn't pay any attention to her, Mary, disgusted, joined Maye in the bedroom. "I could tell this argument was going another place," Maye said. "It was going crazier and crazier."

Then the two men began to tussle with each other. The frightened women stood behind the closed door of their bedroom in silence listening to them. "We didn't know what to do," Maye said. "Then we heard a gun go off."

Stunned, Maye hurriedly took Wells into the bathroom so that they could be as far as possible from whoever had fired the gun. They closed the bathroom door and huddled together against the bathroom's far wall. Maye then realized that she had forgotten to lock the bathroom door. At just that moment, the door began to push open slowly, "just like in a horror movie." The two women, clutching each other with fear, remained pressed against the bathroom wall as the door opened. "Herman Griffin was standing there with blood all over him," Maye said. Griffin stared at them with a stunned look on his face. "What happened, Momma?" he asked Wells, using his pet name for her. Frozen with fear, Wells said nothing.

While Griffin stood there as if paralyzed, Maye found the courage to walk past him into the bedroom and pick up the telephone on the night table between the twin beds. She dialed the hotel operator and said there had been a shooting in the room. When the operator asked Maye if she was able to leave the room, Maye and Wells quickly pulled on blouses and skirts and not much else. "One of us wasn't wearing shoes," Maye remembered. They walked out past West, who was lying motionless on the floor, while Griffin continued to stand frozen in the bathroom. Then the two women walked slowly down the hallway. "You know how hotels used to have those very long halls?" Maye said. "I was so afraid that before we got to the corner of the long hall and got on the elevator we would be shot."

The women, arriving safely in the lobby, staggered off the elevator into the arms of the NYPD. Police officers took them outside and put them in the back seat of a police car. While they were sitting there, Maye said, a photographer snapped a picture of them. She felt that the photographer got a good picture of her, since she considered herself totally innocent and unashamed and made no effort to hide her identity, but Wells hid her face with her hands.

The police then took them to the local precinct house and put each woman in a different interrogation room with just a table and chair for company. "We sat in that police station for so long," Maye said. "Meanwhile they did their detective thing. They would tell Mary what I said and tell me what Mary said. Back and forth. I was so tired I wanted to cry. I put my head down on the table and tried to go to sleep."

Maye said she kept telling the cops that she knew nothing, except that two people had come into their room and one had shot the other over something she didn't understand. She would say nothing else and kept trying to sleep. She said the detectives were laughing because while they were hustling back and forth Maye seemed so relaxed that she was trying to log her eight hours of zzzz's.

Later, Maye was questioned about the incident by legendary Manhattan District Attorney Robert M. Morgenthau. But by then, she had finally gotten some sleep. "I remember sitting in Mr. Mogenthau's office. He was very nice to me," she said.

Robert Bateman, who had arranged for Mary's initial meeting with Gordy and was still in touch with Mary at this time, said the dispute was over whether Mary would sign with Atlantic Records or Twentieth Century Fox Records. Mary insisted on the latter because it was a subsidiary of Twentieth Century Fox Film Corporation and she wanted to go into the movies. But West had apparently taken some money from Atlantic, which also was seeking Wells's services. "He was drinking and was afraid something was going to happen to him if Mary didn't take the deal he had signed her up for," Maye said.

Bettye LaVette, who wasn't present but apparently talked to Griffin later, provided more details on what went on while Mary and Maye were hiding in their bathroom. The dispute between the two men became so heated, LaVette said, that West pulled what she called "his little ragged gun" on Griffin. "Herman ran toward West and pushed his hand back. The gun fired and the bullet went through West's eye and through his brain."

The *New York Daily News* reported that the bullet had plowed into West's head just above his left eye. He was taken to Roosevelt Hospital; amazingly, he survived.

Griffin, accused of assault, was hauled before a Manhattan Grand Jury on November 17, 1964, where Irving Lang, one of Morgenthau's assistant district attorneys, attempted to convince the jurors to indict him. Lang failed, possibly because Griffin told the jury the same story he had told LaVette, and Griffin walked. He was not only free of legal charges but also remained active in the music business.

West said later that all he remembered about the incident was "ending up on the floor" of the hotel room. After recovering at Roosevelt and finding that he was going to be blind in one eye for the rest of his days, he finally decided that struggling against Motown was a losing proposition. He moved to Las Vegas and worked at various jobs, occasionally sending out material about his former musical activities via a post office box, until his death from natural causes in 1983.

14

MOVING TO TWENTIETH

Mary Wells is a talented girl with a special and unique quality of voice; but . . . without the services of persons, including [Smokey Robinson] and other writers, arrangers, and other skilled persons, she would be unable to make successful recordings in the style to which the public has become accustomed.

—Attorney for Motown Record Company,
Wells vs. Motown, 1964

The public purchasing such records places the greatest value upon the vocalist who makes the record.

—Attorney for Mary Wells, *Wells vs. Motown*, 1964

Mary Wells, fresh off a number one song, had avoided injury during the Griffin-West shooting incident. She was also now free from Motown's yoke and searching for a new record company. Corporate talent scouts swarmed around her, hoping to get lucky. Quincy Jones, the famous musician and composer, who in 1964 was vice president of Mercury Records, visited Mary to try to convince her to join forces with him. She also was courted by Atlantic,

MGM, ABC Paramount, United Artists, Warner Brothers/Reprise, RCA Victor, and Twentieth Century.

Helping her deal with the torrent of offers was her new manager, George Scheck. Mary hired Scheck after the arrest of Herman Griffin and the shooting of Robert West had forced her to dispense with their services. She had divorced Griffin in Detroit more than a year before the shooting, but now he could no longer remain her manager either.

Scheck was not necessarily the best choice Mary could have made. He was managing Bobby Darin and Connie Francis, both extremely popular vocalists at the time, and may have had trouble devoting the necessary time to Mary's career. In a way, her experience with Scheck was a repeat of her experience with Johnnie Mae Matthews, Mary's first boss, who also managed Otis Williams and the Distants as well as Popcorn and the Mohawks, and had done more for Williams than for her other clients.

Scheck, however, is universally remembered as a tough and driving manager. Many of his clients also recall his little son Barry running in and out of his father's office while George dealt with them. Later, Barry became a lawyer, and was part of the dream team that successfully defended O. J. Simpson when the football great was charged with murder. He now codirects the Innocence Project, an organization dedicated to exonerating wrongfully convicted people through DNA testing and reform of the criminal justice system.

While Wells's attorneys were fighting Motown for her release, Wells, at the urging of George Scheck and Clarence Avant, made three new master recordings at the New York City facilities of Capitol Records. Former Motowner Robert Bateman, who had left that company and become a freelancer in 1962, produced two of them. Bateman was the man who had connected Wells to Gordy in the first place and, later in the decade, he would produce the first post-

Motown records cut by another much publicized Motown departee, former Supreme Florence Ballard.

While Wells was making these recordings, she was still arguably covered by her Motown contract, and she did not yet have a contract with any other firm. Because of this, the recording sessions were held late at night so there would be less chance of Motown finding out about them. According to author Fred Bronson, "a curtain of anxiety hung over the sessions."

Avant first presented the finished products to Arnold Maxin, president of MGM Records. Maxin noted that one of the records, probably "Jive Guy," was basically a rewrite of "My Guy." He also said only one of them was "acceptable," but it isn't clear which one he meant. Finally, he decided to reject all three. Maxin then told the Wells team he would sign the singer only if she were accompanied by a Motown producer, something that Griffin, West, and Wells had already tried hard to accomplish without success.

Twentieth Century Fox Records, excited by Wells's potential, told the Wells team they liked the records. But the company directed the team to improve them electronically and make additional recordings at Bell Sound Studios, also in New York City. They did so, starting September 14, 1964. Among the songs recorded at Bell were two released later that year by Twentieth, "Ain't It the Truth" and "Stop Takin' Me for Granted," as well as others not released until later: "How Can I Forget Him," "I'm Sorry," "Jive Guy," "My Mind's Made Up," "Say What You Gotta Say" (in which Mary has a hard time staying in key) and a song titled "Memories Are Creeping Up on Me" (the oft-repeated refrain in the actual song is "Memories keep creeping up on me").

Then confusion erupted. In a move to sample the industry reaction to a post-Motown Mary Wells, Morty Craft, the creative director of Twentieth Century Fox, wrote to record distributors throughout the country, including some who distributed Motown records. He stated that his company was about to acquire Wells's exclusive services and asked them "to show your interest in this artist and Twentieth Century Fox Records" by sending in an advance of $3,000 each. The advance would be applied against the distributors' future purchases of Twentieth Century Fox records. Craft obligingly promised to return any advance he received if "the deal falls through."

It's doubtful that any distributors followed up by sending money to Craft, because Motown immediately sent telegrams to Twentieth Century and the other record companies the Wells team had approached, notifying them that Wells was still under exclusive contract to Motown. Motown executives made sure other organizations knew about these telegrams by sending *Billboard* a press release about them. (This is the same release in which Motown exec Barney Ales accurately predicted the success that the Supremes were shortly to achieve.) The subsequent *Billboard* story was headlined, "Reminder Is Issued by Motown."

Although Motown's tone in its telegrams bordered on outrage that other companies would poach on its turf, the court decision that released Mary from Motown was handed down shortly thereafter.

While her handlers negotiated, Wells herself had been seriously concerned about where she would go. She knew that Motown was the only major black-owned record company and that most major white-owned companies had little or no experience with black music. Now, however, she was thrilled by Craft's boldness on her behalf and his previous record with black artists. "I felt like, Wow, this is great," she said. "He's a white guy who knows how to handle black recording artists, business-wise and promotion-wise. I thought it was a great move."

Craft was well known in the music business for his success with black vocalists Shirley Mae Goodman and Leonard Lee (who sang as "Shirley and Lee"), Louis Jordan, Roy Milton, Little Esther, Faye Adams, and Percy Mayfield.

Nevertheless, some cronyism may have been involved in Mary's move to Twentieth. "Craft and Scheck were good buddies. That's why Scheck took Mary to Twentieth," said Mickey Gentile, who worked on Mary's first three songs at that company. Twentieth "had plenty of money and the name, but they weren't on the charts and didn't know how to handle major artists." If he had been handling Mary's career, Gentile said, he would have taken her to Atlantic or Columbia Records.

Mary made the move to Twentieth Century as soon as possible because of its movie connections and because the company paid her a $250,000 advance, tremendous money in those days and the equivalent, when inflation is taken into account, of some of the startlingly large advances paid to recording stars in recent years. She signed a contract with Twentieth guaranteeing her this advance in the fall of 1964.

For someone who had only recently lived in a small Detroit apartment and fed herself on the road on little jars of pigs' feet she bought at a 7-Eleven store, a quarter of a million dollars seemed limitless. Wells had always said she was a great recording artist, and here, finally, was cash to match her status. "I was finally paid a decent salary for my work," she said later. On another occasion she said that "from a financial viewpoint, this is the best deal I ever made."

Gordy was stunned when he heard she was offered $250,000. "There was no way I could compete with the money being offered her," he said. "I couldn't begin to bid against the major labels."

Mary reacted to the quarter million as some would have expected. "We spent it," Maye James-Holler said.

One item Mary spent it on was an apartment at 1245 Park Avenue in Manhattan, on the north side of Ninety-Sixth Street at that street's intersection with Park Avenue. In renting it, Mary seemed to be extending her crossover achievements in the music world to her living situation; Ninety-Sixth Street was the informal border between Harlem, the city's most famous black neighborhood, and the large white residential area south of that street. The building now hosted Mary in one apartment and eight other "Negroes" in various other apartments, according to the *New York Times*, which sent reporter Gay Talese to the intersection to do a story about black people moving into the building.

In his article, which appeared in the *Times* on June 23, 1965, Talese describes Park Avenue south of Ninety-Sixth Street as an area "of poodles and polished brass; it is cab country, tip-town, glass-ville, a window-washer's paradise." The area north of Ninety-Sixth Street was by contrast "shadowed by elevated railroad tracks and wobbling with winos . . . where women's heads, not air conditioners, pop out of windows." The story was accompanied by a photo of Mary's head sticking out her apartment window. (1245 Park Avenue still operates as an apartment house and seems none the worse for wear.)

According to Maye, she and Mary spent the advance on more than the apartment itself. "We had drivers and everything. If you're spending money and not bringing it in, it goes fast." Especially the way Mary did it. Songwriter Micky Gentile told *Unsung* that around this time Mary asked him and her new manager, George Scheck, where she could get a car. Gentile asked her what kind of car she already had, and she replied that she didn't have one. Gentile and Scheck glanced at each other in surprise, because they both knew that Mary had a high-salaried chauffeur on her payroll.

Curtis Womack said his brother Cecil visited Wells and James-Holler at around the same time and reported that they "were living high on the hog. They were paying everybody and going out and doing this and that."

The "this and that" includes attempts by Mary and Maye to continue their social life as youngsters, this time in the Big Apple. One night, unfamiliar with Manhattan, they decided to go to the Times Square area to take in a movie, not realizing that most movie theaters there were porno palaces. They blithely walked into one porno theater, expecting conventional entertainment. Even before they got to their seats, they noticed that all the other patrons were male and, in Maye's words, "the place smelled like piss." Maye also noticed that the theater was apparently where men went "to do what they had to do." The two women looked at each other, told each other, "We've got to get out of here," and rushed back out onto the sidewalk, where they laughed uncontrollably and congratulated each other on their narrow escape.

Later on they visited the famous Rolling Stone club in midtown Manhattan where they danced just like they had at Detroit's Greystone. Maye said she danced with actor Steve McQueen. He tried to get better acquainted with her, but Maye was too shy to deal with him. Meanwhile, "Mary was unable to have a good time because everybody kept asking for her autograph."

15

JACKIE WILSON AND CARL DAVIS

Mary sure liked her men.

—Maye James-Holler, 2009

Although happy to leave Motown for good, Mary still needed to settle one crucial detail—she didn't want to abandon the man she had said was her boyfriend, Brian Holland.

After Wells left the company, she said, she called Holland from New York and asked him, "Why don't you leave there? Then we could work together and build something together." Wells wanted Holland to join her in New York City and help her advance her career. "We were young, and he had talent, and I had my talent."

According to Mary, Holland, still hoping to rise with H-D-H at Motown, refused. Holland says he was dedicated to Motown and never thought of leaving it. Meanwhile, Wells said, she missed him terribly. "I went through a lot of pain because I was missing him. I loved him. I was still a girl, and I needed him with me." After agonizing for a while, however, "I got the courage to pull away from him," Mary said.

Telling Holland "we could build something together" was the essential Wells. As her longtime friend Randy Russi said, "Mary had a big problem: she wanted men with her. They had to work with her or for her or tag along." Will Porter, her bandleader in her later years, noted, "Mary was always used to being handled by a man." When Mary's mother died a few years later, "Mary was very impressed that Mary Wilson showed up at the funeral by herself" without a man, Porter said. As much as possible, Wells went from one man to another.

Eventually, H-D-H decided that Wells had been right. Although they had written no fewer than twenty-five top ten pop songs for Motown from 1963 to 1967, making them history's most successful rock 'n' roll songwriting team, they were not as rich as they thought they should be. In 1968, they left Motown and founded the Invictus and Hot Wax record labels. But by that time Mary had moved on to new men and new record companies. The team's tardiness angered Wells. "They saw things much slower than I did," she said to Steve Bergsman. "I really got hurt real bad by that, because I truly thought we [Wells and Brian Holland] would have been a good couple."

According to Mary, Holland apparently thought so, too. Mary said he once again proposed to her during this period and was angered when she refused him a second time. "He figured that during those months that I was missing him I should have just waited until he saw the light," the somewhat embittered Wells said. Holland denied proposing to Wells on either occasion.

By her own account, however, Mary, always a hard charger, was not the kind of woman who would wait for Holland or any other man. "Anger built up in me, confusion, and I got involved with another guy, Jackie Wilson, to get Holland off of my mind," she said.

Wilson, the man for whom she had written "Bye Bye Baby," had been her first crush. "I idolized him," she said. "I grew up with his music." In 1965, while she and Maye James-Holler were staying at the Sheraton Hotel in Manhattan waiting for their luxury apartment to be decorated, Wells decided to go to a Jackie Wilson concert. Because she was now an international superstar, Wilson's handlers couldn't help noticing that she was in the audience. Since they also knew that she had written her first song for Wilson, they would have been terribly remiss had they not invited her backstage after the show. Wilson reminded Wells of how much he admired her singing. Wells reminded him sincerely that she thought he was a great artist and that she had admired his music for years. Not one to miss a cue, Wilson, who was separated from his wife, immediately invited her to dinner. She accepted, and they went out to a fancy restaurant. He immediately heightened his appeal to Wells by educating her on what he saw as some of the nuances of high living, a likely turn-on for the semi-fatherless girl from inner-city Detroit.

When Wilson asked Mary if she would like a drink and she suggested scotch and water, he told her a lady always drinks pink ladies and raspberry daiquiris and ordered her one of each, so she could choose. After she picked one and drank it, he told her, "This is as far as I ever want you to go, just a small drink every night." From Wells's point of view, "He had finesse, he had . . . class. He knew the best places to eat. He knew how to conduct himself as a gentleman." To top it all off, over the next few days, she said, Wilson bought her $25,000 worth of clothing.

They started dating regularly, with Wells becoming more and more enamored. After three months, he suggested that she move into his apartment until her apartment was ready. Then the trouble began.

First there were the drugs. Wells saw Wilson "messing" with a white powder, which he told her was cocaine. "I'd never seen any cocaine before," she said. "So I said, 'What is that you're putting in your nose?'" After he told her she said, "I wouldn't dare put anything like that in my nose," and didn't participate.

Then there was the alcohol—lots of it. "Jackie was drinking hard," she noted. "He's the only man I know who could take drugs and drink the way he did."

Wilson also turned out to be extremely jealous and possessive. When Mary tried to leave his apartment without him at the end of their first week of living together, he told her, "You don't go nowhere. You stay in this apartment. It's a beautiful place."

Wells had had enough. When Wilson left the apartment on business, she called Maye James-Holler, who was still living in their suite at the Sheraton, and said, "I'm coming home." Wilson came back, found out she had decamped to her hotel, and became furious. He barged into the Sheraton suite, where Wells, forewarned by the front desk, was hiding under the bed. "You tell her that Jackie came by here to get her and I *will be back*," Wilson told Maye.

Wilson was well known for his drug use, drinking, and womanizing. Wilson biographer Tony Douglas, in his book *Jackie Wilson: The Man, The Music, The Mob*, refers to the singer's "untold affairs with women both married and single." Among these women were both Wells and Joyce Moore, before her marriage to Sam Moore (of Sam and Dave). The two women later compared their experiences.

Wells's analysis in retrospect was that by linking himself with her, Wilson was trying to get back at his wife by moving in with a young girl. She didn't see Wilson again until after her second marriage.

Mary's second romantic entanglement in New York was with the talented record business pro she finally hired as her producer, Carl Davis.

Davis said he didn't know Wells was looking for a producer until one of the artists he was already handling, Gene Chandler, best known for his hit song "Duke of Earl," was appearing at the Apollo with Wells. Wells told Chandler she was leaving Motown and would need a producer, and Chandler, aware of her talent and struck by her general attractiveness and needy look, suggested that Davis visit Wells to discuss that possibility.

Davis, a Chicago resident, flew to New York to see Wells and visited her at the now fully decorated Park Avenue Apartment she and

Maye James-Holler were sharing, an elegant two-bedroom suite with a marble foyer, white and lavender rooms, white carpeting, a piano, and what Davis called "a gorgeous Afghan hound." More important, a gorgeous Mary also was in the apartment.

"Like anybody else," Davis said, "before I would agree to produce somebody, I wanted to get to know her. So I wanted to meet Mary and find out what kind of person she was. I found out she was a wonderful person, a lovely, beautiful, talented lady, and a great artist."

They soon started a romantic relationship as well as a professional one. "She was gorgeous and a really sweet person," Davis said. They were together for at least a year, working and vacationing. "Carl was absolutely drop-dead in love with her," Joyce Moore said.

However, Davis said, their relationship was plagued by jealousy. On one occasion, it was *his* jealousy problem. He heard a rumor that Wells was cheating on him with one of the Four Tops, "so I broke up with her over the phone," he said, then flew to Houston for the first ever national R&B convention. Wells, in a fighting mood, called him there and told him, "I didn't do anything wrong, and if you want to break up with me, do it to my face." She immediately flew to Houston, and when she walked into the airport terminal, Davis said, "She was so beautiful I forgot about the problem." Soon, Davis and Wells were engaged to be married and Davis had given her an engagement ring.

On another occasion, the jealousy was all Mary's. Davis was producing a record by a group called the Peaches in his Chicago studio when Mary visited him, "looking as good as can be, with long pretty hair," according to Davis's account of the incident in his autobiography, *The Man Behind the Music*. Then she saw the Peaches. "She started fussing at them," saying, "I don't want any of you-all flirting with my man, because you-all can't afford him," he wrote. She then started telling them what they were allowed to do and not allowed to do. Davis objected, resulting in a major fight between Wells and Davis. Although the couple later kissed and made up, Davis did note that some time later he married one of the Peaches, so perhaps Mary's fears were understandable.

They weren't able to solve their next breakup so easily. Davis went to work for Columbia Records and flew out to California to promote an appearance by R&B singer Major Lance on the TV program *Shindig!* While he was there, a female colleague of Davis's came over to his hotel room to help him work out a plan for promoting Lance. Noting that the colleague was a "really nice lady and very professional" but that she "just wasn't my type," Davis said nothing untoward happened in the hotel room.

Mary had traveled to California to visit Davis, however, and "thought something was going on between this girl and me," he said. Mary visited him in his room, broke a glass, and attempted to cut him with the jagged edge. He avoided injury but had his room changed so she couldn't try to assault him again. He also instructed the hotel staff not to give her his new room number. When Wells recovered her composure and began feeling sorry for her actions, Davis wrote, she ran around the hotel looking for him, yelling, "Carl! Carl, come back baby. I'm sorry!"

When Davis returned to New York after the promotional trip, however, Wells became angry again, and, in his words, "had a hissy fit." She also threw at him "the three-and-a-half carat engagement ring that I had paid $20,000 for." He caught the ring in the air, but it wasn't the ring that he wanted, it was Wells. Shortly thereafter, he flew to meet her in Cleveland, where she was performing, "to see if we could work things out." He tried to reason with Mary, pointing out that "the girl she thought I was having an affair with was not very attractive. I don't know why she would have thought I had done something like that."

Davis said he "never could figure out why" Mary was so jealous. Perhaps she hadn't told him about some of her previous experiences, such as her betrayal by Griffin.

The relationship ended when Davis ran into Cecil Womack, with whom Mary was beginning to get involved, in Cleveland, and had his own hissy fit. "If she wanted Cecil Womack or anyone over Carl Davis, that was a bad decision," he said. "I didn't want to have anything more to do with her. When I walked away from Cleveland, I never spoke to her again and never listened to her again."

16

SINGING FOR TWENTIETH

Lots of acts with any label have a sad story to tell.

—Will Porter to *Unsung*

The first thing I look for [in potential Motown vocalists] is personality and character. . . . Sometimes you will get a man who has talent but nothing else and you will nurse him along to the big time. Then he goes, say, to New York and others . . . promise him movies and TV and all. . . . No loyalty, no character. It can be very serious.

—Berry Gordy in an interview with the *Detroit Times*, February 25, 1960

Mary's rock 'n' roll stardom not only affected her ability to move about unnoticed in public, but it also inflamed her ambition and made her believe she could be a movie star as well as a music star. Twentieth Century Fox Records fit perfectly into Mary's scheme, because it was a subsidiary of the Twentieth Century Fox Film Corporation. Mary's movie ambitions also may have been another reason for her choice of George Scheck as her first post-Motown manager after Herman Griffin. His major client, vocalist

Connie Francis, had moved successfully into Hollywood semi-stardom, appearing in films such as *Where the Boys Are*, *Follow the Boys*, and *Looking for Love*.

Although Craft had treated Wells with warmth and courtesy when he was trying to recruit her for his label, he didn't turn out to be the friendly mentor Mary was hoping for. During their negotiations, Mary told him she wanted to be a movie star, and he promised to make her one. That promise "wasn't in the contract, of course, but why should I feel sorry I tricked her?" he told Charlie Gillett, who quoted him in his 1975 book *Making Tracks*. "If she's so crazy with overblown ambition, she deserves what she gets."

Wells, apparently embarrassed by the eventual failure of her plans for a film career, and probably having heard what Craft had said about her, told Bergsman years later that although she had indeed harbored movie ambitions, she didn't talk to Twentieth Century about them. "I thought that with the hit records that I was making over at Motown, I could do it with Twentieth and then eventually get into movies," she said. But all Twentieth Century Records promised her was "what I asked for. I asked for a record deal, a production deal, and they gave me a good one." One reason she "didn't talk to them about acting was because I figured I had to go to school for that. I wanted to be really great, like I was as a singer, and I figured school would be better."

Wells's longtime confidante Maye James-Holler put it more bluntly and truthfully in 2011: "Twentieth Century did Mary wrong," Maye said. "They told her she was going to do movies and TV."

Although Mary never made a movie at Twentieth, she was quick off the mark as a Twentieth Century vocalist. "I was a hit machine they thought could sell anything," she said.

Twentieth Century was a relative newcomer to the record business and anxious to succeed. It previously had produced only one Top 10 pop hit, "Navy Blue" by (white) vocalist Diane Renay.

Hoping for another success, the company released Wells's first post-Motown record, "Ain't It the Truth" backed with "Stop Takin' Me for Granted" in October 1964. Mary did a good job with these new songs, in part because they were similar to her Motown tunes. They were in fact produced by former Motown record producer Robert Bateman, who made a habit of hiring other present or former Motowners to help in the production process.

Bateman seemed unsure which of Mary's two Motown paths he should take, however. "Ain't It the Truth" was a finger-snapping rhythm and blues tune with gospel-style backing vocals. Although Mary's voice while singing it was smooth rather than gritty, "Ain't It" sounds similar to "Bye Bye Baby," her first Motown song.

By contrast, "Stop" is very similar to the coy and vulnerable hits Wells had produced with Smokey Robinson after Robinson had decided those qualities were among her major vocal assets. The song is distinguished by a dramatic gap between the words "Stop" and "takin' me for granted," which made it memorable for thousands of listeners.

The pop chart results for both songs were confusing. Although her vulnerable songs had done better at Motown than her blues style tunes, in this case the reverse occurred. "Ain't It the Truth," the blues-style tune, rose to number 45 on the *Billboard* pop chart while the relatively shy-sounding and understated "Stop Takin' Me for Granted" stopped at number 88.

Mickey Gentile, who wrote "Stop Takin' Me for Granted" with his wife Jennifer Lambert, said "Mary sang the song perfectly" and he had thought it was going to reach at least number five on the pop charts. While admitting it wasn't as good as "My Guy," he called "Stop" a "very nice soft R&B pop song," very much like the successful songs Mary previously had recorded. Critics said, however, that neither tune was as good as her final records for Motown.

Twentieth Century kept trying. Andre Williams, who produced Wells's next record, created another Motown-soundalike, "Use

Your Head." Released in 1964, it reached a respectable number 34 on the *Billboard* pop chart, number 41 on the *Cash Box* pop chart, and an even better number 13 on the *Billboard* R&B chart, all in late January and early February 1965.

Carl Davis produced Wells's next song, "Never, Never Leave Me," a wistful nightclub-style ballad that Twentieth Century released in 1965. Originally written by Gentile and his wife for Dionne Warwick rather than for Mary, "Never, Never Leave Me," backed with "Why Don't You Let Yourself Go" reached number 53 on the *Cash Box* pop chart, number 15 on the *Billboard* R&B chart and number 54 on the *Billboard* pop chart.

Some critics complained that the record made Mary sound as if she was trying to imitate Warwick, rather than stick with her own attractive vocal style. But Gentile argued that popular vocalist Dusty Springfield and others also sounded like Dionne Warwick—and had climbed the charts by doing so. He and Mary obviously thought the song was a success, because Mary performed it for years at concerts. As late as 2010, it was still putting money into Gentile's pocket through his songwriter's royalties.

Many people see Mary's inability to produce an exact replica of her Motown sound after leaving that company as the root of her failure to ever make it to the very top of the charts again. Nevertheless, Gordy and Co. were so impressed with "Stop Takin' Me for Granted" and "Never, Never Leave Me" that they called them "Motown songs made by another company," the highest compliment of which they were capable, and immediately hired Gentile for Motown. Gentile said Mary half-seriously scolded him for this desertion, telling him, "I knew you were going to abandon me for Motown after writing those songs."

Twentieth Century then put out its first Wells album, titled *Mary Wells*, in 1965. A mix of show tunes and pop tunes, it includes

"Time After Time," which uses a big band behind Mary's singing, plus "How Can I Forget Him," "My Mind's Made Up," "We're Just Two of a Kind," and "He's Good Enough for Me." Although Wells said the company spent less than $5,000 promoting the album, it rose to number 145 on the *Billboard* album chart in May 1965, making it the fifth album by Mary to hit that chart.

Meanwhile, Craft, who had recruited Mary for Twentieth Century, was fired after just three months in his job. Gentile said he thought Craft was fired because Mary had failed to score a huge hit. Mary later expressed bitterness about Craft's quick departure, telling Steve Bergsman that Twentieth Century "had this guy who was supposed to be good at promoting black artists, but then they fired him. I was stuck there for a year and a half."

Although it had bounced Craft, Twentieth Century didn't change its policy toward Wells, which was to imitate her Motown past even to the point of having her mention her Motown songs while singing Twentieth Century songs. Bateman produced her next release, "He's a Lover," which opens, after the background vocalists sing the song title, with Wells singing "Some people talk about my guy" with emphasis on the words "my guy." Some fans called this phrase ironic while others called it "vomit-inducing." The tune, backed with "I'm Learnin'," failed to chart on *Billboard* but rose to number 82 on the *Cash Box* pop chart.

This performance was substantially below Mary's previous singles for Twentieth Century and a long way below number one. In general, none of her Twentieth Century records had come near to equaling her Motown records in popularity, and the momentum of her hit-making career was lost.

Critics argue that Wells's problem at Twentieth Century wasn't the songs the company produced but its lack of ability to promote black music. That was Wells's opinion also: "Twentieth Century Fox had very few black artists. No real soul or R&B acts had signed with the label. It was too uptown. They were mystified by me, and they didn't promote me," she said.

Gentile agreed. Twentieth "paid a good price for Mary. They really wanted someone of her stature. But it was a big mistake for them. They didn't know what to do with her, and promotionally they crucified her." The company, he said, had plenty of money and a name but didn't know how to handle major artists, especially black ones.

Gentile said that after Mary's first records at Twentieth were released, he called the big stations himself to make sure they'd be played. He was shocked to discover the DJs didn't even know the records existed. Twentieth had a promotional staff but "didn't have R&B promotion."

As CBS president Larkin Arnold later told *Unsung*, to get R&B records played and purchased, "You have to have people who know the music directors, know the disc jockeys, and know the stores" that specialize in black music and who socialize and communicate with those audiences on behalf of individual records. Gordy and Motown had worked hard to build a promotional staff that had this knowledge and experience and were willing to work relentlessly to capitalize on it. Twentieth Century had not.

Wells also complained that Twentieth Century execs refused to listen to her ideas about how to better produce and promote her records. While Motown executives had listened to her, "giving ideas to different record executives or producers outside of Motown was like talking to a brick wall."

Some of Mary's fans, unable to believe that a singer who was a megastar at one company could be less than a star at her very next company, began spreading rumors alleging that Motown execs, furious at Mary for leaving them in the lurch, had sabotaged her future career, beginning with her work for Twentieth.

According to one such rumor, as soon as Mary left Motown, Motown promo people began denouncing her to black DJs for moving from a black-owned company to a white-owned one. Another rumor had it that Motown promoters told the DJs they would not be given new Motown records if they played Wells's non-Motown records. As a result, the black DJs allegedly cut back on airplay of her Twentieth Century releases, causing those records to be less popular than her Motown recordings.

A more virulent strain of gossip had it that Motown actually threatened both black and white DJs with more hurtful "unwanted consequences" if they played her records. A British magazine quoted Mary's manager, George Scheck, as claiming that DJs had been warned of "possible involvements if they programmed material Wells might release" on non-Motown labels. Scheck was quoted by others as making the same statement. But he made it during the court dispute over Mary's move to be released from her Motown contract, when she arguably was still contractually committed to Motown and subject to legal action if she signed with another firm. After the case was concluded, Scheck told an interviewer it had become possible for her to record for any company without "involvements."

Mary believed and circulated some of the rumors. She told one interviewer in 1989 that Motown did everything it could "to stop the black disc jockeys from playing my records."

There's no evidence supporting the rumors, and Motown has denied them. There's also not much of a motive for Motown to indulge in such behavior. In line with the terms of the court settlement under which Mary was released from her Motown contract, a percentage of her royalties on her Twentieth Century recordings, and all of the royalties on her Motown records, went to Motown itself. Considering Gordy's warm, lifelong relationship with money, it's extremely doubtful that he would have cut himself out of this action for revenge's sake.

In spite of Wells's unspectacular performance for Twentieth, the company still had hopes for her. Twentieth Century executives decided to try a new tack with Wells, issuing the surprisingly upbeat "Me Without You" backed with the wistful "I'm Sorry" in September 1965. Mary did well on "Me Without You," but it didn't hit the *Billboard* charts and rose no higher than number 99 on the *Cash Box* pop chart. "I'm Sorry" didn't hit any chart. Neither side did well enough to convince Twentieth to keep heading in either of those directions.

Instead, influenced by the Beatles' high opinion of Wells and Wells's success while touring with the Fab Four, the company had Mary sing a bunch of Beatles tunes and put them out on an October 1965 album titled *Mary Wells Love Songs to the Beatles.* Mary complained to no avail that the song arrangements were "unhip" and that the producers were trying to "middle-of-the-road" her. The album failed to chart on *Billboard.* Mary told a later interviewer that once again, in terms of promotion, Twentieth Century "didn't know what to do with the LP, so they did nothing."

At the same time, Twentieth released a Wells single with "I Should Have Known Better" on one side and "Please Please Me" on the other. Neither song charted.

Soon, Mary's youthful tuberculosis reoccurred, requiring her to stay in bed for several weeks. Then, repeating her pattern at Motown, she became the one who wanted to leave the label while the company wanted her to stay. Although Wells hadn't brought the company major fame and fortune, she was its most successful singles artist while she was there. Also, Twentieth had certainly not earned back the $250,000 it had somewhat rashly advanced her. When she left in October 1965, the company laid off a number of employees and tried to play catch-up by launching a budget label called Movietone. In 1966, on the Movietone label, Twentieth also rereleased the first album Wells did for the company under the title *Ooh!* It failed to chart.

Although displeased with Twentieth, Mary told one interviewer some years later that "I think the move was a wise one. I learned from it to take care of myself and to take care of my business myself."

That included touring and performing on her own. Although she had been on the road since she was seventeen, appearing in a chaperoned, directed Motortown Revue must have seemed easy compared to the situation she had to deal with as soon as she moved to Twentieth. Without direction from Motown headquarters in Detroit and without their army of musicians, backup singers, drivers, negotiators, and money handlers, Mary encountered a whole new world of economic uncertainty, bloodshed, and near-disaster. But she also gave dazzling performances before audiences whose incredible enthusiasm for her music made her feel as though she would be everlastingly popular on stage.

Mary always brought style to her stage appearances. Performing in 1965, for instance, she wore a long black wig and a white sequined gown and was backed by six female singers and three male dancers. Randy and Tony Russi saw and heard Wells dazzle a crowd when she was costarring with Joe Tex at the Joe Tex Show at the Orlando (Florida) Municipal Auditorium in 1966. Also on the bill were Mabel John, Barbara Lewis, Pigmeat Markham, Howard Tate, and Clyde Williams. Tony Russi was fifteen at the time. "There was no assigned seating, so you got there early, bought your tickets, and rushed in," Tony said. "I tried to go backstage to see the performers, but the police were not very nice back then." When he and his friends got up to dance at their seats, the police would come over and push them back down with billy clubs. He concluded that "maybe those redneck cops didn't like us because we were the only white kids up close."

For the Russis and most of the rest of the audience, Wells dominated the show. "While Pigmeat Markham was doing his thing, I could see these gold sparkly high heels under the curtain, and when Mary came out she looked beautiful, with her long black hair and orange gown," Tony said. "The bottom of it swayed as she sang." She performed five songs and was applauded wildly.

But the applause was mainly for her Motown songs, not for the tunes she had recorded for Twentieth Century, which were unpopular by comparison. As a result, Wells continued to feel that she had been mishandled by Twentieth. This feeling was vindicated when she jumped to Atlantic Records and scored her biggest post-Motown hit yet.

17

SWIMMING THE WIDE ATLANTIC

I'm pushing on when dawn's a-breakin'
Goin' 'cross the wide Missouri,
Where my love, she stands a-waitin'
For me.

—"Across the Wide Missouri,"
traditional American folk song

Although Wells originally had spurned an offer from Atlantic Records after seeing the color of Twentieth Century Fox's $250,000, Atlantic was actually more of her kind of company. It was doing well with black vocalist Barbara Lewis, whose recording "Hello Stranger" had climbed to number 1 on the *Billboard* R&B chart and number 3 on the *Billboard* pop chart in 1963; her "Baby I'm Yours" and "Make Me Your Baby" would both rise to number 11 on the *Billboard* pop chart in 1965. The company also had scored several R&B chart and pop hits from 1961 through 1964 and would score more in 1965 with Carla Thomas, Mary's sometime rival for the "Queen of Soul" crown. Also starring at the company were other black female singers, including Doris Troy, whose 1963 pop song "Just

One Look" had climbed high on both the white and black charts, and Patti LaBelle. And, as Wells noted later, Atlantic Records boss Ahmet Ertegun and executive Jerry Wexler "really showed an interest in what I was doing." The stage was set for a Wells comeback.

Carl Davis continued as her producer when she moved to Atlantic in late 1965 and began recording for its Atco label. Davis recruited former Motowner Sonny Sanders to assist him. Sanders, a Motown singer and trumpet player, had been frozen out at Motown because he was dating one of Gordy's ex-wives, which annoyed Gordy.

Davis, who was producing Mary's records in Chicago, also paid the famous Motown house musicians known as the Funk Brothers to visit Chicago from Detroit one weekend to play the rhythm track on one of Wells's tunes. Gordy was furious when he found out about their participation, but due to his dependence on their work, he had to restrict himself to fining them for aiding a Motown rival.

Wells had to have coaching in the studio, according to Davis. "She needed someone to tell her the flavor of the song. She might sing it too smooth. I'd say, 'You gotta be bouncy with it, follow the guitar licks. The guitar licks will always tell you where to go.'"

He also said something that many others repeated about Wells throughout her life. Even though Wells had fallen from her Motown peak in commercial terms, "I don't think she thought she had fallen at all," Davis said. "She believed in herself and knew she was good."

Wells's first studio session for Atlantic, on November 26, 1965, produced five songs, including "Dial L for Loneliness," which was never released and may have been destroyed in a subsequent fire. It also resulted in the songs for her first Atlantic record, "Dear Lover," backed with "Can't You See (You're Losing Me)."

Davis and cowriter Gerald Sims wrote "Dear Lover," Davis produced it, and Sanders arranged it. "Mary wanted a song in the same flavor of the ones that made her a star," Davis said of the ebullient, breezy "Dear Lover." "That's what we tried to do." Davis, Sims, and

Sanders said they listened to a lot of Mary's old songs before creating "Dear Lover" and "tried to make the record sound as close to Motown as we could."

They succeeded. Released in 1966, in February of that year "Dear Lover" reached number 6 on the *Billboard* R&B chart, number 51 on the *Billboard* pop chart, and number 45 on the *Cash Box* pop chart. On the R&B chart, "Dear Lover" was Mary's biggest hit since 1963.

"'Dear Lover' got her back on track so she could go out and perform in public for the money she was used to getting," Davis said. This was important to Wells. From the very beginning of her Motown career through the end of her life, much of her income came from performing several nights a week whenever she could.

Davis notes in his autobiography that "Dear Lover" is similar to the song "Hello Young Lovers," a show tune from the musical *The King and I*. Paul Anka had sung that tune as a paean of praise and encouragement to youthful lovers all over the world and had succeeded in pushing it to number 23 on the *Billboard* pop chart in 1960.

According to Davis, he and Sims distinguished "Dear Lover" from "Hello Young Lovers" by "slightly rearranging the opening melody" of "Hello Young Lovers" and adding an R&B sound to "Dear Lover" as opposed to the big band sound used in "Hello." Despite these changes, the melodies of the two songs are quite similar. But the general theme of "Dear Lover" and Mary's treatment of it give it an independent life. (Mary is hoping her boyfriend will answer a letter she is sending him.)

"Can't You See (You're Losing Me)," on the record's B-side, didn't hit the R&B chart but rose to number 91 on the *Cash Box* pop chart. Although it is a bluesy, fast-paced dance hall stomper rather than the subtle plea for romance that usually worked best for Mary, "Can't You See" helped the record's overall sales with its appeal to the English soul music fans known as the Northern Soul crowd.

Perhaps the success of "Dear Lover" reminded Gordy of the commercial potential of the Robinson-Wells tracks that Motown had not yet released. In November 1966 Motown released an album of Wells tunes accurately titled *Vintage Stock*, which, although bouncy and attractive, did not chart on *Billboard*. The album contains several songs of Mary's that Motown already had released: "The One Who Really Loves You," "Two Lovers," "My Guy," and "You Beat Me to the Punch," the girl group–like "He's the One I Love," in which Mary was strongly aided by the Supremes as background singers, as well as some of her previously unreleased Motown tunes: the bouncy, surprisingly upbeat "When I'm Gone," "Guarantee (for a Lifetime)," "Honey Boy," "Everybody Needs Love," the minor-keyed, jazzy "I'll Be Available," the hallelujah-accented "One Block from Heaven," and the part-mournful, part-jaunty "Goodbye and Good Luck."

The album was so good it should have charted, but its popularity wasn't helped by its cover, which is dominated by a photo of a wine rack in what appears to be the basement of a Parisian wine store. Although somewhat subtle notices for various Parisian nightclubs decorate the wine rack, nothing on the cover, except Mary's name in the upper left hand corner, connects the album with Wells. Her picture appears nowhere on it.

Intrigued with the success of "Dear Lover," Atlantic had Mary record another two songs in Chicago for her second release for the company. She might as well have recorded them in Detroit, because they sound like Motown knockoffs. Wells put the *S* in sultry while recording "Such a Sweet Thing," which is backed with "Keep Me in Suspense." Critics said Mary sounds "elegant and confident" in the former tune, but it only reached as high as 93 on the *Cash Box* pop chart, and neither song reached the *Billboard* R&B Top 100.

Thus, from one point of view, the Atco-based Wells was a moderate success with three Top 100 hits on the pop charts, including one Top 10 R&B hit, in one year, 1966. Unfortunately, with the exception of "Dear Lover" among R&B records, those songs didn't climb as high on the charts as her Motown hits, although Atlantic took out a full-page ad promoting them in *Billboard*. Neither did her next single for the company that year, the yearning "Fancy Free" backed with "Me and My Baby," with both tunes failing to make either the R&B chart or the pop charts.

Atlantic executives decided it made no sense to continue along this road. They turned to a tactic that they and other record companies were adopting at this time with other soul songstresses on their roster: putting out an album of the vocalist singing standard tunes, rather than newly written numbers. The tactic had been used by, among others, Wells's former boss Berry Gordy, who put out an album of Supremes songs in 1965. Half of those songs were standards the group performed at New York's Copacabana nightclub.

But because Wells had made some headway performing new tunes, Atlantic didn't want to make her totally a singer of standards. It decided she should maintain a presence in both the old and the new.

On one side of the resulting 1966 album, *The Two Sides of Mary Wells*, Mary performs, among other songs, two white soul singers' tunes, the Rolling Stones' "(I Can't Get No) Satisfaction" and the Young Rascals' "Good Lovin'." Both of them are enlivened by what sound like farts from a low-pitched tuba. She also sings an R&B standard, Wilson Pickett's "In the Midnight Hour," and a Motown hit, "My World Is Empty Without You," which the Supremes had only recently recorded. One critic said accurately that Wells's "yearning, almost sultry performance on 'My World Is Empty Without You' effortlessly beats Diana Ross." Tripping along at the end of this parade is Wells's "Dear Lover," her recent Atlantic hit.

On side two is a group of show tunes and standards including "The Boy from Ipanema," which one critic noted was "boosted by Mary's playful Motown-styled vocal." Accompanying "The Boy" are

"Sunrise, Sunset," on which Wells displays her full emotional range, "Shangri-La," "Where Am I Going?," "The Shadow of your Smile," and "On a Clear Day (You Can See Forever)."

Critic Doug Sheppard said that listening to side two was "like witnessing Mary live in an upscale dinner club, circa 1966. One can imagine her taking the stage with the glimmer of the spotlight reflecting off her sparkling gown and the brass section, delivering 'The Shadow of Your Smile' and 'Sunrise, Sunset' with a radiant smile adorning her face."

A *Detroit Free Press* reviewer, after actually seeing Mary perform both her rock hits and her show tunes at a club, noted that the show tunes were "still new and strange to her" and that she sounded like Gwen Verdon when she sang "Where Am I Going?" She had her hair done "in an ear-top-eyeball-level–chop-off that hides her eyes and only lets the sparkle come through" and her dress was "a white floor-length with an Empire line and a big pink bow." Somewhat alarmingly, considering her earlier wardrobe malfunction, the top of the dress was "slashed to the big bow, and sometimes it seems possible that she might jump out of it on her big-beat numbers."

Billboard's *Pop Spotlight* column called "Satisfaction" and "Good Lovin'" the "highlights of the rock side of the album" and said that a "smooth 'Shadow of Your Smile' stood out in the ballad half." The column went on to predict that "outstanding performance and arrangements will make this a top album." But the album failed to chart.

As a result, Atlantic started losing interest in Wells. Although Mary kept recording for the Atco label, it didn't release any more of her tunes until she married vocalist and songwriter Cecil Womack and the two began to collaborate on writing and producing her songs. Atlantic was briefly pleased enough to release, in 1967, one of the resulting records, "Coming Home," backed with "(Hey You) Set My Soul on Fire." But neither song charted in the United States or the United Kingdom. In a demonstration of how diverse both the recording business and the world were becoming, however, "(Hey You) Set My Soul on Fire" became a Top 10 record in, of all places, the Philippines.

In that same year, however, another discouraging note was sounded when Mary sang an original song for the soundtrack of the film *Catalina Caper*, which tells the story of a comical theft off the California coast. The song, "Don't Steal Anything Wet," is heard over the film's closing credits. Released by Crown International, the movie also features Little Richard Penniman performing the song "Scuba Party" on screen. Wells's song is haunting, but critics panned the movie and Wells called the film "embarrassing."

The silent reception that "(Hey You) Set My Soul on Fire" received everywhere but in the Philippines contributed to an Atlantic decision to devote a good portion of its future publicity efforts to another of its artists, newly signed soul singer Aretha Franklin.

Atlantic "was very honest with me," Mary told an interviewer. "They told us how they were compelled to give Aretha's first record that extra push and that they wouldn't be able to concentrate on my record. Sure, I was disappointed because I thought this was going to be a long and happy stay with Atlantic, but I'm also pleased that they leveled with me and told me straight how the situation was."

The Atlantic execs delivered versions of the same message to the other soul sisters at the company, including Patti LaBelle. Perhaps as a result of the extra effort Atlantic made for her, Aretha Franklin's songs suddenly took off up the charts while the tunes sung by Wells and the others languished at the starting gate.

Franklin's success at Atlantic also was due to Atlantic exec Jerry Wexler's decision to record her as a soul singer, rather than repeat the mistake her previous record company had made. That company, Columbia, had restricted Franklin to recording mainly middle-of-the-road standards.

Wells left Atlantic shortly thereafter. "Once again, I was on my way," she said.

Wexler, who had signed Wells to the company, tried to avoid accepting the responsibility for repeating Mary's cycle of success followed by failure. In his autobiography, *Rhythm & the Blues,* he wrote, "We soon realized we could do nothing with Mary. The fault wasn't hers nor was it ours; she was an artist who required the idiosyncratic Motown production, which was simply out of our ken. There was something unique about that little Detroit studio—the attitude, the vibes, the energy—that couldn't be duplicated elsewhere."

This was only half true. If everything depended on "the idiosyncratic Motown production," why did Wells start off so well at Atlantic and at the other record companies that hired her after she left Motown? The real problem was that no one other than Smokey Robinson, and Motown's promo men, could figure out how to score a homer off the softball of initial success that Wells obligingly pitched them at or near the beginning of each game.

Atlantic partner Ahmet Ertegun was more honest about their problems in trying to compete with Motown. Ertegun, quoted by author Robert Greenfield in his biography, *The Last Sultan*, said of the Motown sound, "I didn't know how to reproduce it, and it scared the shit out of me. We didn't understand how to write it; we didn't understand how to play it; we didn't understand how to sing it. It was newer and hipper than what we were doing, and it got to the public in a very heavy way and became pop music."

18

TWO BROTHERS AND I AIN'T ASHAMED

All the brothers had feelings for me. They all could have liked me. . . . I've tried to make my marriages work. I don't think I could have done any more, and when I go to meet my maker, I want Him to say I've done my part. I've stood by my husbands through thick and thin and went completely by the Bible.

—Mary Wells, 1991

Mary had divorced Herman Griffin in 1963 and had subsequent affairs, she said, with David Ruffin, Brian Holland, Benny Mullins, Jackie Wilson, and Carl Davis. After breaking up with Davis, but before leaving Atlantic in 1967, she had been on the lookout for a new relationship. "It was a very lonely point in my life," she said. "My record sales were down; I wasn't working as much. . . . I was in a slump about my career."

She languished for six or seven months in 1965 and 1966 without seeing anybody. "I didn't go anywhere," Wells said. "I stayed in my bedroom most of the time and read a lot of books."

Maye James-Holler, her friend and aide, had observed Mary during previous hiatuses in Mary's social life. Maye would go out on weekends and try to convince her to come along. "Sometimes I would go, but very seldom," Mary said. "I would just stay there and read."

"If Mary had a guy, she was always happy," Maye said. "But if she didn't, she didn't do much besides stay in her room." There, Mary would read "positive thinking" books and magazines, but also just mope a lot.

Due to her long childhood illnesses, Mary had become accustomed to being alone and was never really a party person. By the time she was nearing twenty years old, when other young women would have been going out with boys and socializing, Mary, a guarded rock 'n' roll star, was on the road with national tours. She never developed the habit of going out to clubs or theaters for entertainment and often spent days and nights at home, alone or with just one friend. In Maye's words, "Mary went from being a kid to being a star on stage" and beyond recreational dancing, "never had a chance to find anything else she wanted to do in life."

Randy Russi said Mary liked to go to movies but that he never saw her engage in any other outside activities. He once had tickets to *The Merv Griffin Show* but was unable to talk Mary into leaving her apartment to accompany him there, he said. Randy's brother Tony Russi, who lived in Los Angeles with Mary and her second husband for a while, said he was never able to convince Mary to go out with him to a club and see what other musicians were doing.

Looking back on it in 2010, Maye said the main cause of Mary's moping in the mid-1960s "was probably depression," which she believed was caused not only by the languishing of her career but by a lack of male companionship. Although Mary would "come out of her room and laugh and talk and would love it when people came over, she was basically always looking for a guy to love. Sometimes she'd get a guy, then they'd break up, and she'd be depressed again.

She was always looking for love on the outside, and you have to look for it on the inside."

Mary's loneliness, combined with her celebrity status, had caused the few problems that had arisen between her and Maye. "I wanted a little time for myself," Maye said, "but Mary was a very needy, needy, needy person. She needed . . . somebody she could talk to. But she was too huge a celebrity to go out like a normal person." (Wells would be mobbed at bars and dance clubs.) One night when Maye wanted to leave early to spend an evening with her own boyfriend, Mary objected, "and I went ballistic. I just wanted to dance and have fun."

Slowly, however, Mary became deeply involved with the Womacks, a family that didn't let her alone for the rest of her life. She didn't let them alone, either.

The brothers Friendly Jr., Curtis, Robert (known as Bobby), Harris (known as Harry), and Cecil got their musical start singing gospel as the Womack Brothers under the direction of their father, Friendly Sr., and their mother, Naomi. Later, they sang rock 'n' roll as the Valentinos and the Lovers.

Friendly Jr. and Curtis were born in West Virginia, and Bobby, Harry, and Cecil were all born in Cleveland. Curtis was the group's lead singer from age nine on but eventually was replaced by Bobby. As the Valentinos, they scored a number 8 R&B hit in 1962 with "Lookin' for a Love" and a number 94 R&B hit in 1964 with "It's All Over Now." Both songs rose to number 63 on the *Cash Box* pop chart. When covered by the Rolling Stones, "It's All Over Now" became a number one hit in the United Kingdom and a number 26 *Billboard* pop chart hit in the United States. Bobby later became a major solo star, recording four Top 40 pop chart hits and thirty-nine Top 100 R&B hits. He was inducted into the Rock and Roll Hall of Fame in 2009.

Even before Mary had met any of the Womacks, the Womacks were aware of Mary, not only because she was a national singing star but because they had heard about the performance she gave where one of her breasts jumped out of her dress. But they didn't see it. "We didn't go to any shows," Curtis Womack noted. "We were just church boys singing." Their mother and father accompanied them on tours, with Mrs. Womack's major function being to "make sure the money got back home." The boys later went into pop music because they "thought if we sang rock 'n' roll we could keep some of the money."

Vocalist and record producer Sam Cooke, attracted by the Womacks' increasing popularity, recorded them as the Valentinos on his SAR Records label beginning in 1962. During a break in the recording sessions, Cooke told the Womacks that he was bringing Mary with him to Cleveland and that the two would be performing at the Pla-Mor Ballroom there. "Have you ever seen a rock 'n' roll show in person?" he asked them. "No, but we sure would like to," they said.

Even though Mary had not yet recorded her mega hit "My Guy," she had already ridden "You Beat Me to the Punch" and "Two Lovers" to wide popularity. "She was every young girl's idol, and all the guys . . . wowee," Curtis said. "We were like, 'Oh, man, Mary Wells.' That was big. That was major."

Curtis and his brothers enjoyed the Pla-Mor concert, although they didn't meet Mary personally at that time. They asked Cooke why he and Mary performed together. "She's a crossover artist," Cooke replied, referring to her stunning success in appealing to both white and black audiences. Curtis, whose family's gospel songs were aimed at a purely black audience, said he had never heard the term crossover before.

The Womacks didn't meet Mary face to face until, as the Valentinos, they were performing their hit song "Lookin' for a Love" at the Apollo in 1962. Mary was appearing there too. Seeing Mary on stage for only the second time in his life, Curtis noted with amazement that she was dancing full-speed while singing. "How could she dance like that and not get out of breath?" Curtis said in an interview in West Virginia, where he now lives. "And she was singing all her notes, even though the band was right on top of her, jamming, and she was talking to the people, doing her thing." Obviously, he was impressed.

Noticing the impact Mary was having on Curtis, Cooke mentioned to him that the two young people were the same age. This shocked Curtis. "I thought Mary was a grown-up woman," he said. "When you're a kid, girls mature faster. She had on this gown and she was all glamorous." Cooke invited the Womack brothers backstage to meet her. "She had on these heels, and she was acting and talking like the star she was," Curtis said, "and we were all tongue-tied."

Mary had seen Curtis performing with the Valentinos and singing the ballad "Somewhere There's a Girl," a romantic song, at the Apollo and had told Maye "I like him! I like him!" She called him "the little cute one." Attracted to Curtis but noticing his youthful shyness, Mary arranged a second meeting. She commissioned Maye to tell him that "Mary likes you." Curtis's reaction was "What? No way." To his extreme amazement, Maye added that Mary "sneaks into the audience and watches you when you sing. She likes your singing." Curtis didn't know how to react. "I was pretty bashful," he said years later.

Maye took Curtis up to Mary's dressing room, but Curtis was more dumbfounded than expectant. He took the idea of a rock 'n' roll hierarchy very seriously. "Believe me, I had no idea what to say to her," Curtis said. Mary was a superstar. "I thought if I did talk to her I would have to be a little higher up than where I was then. Even being with the Valentinos, that wasn't going to do it." Curtis stayed mostly silent and didn't go near her, unable to overcome his awe. "I said hello and then I said goodbye and then I left. I was scared of her."

Mary continued to find Curtis attractive and kept reaching out to him as both groups continued on the concert circuit year after year. "Curtis and I used to look at each other backstage a lot and give each other eyes," Mary said.

The Valentinos and Mary continued to appear on the same shows, and on Mary's birthday in 1963, she invited the boys to a birthday party in her dressing room. It was really Curtis she was after. Maye called Curtis and told him, "Mary sure wants to see you," Curtis remembered.

Although Curtis probably had matured enough by the time of the birthday party to dare to begin a relationship with Mary, it was too late. He had already married his first wife, Donice, who had become pregnant with his child. He said he worried that if he attended Wells's party, he "might mess up" by taking up with Mary. So he didn't go. His brothers Cecil and Harry did, but far from paying any attention to them as individuals, Mary talked to them about their brother Curtis. Later in life, Curtis commented to *Unsung*, "Wow, what a missed opportunity that was."

Mary's version of the failure of what amounted to her courtship of Curtis was that they were both too shy to approach each other. Curtis and Donice, who wed in 1962 when he was nineteen and she was fifteen, were married for more than twelve years and had four children: Curtis Jr., Kevin, Robin, and Angel.

Curtis's marriage wasn't the only obstacle between Curtis and Mary. Curtis's younger brother Cecil had begun his pursuit of her.

Cecil's first step was to follow Mary to New York when she journeyed there on tour. This shocked the other Womacks, since they were so bonded as a team that very rarely did one brother go off on his own. Mary was surprised, not only by Cecil's solo stepping-out, but also by his persistence in courting her. Calling Curtis from

New York, she told him, "I can't get rid of your brother," despite falsely telling Cecil she was the mother of several kids (she had no children) and giving him an incorrect hotel room number when he asked for hers. "Cecil didn't let any dirt get underneath his feet concerning me," Mary said. "He was on me every minute to go with him. . . . He was running behind me like mad." Mary was surprised, however, when Cecil made it clear to her that he was pursuing her as a marriage partner as well as a sex partner.

Curtis was astounded by Mary's call about Cecil. He told her, "He's up there? He's got more nerve than me." Still insistent that she much preferred Curtis to Cecil, she told Curtis, "This boy is crazy. I'm not going to marry him."

When Mary returned to Cleveland in 1965, she attended a Womack family gathering. She danced with Curtis all the time, and when the slow, romantic records came on Curtis and Mary continued dancing, provoking Cecil to complain to their mother that Curtis was trying to take his girlfriend. Mrs. Womack told Curtis not to harass Cecil because Cecil, five years younger, was "just the baby." Curtis said he obeyed and did not interfere any further with Cecil's pursuit of Mary.

The combination of Curtis's marriage, Cecil's unending courtship, and Mary's susceptibility to forceful men finally broke her resistance. She accepted Cecil's proposal.

Maye James-Holler told *Unsung* that when Mary told her she was going to marry Cecil, she started laughing. "I thought she was kidding," partly because Cecil was nineteen and Mary was twenty-three. "Cecil practically forced me to marry him," Mary said years later. "You don't know what type of person I am. You can practically stay on me long enough and I'll do almost anything." Wells claimed Cecil was so forceful, "he had me walking down the aisle without me even knowing how I got down there." She had reservations she could barely hide on the day of her wedding ceremony, which took place at Olivet Institutional Church in Cleveland in August 1966. In the church dressing room that day, Mary told her friend Maye, "I don't want to go through with this. I really want to get the hell out of here and run and never look back." Maye replied, "It's your choice, because it's your life. All you've got to do is get up and walk out of here." But Mary pointed out, "All his family is out there. My family is out there. How in the world am I going to get out of this?"

Curtis, assigned to light a candle as part of the ceremony, failed on his first attempt. When he tried a second time, his hand was shaking so badly that the audience started laughing. Afterward, people kept asking him how he could be so nervous, considering that he routinely performed in front of thousands of people and that Mary and Cecil were married in a church that held far fewer.

Summing up this second marriage, Mary said shortly before her death that "I asked the Lord, because I had been very lonely, to please send me someone to love. . . . I think it was supposed to have been Curtis. But He sent Cecil."

Whatever her reservations, one of Wells's major motivations for marrying was to have children, as she had told Maye James-Holler a few years before. "That was one thing dear to her heart," Maye said.

Cecil Womack and Wells remained married for eleven years and had three children: Cecil Demetrius Womack Jr., named after his father and now known professionally as Meech Wells, born December 29, 1967; followed in 1969 by Stacy Womack, their only daughter, now known as Noel Wells; and on February 10, 1975, by Harry James George Womack, now known as Shorty Wells. He was named Harry James after his uncle, who had been stabbed to death by his girlfriend in 1974.

During their marriage, the couple uprooted themselves several times. Soon after their wedding, they moved from New York to Rolling Hills, California, in the Los Angeles area. Moving to California, a record- and movie-industry hub, was a no-brainer. In 1972, the couple moved from L.A. to the Miami area, because Miami was just emerging as a big music scene and was within touring distance of other large East Coast cities. But in 1975, shortly after Harry was born, they returned to Los Angeles.

During her long interview with Steve Bergsman, Mary spent much of her time telling him how little she loved Cecil and how bad their marriage was. Bergsman found this difficult to believe, considering the length of their marriage and the number of children they had. When he asked why she had three children with Cecil if she didn't really want to be married to him, she replied, "Well, you can get pregnant without enjoying it. Especially if you're a breeder." She noted that her grandmother had had twenty-two children. When Bergsman pointed out that she was married to Cecil for eleven years, she responded, "I was with Curtis for thirteen years."

Wells said Cecil dominated her after marriage just as he had during their courtship. "His love was so overbearing that I couldn't talk to anybody."

As Bergsman continued to question her, Mary finally admitted, "I loved, I learned to love Cecil." But "I learned to dislike him too, because he was extremely jealous. Like you and I sitting here talking—I couldn't dare sit down and talk to a man this long, or a woman. He was jealous."

Mary said the honeymoon was over on its second day when her friend Ida, a model, and Ida's husband, a movie producer, came over to visit the newlyweds. "I was sure [the husband] had eyes for me, but I never gave him any come-on. I just treated him nice," she said. Then Cecil started flirting with the wife but told Mary not to talk to the husband. "I said if you're going to talk to her, and flirt with her, and this man's just talking to me like 'Mary, I would like to do a production of you and "My Guy" for the movies or television,' in a business way, he wasn't flirting."

Cecil allegedly replied, "You don't need to be around people. I have to be very careful with you being around people, because you're like a kid. You don't even know when someone's flirting with you."

After this, Mary said, Cecil usually made it clear without words that she couldn't talk to any other people, especially men. "It was the way he reacted when I spoke to others. The look on his face. The fear I would feel. 'You don't talk to any man; you don't talk to any women; you don't talk to anybody.'"

Some of this may have been in play when Mary, Cecil, and their children moved back to Los Angeles from Florida and stayed with Cecil's brother Friendly Jr. and Friendly's then-wife Sally in that couple's three-bedroom apartment. According to Friendly, all Mary and Cecil would do was stay in their room rather than look for another place to live or communicate with anyone. "They'd come out, get a tray of food, and then take it back into their room." They stayed with Friendly and Sally for a year, Sally said. Finally, under pressure from Sally, Friendly found an apartment for them and suggested they move into it, which they did.

Sally Womack noticed some other oddities about their life. Whenever one of them went to use the bathroom, she said, the other one would go into the bathroom also. And, when she was cleaning up after the couple and their children had left, Sally found Pampers that had been soiled by Harry hanging in their room. Short on funds, Mary and Cecil planned to reuse the cleaned Pampers after they had dried.

When at home with Cecil, Mary said, she felt like she was living in a prison cell. Describing her day, she said she would "just automatically get up, clean the house, feed the kids, feed him . . . I had everything routine, put on my clothes, cook, wash, and when there wasn't anything else to do, I'd just go and lay on the bed." Curtis later told *Unsung* that Mary told him, "Your brother thinks he is going to pump me full of kids and keep me barefoot at home." Mary eventually moved her own mother, Geneva, to Los Angeles, where Geneva lived with Mary and Cecil and helped them with child care.

Wells said that when she was home and Cecil went out somewhere, "mentally, without him telling me, I knew I was supposed to stay in the house, maybe in the bedroom." She admitted, though, that "after a while I got used to it. I think I liked it."

Mary may have been able to tolerate, or perhaps enjoy, the home life she described with Cecil because she retained her professional life. She needed to do so to help pay the family bills. Although she took some time off after she had her second child, she soon began performing as a singer again, on stage and in clubs, on a regular basis. She said, however, that she did this over Cecil's resistance. "He didn't really want me to work or be an entertainer," she said. "He was supposed to help me with my career, but he put it into a slump."

Cecil Womack did not respond to requests for an interview for this book.

Mary's charges that Cecil wanted her to stay at home all the time and didn't want her to resume her singing career may be an attempt to rewrite her personal history because of the guilt she felt later over the eventual failure of the marriage. Her criticism ignores Cecil's attempts to help her develop her career at Atlantic Records and at her next company, Jubilee Records, as well as the work he put into cowriting and producing many of her songs and arranging many of her performance dates. It also ignores the energy Cecil put into backing her on stage with his bass guitar. "It's nice to have his guitar behind me," Mary told the British publication *Melody Maker* in 1967.

Along with all his other contributions, Cecil also set up a music publishing firm called Welwom, through which he marketed the couple's jointly written tunes, many of them labeled as written by "C

& M Womack" or "Cecil and Mary Womack." These songs include "Sweeter Than the Day Before," "Baby Girl," "Let's Get Together Again," "Soul Train," "Two Lovers History," "Can't Get Away from Your Love," "The Doctor," "Don't Look Back," "Woman in Love," "Love-Shooting Bandit," "Mind Reader," "Sometimes I Wonder," "Dig the Way I Feel," "Hold On," "Sweet Love," "Mister Tough," "Never Give a Man the World," "It Must Be," and "Love and Tranquility," many of them recorded on Jubilee.

Many music fans, in fact, refer to Cecil Womack and Mary Wells as the first Womack & Womack. (Cecil and his second wife, Linda Cooke, the daughter of Sam Cooke, became the second Womack & Womack.)

Mary always insisted that even though Cecil was not faithful to her during their marriage, she remained faithful to him—until Curtis came back into her life. (Cecil has told interviewers he was faithful to Mary.)

Meanwhile, her professional pride and her financial needs required her to make another stab at recapturing her former popularity as a singer.

19

THE YEARS OF JUBILEE

I hear the angels sing
I see the lamps burn low
I know it's now the kingdom coming
And the Year of Jubilo.

—Traditional African-American folk song

At Jubilee Records, to which she moved in the spring of 1968 after leaving Atlantic, Mary was determined to break her post-Motown pattern of one or two pop hits followed by a decline. She also was resolved to continue to produce and write her own songs, with Cecil's help. Together, they produced forty Mary Wells songs for the company, sixteen of which also were written by the couple.

Jubilee was certainly glad to have her. The company placed ads in music publications proclaiming that "Jubilee Records takes great pleasure in announcing the acquisition of one of the greats in the recording industry." And, as most people familiar with Wells's recording history would expect by now, the first Wells tune released by Jubilee was a hit. "The Doctor," released in 1968, reached number 22 on the *Billboard* R&B chart, number 65 on the *Billboard* pop chart, and number 79 on the *Cash Box* pop chart that year, featuring, as one critic put it, Wells's "slinky . . . honeyed tones, now spiced with just a dash of vinegar."

On the B-side of "The Doctor" is the Mary-and-Cecil song "Two Lovers History," which is about them as a couple. In a way, "The Doctor" a pleasant, mid-tempo tune, also is about their relationship: Wells said Cecil imitated her perfectly as he sang her undertones on the song. He added even more to the record by introducing it with some soulful guitar licks.

The record's success was aided by Wells and Womack's ceaseless efforts to get it played. Frustrated by what they believed had been inadequate promotion at Twentieth and Atlantic, they had decided to take on this function as well.

Jubilee, pleased at the success of "The Doctor," soon released an album of Wells tunes called *Servin' Up Some Soul*, which contains "The Doctor" and thirteen other songs. Unfortunately, not only did the album fail to chart, none of the thirteen non-"Doctor" tunes recorded on it did either, meaning that Mary's post-Motown up-and-down recording pattern was continuing with a vengeance. Among the failing tunes on the album are the plodding "Woman in Love" backed with the tuneless "Can't Get Away from Your Love." Also headed for failure was "Don't Look Back" backed with the standard "500 Miles," sung at a very slow tempo, which includes a line about "reaching the mountaintop someday," a reference to the recent assassination of the Rev. Dr. Martin Luther King Jr.

The album also includes a jazzed-up, funky remake of "Bye Bye Baby," the first song Wells ever wrote and recorded and the one that had launched her toward Motown fame. Before starting to sing it, she says, "Here's a song I did way back in 1960. So many people tell me 'Sock it to me one more time.'" Not enough people, apparently.

There was a slight uptick in 1969 when Jubilee released the single, "Dig the Way I Feel." Once again cowritten by Mary and Cecil and called a "perfect summer ballad" by one critic, "Dig the Way I Feel" was unfortunately released in the winter, possibly damaging its potential. Although it reached number 35 on the *Billboard* R&B chart, it made it only to number 80 on the *Cash Box* pop chart and to number 115 on the *Billboard* pop chart in February 1970. It was backed with "Love Shooting Bandit," which didn't make any chart.

In 1969, Mary's career seemed like it might lift on yet another updraft when Jubilee released "Mind Reader," backed with "Never Give a Man the World." While "Mind Reader" completely failed to chart, "Never Give a Man the World," while not making a dent on any pop chart, rose to number 38 on the R&B chart. The song features Mary singing subtle *ha-has* and *ho-hos* in the background, a throwback to the *ho-ho-hos* in her Motown tune "Laughing Boy."

The next year, Jubilee released "Sweet Love" backed with the driving "It Must Be," both of which also failed to hit any chart. In a final effort, the company released "Mr. Tough," backed with "Never Give a Man the World," the tune that had already backed "Mind Reader" the year before. Neither song charted, rounding off a dismal Jubilee singles career for the former Motown great.

Although Jubilee had been planning a second album for Mary, originally titled *Come Together* and later titled *Love & Tranquility*, most of the singles planned for it that the company already had released had done so badly that Jubilee canceled the album. It wasn't released until after Wells's death. That's a shame, because it's a pleasure to listen to. It includes the bouncy tunes "Sometimes I Wonder" and "Hold On" plus a critically acclaimed "achingly vulnerable" version of "Leaving on a Jet Plane." Among the other standouts on the album are an amazingly sensual rendition of "Come Together," a version of "Raindrops Keep Falling on My Head" that adds a verse urging "let it keep raining, let it keep raining, I'm not worried," and "Love and Tranquility," a socially conscious song accompanied by Asian musical notes and harmonies.

When she wasn't working on her own tunes, Wells spent some of her time at Jubilee helping to produce the Valentinos, whom the company had allowed Cecil and Mary to reunite and record again. This may have helped the couple remain somewhat upbeat about Jubilee. Whistling while walking past the graveyard, Cecil told an interviewer later on that his and Mary's days at Jubilee "were some of the best. We faced all sorts of different problems from any we'd faced before, and it made us both bigger and better people."

But Mary always remained puzzled by her experience at Jubilee. "I couldn't understand why I couldn't have any [major] hits" there, Wells said. "I guess there were too many companies into black music at the time."

Competition in black music certainly had increased since the time when Wells was among the few active soloists on the distaff side of the genre. By 1970, companies such as Stax and Atlantic were producing soul sisters en masse. The underlying problem, however, was that although Mary did very well as a vocalist on much of the Jubilee material, she and Cecil were no match for Smokey Robinson in the songwriter category.

Wells also had another explanation for her post-Motown decline, telling friends she might be on some sort of industry blacklist because Gordy was still angry at her for endangering Motown's early success. "I don't think Berry Gordy has really forgiven me for leaving the company," she told author Sharon Davis in the late 1980s. "It has been a long time, but he hasn't forgotten. I have tried to speak to him, but he will not speak to me."

As Mary's remark about Gordy indicates, she felt strongly nostalgic about her Motown days. In the late 1980s, when she was performing in England, a fan played her a tape of a duet that she and Marvin Gaye had recorded at Motown. Saying she had not heard the song since it was recorded in 1963, Mary started crying. She then sang along with the entire tune with her eyes closed.

Wells was so discouraged by her performance at Jubilee that she left in 1970, announcing that she would cut back on recording and concentrate on giving live singing performances and being a wife and a mother. "I'd lost faith in record companies," she said later. (Nevertheless, Mary was a prolific performer and helped keep the family afloat with her concert earnings; Cecil was also employed by various record companies.)

At first, that didn't mean giving up recording completely. After leaving Jubilee, Mary did three recordings for Warner-Reprise on separate contracts. The first one, "I See a Future in You," backed with "I Found What I Wanted," both George Jackson tunes, was produced by Rick Hall and Sonny Limbo at Fame Studios in Muscle Shoals, Alabama. Released in 1971, the record failed to chart.

Her second Reprise recording, "If You Can't Give Her Love (Give Her Up)," backed on its first pressing by "Cancel My Subscription," was written and produced by her brother-in-law Bobby Womack. Released in 1974, it made it onto the R&B chart that year but only to number 95. On this song, a discouraged Mary seems to be retreating to the style that had first made her popular: she sings it as a gritty-voiced soulful shouter.

She and Reprise tried once more with "If You Can't Give Her Love (Give Her Up)," backed in its second pressing with "Don't Keep Me Hangin' On," also produced by Bobby. It failed to chart, with Wells complaining once again about inadequate promotion.

She recorded no further records until 1981 but continued performing. Unfortunately, many of Mary's post-Motown concerts were underfunded, and she often was nearly broke. That may help explain an incident Tony Russi recounted: Mary's manager, George Scheck, called him once at Mary and Cecil's home in California, where Russi was staying and helping them line up gigs, and asked him to tell Wells that Scheck had landed a concert date for her at a US Marine base in the southeastern United States. Russi passed the message on to Wells and was surprised when Cecil and Mary took off for the date by car, apparently to save money. Scheck called back a couple of days later wondering where they were and was angry to find out they were driving, not flying.

Lacking savvy direction from Motown, Mary and Cecil also were sometimes deceived in their eagerness to continue the concerts that provided much of their income. Tony Russi remembered one alleged promoter who approached Wells and Cecil at a Los Angeles TV station where they were waiting to be interviewed in 1976. The man claimed to have landed high-level bookings for the Platters and the Coasters and said he could get similar gigs for Wells.

Wells and Womack "actually let this guy stay in the living room of their apartment for a couple of nights," Russi said. "They were too kind." Then, Wells assigned Russi to drive the promoter to night-clubs all over the area. "I was embarrassed to be seen with this guy," Russi said. "The people at the clubs would come up to me behind his back and ask me what I was doing hanging with him."

As it turned out, every one of the performance dates the "promoter" claimed to have set up for other groups, including the Platters and the Coasters, turned out to be fictional. The episode ended when Russi was using the bathroom at Wells's apartment and Wells yelled at him through the door. "You've got to come out here," she said. The man was crying and tearfully admitting to all of them that he was a phony.

To Mary's credit, however, she tried to stay positive about her situation. "My life goes on," she said. "I work still. I perform a lot. . . . Motown goes on. Life is still great." She also continued to express hope. "I think I can make it without being on the Motown label," she told Sharon Davis more than twenty-five years after "My Guy." "After all, Diana Ross and Michael Jackson have managed it." Only rarely did Mary complain about her obviously flawed decision to leave Motown.

Mary's life did indeed continue and so did Motown's, but Mary and that company had become separate entities in more than contractual terms. While Motown records continued to rise high on the pop charts, which reflected the taste of both white and black Americans, most of Mary's post-Motown records ascended only on the R&B chart, which mainly reflected the taste of black Americans.

This was the gap that Motown had been created to bridge. After leaving Motown, Mary, in spite of her best efforts, was no longer participating in this grand enterprise.

Before returning to the recording studio in earnest, Mary had to settle a few love problems.

20

CURTIS WOMACK

I don't think the Lord even thought about me getting married or being a wife or a mother. A lot of those things I had to learn myself. But it looked like I was made for just that.

. . . I'm too sensitive. I can't take abuse. I've been in too much pain all my life. You know you have to handle me with love, because I fall apart; I break up.

—Mary Wells, 1991

During Mary's marriage to Cecil, she and Curtis would see each other, as sister-in-law and brother-in-law, as much as three times a week. Although they gravitated toward each other during family gatherings, Mary said, they would never look each other in the eye. They would never dance together like they had years before. Curtis told her he loved her on many occasions, but for a while she didn't want to believe that he was referring to romantic love between a man and a woman rather than the love that two relatives might have for each other.

Mary noticed that Curtis's attitude toward her meeting other people in the record business was totally different than Cecil's. While Cecil, she said, was hiding her "so I wouldn't be meeting anyone or anything," preventing her from getting to know other people in the business who could help her advance her career, Curtis was always introducing her to different record people. "I felt like Curtis was really in my corner," Mary said, "and I got concerned about him and his life."

Mary insisted Cecil became more and more controlling in his attitude toward her as the years went by.

On a much less important but symbolic level, while Cecil didn't pay much attention to his own clothing or hairstyle or those of others, people became accustomed to hearing Mary and Curtis discuss fashion or hair and were not surprised at seeing the two of them combing each other's hair in the bathroom. "I used to tint her hair myself," Curtis added. Others told him that Mary wouldn't let anyone but him comb her hair.

Eventually, things got to the point that the two couldn't even talk together without, as Mary put it, becoming "too steamed up." Curtis said Mary visited him at his house one day and "got mad and ran out of the house because she never could totally control her emotions." As author Tony Turner put it, "Mary had great, great difficulty with the drama of her personal life."

Mary, talking to Steve Bergsman about Curtis, said, "He would leave and go away for a month or two and come back and visit again, but I had no idea for the longest [time] what was going on. Evidently I blanked it out of my mind. We must have needed some kind of relationship in order to survive the pain we were going through."

Then one day, during the eleventh year of her marriage to Cecil, Curtis, who was separated from his wife, "just begged me to kiss him," Mary said. "He said, 'Mary, please just kiss me one time.'

"I said, 'Curtis, I can't do that, I'm married,' and he said 'Please, kiss me one time and you'll never have to do it again.' So I gave him a *quick kiss*. Then he started needing more, and I must have felt really bad for him, and then, after about a month of involvement, you know, I brought myself to try to help him, to ease his pain." The kissing led to sex, which, "really just opened up the doors, because we were really already into each other mentally."

Curtis said that Cecil knew Mary and Curtis were sweet on each other in a platonic way but thought, "Well, it could be somebody else, and if she kind of liked me he didn't [need to] pay any attention to it." That, Curtis said, "*was very wrong.*"

"We had a whirlwind romance together," Wells said of the new affair. "Sometimes we'd leave and be gone for a few days. We'd check into a motel and go walking on a beach, and then we'd go play tennis and have a lot of fun together."

Mary said she hadn't known how to play tennis until Curtis taught her and that he was constantly thinking of new places to go "because he was always trying to please me." She described him as "a real sporty man, an outdoor man, a lot of fun. He brought me a lot of excitement."

Mary said that although she felt bad about interfering with Curtis's relationship with his wife, she finally told herself, "Oh, just be involved with it. I think he really wanted me and needed me." Mary didn't mention at this point that she had previously shown her desire for a relationship with Curtis by aggressively courting him before her marriage to Cecil.

At times during her interview with Bergsman, Mary also insisted that as her relationship with Cecil had been deteriorating, Cecil himself had suggested they start seeing other people. She never suggested, however, that Cecil had his older brother Curtis in mind for her.

The two in-laws tried to keep their relationship secret. Curtis rationalized that "if nobody really knew it but me and her, it wasn't hurting anyone." But eventually both of them were away simultaneously on so many occasions that their affair became obvious to others.

As reality sank in, the rest of the Womacks began to pull away from Curtis and Mary. "What in the world is happening? How is this going to end?" various family members asked Curtis. Mary said she had been "pretty close with the family, but they stopped communicating with both Curtis and me. Curtis stopped coming over, although we'd sometimes talk on the phone. And I wasn't with Cecil either." Mary also felt terrible about the impact all this would have on the three kids she had had with Cecil. Curtis said he had a migraine headache that wouldn't go away. "I thought my brain was going to bust," he told *Unsung*.

Being estranged from the rest of the Womacks may have bothered Mary even more than it bothered Curtis. She told Bergsman that when she had become involved with the Womack family by marrying Cecil, she had resolved to be a functioning part of it. Families were important to her because she came from a situation in which her church was her family, then went to Motown, "which was another family situation, an organization of singers and songwriters and producers working toward something. I grew up with that kind of system."

The process of hurting two brothers and gravely disturbing other family members was devastating to Wells. Cecil finally confronted her. "He told me to let him know [about any other relationship], to let him get out of the darkness," Mary said, "to let him know, and then he wouldn't be mad. And like an idiot, because I had never hid anything from him before, I'd always been honest with him, I told him the truth." Cecil and Mary then separated.

The other Womacks immediately put tremendous pressure on Curtis and Mary to break off their relationship. "They were telling me to leave her," Curtis said, "and I said, 'If I do, she might commit suicide.' They said, 'Just take a chance on it; just break up with her.'" He refused.

Mary's first reaction to the family pressure was to validate Curtis's fear by indeed attempting suicide in 1977, at age thirty-four. "I tried to kill myself from the guilt," she said. "I just couldn't stand the pain. I just couldn't take it. I mean, Cecil was suffering; Curtis was suffering; I was suffering. I just couldn't deal with it." She took an overdose of sleeping pills, closed her bedroom door, and passed out. Luckily, her mother, who was living with her, grew suspicious, opened the door, and called 9-1-1. Mary was taken to Los Angeles County–USC Medical Center.

According to Mary, the doctors at USC told her later they worked hard to keep her alive and were aghast when she stopped breathing for a few moments. Curtis said she remained unconscious for three days. Mary quoted the doctors as telling her when she woke up, "How could a woman this pretty and this talented want to kill herself? She has so much going for her." They insisted that if she tried it again, they'd make sure she saw a psychiatrist.

Mary's suicide attempt shocked Curtis. He decided to stay with Mary and end his marriage to Donice. The aftermath of Mary's desperate act also killed her marriage to Cecil. The Womacks, blaming Curtis for the suicide attempt, went to see her in the hospital and forbade Curtis from visiting her. Curtis went anyway and stood in the hallway looking in on the rest of his family, including Cecil, talking to the hospitalized Mary. "I saw the family and I didn't want to be fighting or arguing with anyone because I'm older than Cecil and he's my little brother. . . . I understood his feelings, so I just didn't say anything," Curtis said. Finally, though, he couldn't take it anymore and walked in, sat on the bed, and started talking to Mary. Cecil told Curtis to "get off the bed" and Mary said, "Don't talk to him like that." Cecil responded, "OK, that's it. I'm gone; it's just you and him," and stormed out. Cecil and Mary were divorced in Los Angeles in 1977.

To Mary, the confrontation came as a great relief. "It released me, because here I was torn between both of them and I didn't want either one of them to be sad," she said. "But this way when he [Cecil] released himself, that released me from him."

This was not completely true, for either Mary or Cecil. Later on, when Mary found out that Cecil had taken up with another woman, she was so upset she ran out of the room. Cecil also was badly hurt. Friendly Womack Jr. recalled, "When Mary moved to Curtis, Cecil and me got closer because I was worried about him. I started a production company with him. I introduced him to a couple of girls. You can give the divorce, but you can't turn off the feelings."

Curtis claimed, however, that Cecil was less affected by the breakup than the others thought. "It wasn't like he was jealous of us. It was like he just felt it was strange that his brother and his wife were together."

This isn't terribly surprising. Many people are very resistant to the idea that one woman should marry, or live with and have children with, two brothers in the same family, one after another. The plot of *Hamlet* revolves partly around Hamlet's violent disgust that shortly after his father had died, his mother married his father's brother. And this attitude is far from dead. Vandella Annette Helton remembered in 2011 that she thought at the time, "Oh Mary, no no, you just don't go through the family."

"You don't marry brothers when they're both alive," former Motown vocalist Brenda Holloway said from Los Angeles that same year. "It's incest." Holloway added, "Mary was very weak. And she was a lady with a lot of different passions and confusions, mental and sexual. But you can't let your passions get the best of you."

Mary's old friend Maye James-Holler was equally scathing about Mary taking up with her husband's brother. "Why didn't she find *another* man?" Maye asked. "Why go with your brother-in-law?" Also in 2011, referring to Mary taking up with Curtis, Maye said, "I'm still shocked. . . . I just can't believe it."

Maye quoted Mary as saying that Curtis "helped her and was nice to her and listened to her." Without referring specifically to

Cecil or Curtis, Maye strongly implied that Mary was naïve. "When men are trying to capture women's minds, they always seem helpful and ask them about their ideals. . . . Then they show their butts," (i.e., their bad sides).

Other friends of Mary's have argued in response that because of the security bubble surrounding music celebrities, it is very difficult for them to get to know anyone well enough to wish to marry them unless that person also is a celebrity or a member of their own extended family.

Cecil predicted darkly, and understandably at the time, that the liaison between Curtis and Mary "was going to ruin Mary's career, and they were going to run Mary out of the country like they did Jerry Lee Lewis." (In 1958, it had been reported in London that rock 'n' roller Lewis's third wife, his first cousin once removed, was thirteen years old. Lewis, then twenty-three, insisted she was fifteen, but his European tour was canceled and his career nearly ended.) The problem with Cecil's analogy is that Lewis's marriage violated child abuse and marriage laws in many jurisdictions. But Mary, Cecil, and Curtis were all adults.

For a long time after the hospital room incident, the rest of the Womacks kept trying to convince Mary and Curtis to break up. According to Mary, Bobby Womack suggested that she and Curtis move somewhere far away, specifically mentioning Egypt. She insisted he was serious about this.

Paradoxically, such family opposition strengthened the bond between the lovers. "They were trying to get us apart," Mary said. "And we were fighting to stay together." Friendly Sr., the Womacks' father, "eventually accepted it more than anybody else did."

The other Womacks also finally softened. Ironically, Mary later claimed that by doing so, they hurt the relationship between her and Curtis. "Their lack of opposition damaged it," she said. "We had a lot of fights and tore our relationship down." Mary and Curtis would be discussing something and an argument would begin in which "there was a lot of animosity, and, temporarily, hatred in the air for that other person. It never lasted long, but it was always underneath."

Sometimes the animosity was brazenly out in the open. "He beat me more than once," Mary told Bergsman. "Two black eyes, a puffed-up nose, and my caps knocked out, my lips swollen . . . ." She hated physical fights with Curtis "because I had seen my mother under those conditions, and it worked with me mentally very bad, just pulled me apart from him."

Curtis told *Unsung* he fought Mary in self-defense. "You didn't start no stuff with Mary," he said. "You will be fighting her to . . . make sure she didn't . . . really mess you up."

During one argument, Curtis said, Mary started "dancing around like Muhammad Ali," encouraging him to fight her. When he started laughing at her, he said, "she got real mad," pulled him by the hair, split his earlobe by pulling off an earring he was wearing, and then ran out of the apartment.

He said that when the couple argued they "would get into wrestling and scuffling matches. . . . Mary was a strong woman, you know." If she put something in her hand that she might hit him with, he said, "I would run out the door."

About a year after Mary and Curtis moved in together, and after, in Mary's words, having "an argument and some physical fights" with him, she tried suicide a second time. "I was just torn down and depressed. I still wasn't able to cope with how we had gotten together. Cecil and Curtis and me, the triangle, was still in my mind. I couldn't deal with it." Not only did Mary feel guilty, she had started taking prescription drugs, including sleeping pills again, to ease the pain. They didn't help. "So I took some more pills," she said. This time Curtis was in the house when Mary went into the bathroom to take a shower, took some pills, and collapsed. Curtis at first thought she was faking but then saw her getting sleepy and ran the shower on her until the ambulance arrived. She woke up in Cedars-Sinai Medical Center in Los Angeles.

As in her previous suicide attempt when she overdosed on pills while her mother was in the house, the fact that another person was at home at the time of this incident shows that Mary may not have really wanted to kill herself. She could have rented a motel room, locked the door, and killed herself with no one present. But she insisted to Bergsman, "I really wanted to die. . . . You can only bear so much pain. That pain was really bad on me. I just could not deal with it."

In spite of their verbal and physical battles, Mary and Curtis were together off and on almost to the end of Mary's life. During their first ten years, the couple broke up three times for as long as three months on each occasion. Nevertheless, Mary said, they always got back together after their breakups. Each reunion occurred because she thought Curtis had changed, although she didn't specify in what way. However, their life together remained rocky.

It also had its high spots. At one point during their years together, when they were living in the L.A. area, Mary proposed to Curtis that they move to West Hollywood. "She liked this beautiful apartment there that had this Hawaiian garden look to it," Curtis said. "When we got there, it had a hairdresser in it, and all these guys were jumping in the pool and waltzing around in there. I was thinking, 'Where's the women? Where's the women?' Mary was saying, 'Isn't this beautiful?' and I was saying, 'Yeah, but there's something about this place I can't put my finger on.'"

When Curtis told others that he and Wells had moved to West Hollywood, they said, "West Hollywood! Womack, you ain't turned over, have you?" He responded, "Say what?" and they told him, "That's a gay area, man. The mayor's even gay." Curtis found all this amusing and told Wells, "It would take you to find a place like this and look just at the beauty of it." They lived there for years.

Mary especially felt very comfortable there. One weekend night when they were in their apartment in the complex, a "butt-naked" Mary told Curtis, "I'm going to go out into the hall." Curtis said he didn't want her to be out there like that. In response, she opened the door and ran down the hall without a stitch on. Although it turned out that no one else was in the hallway at the time, Curtis coaxed her back into the apartment as soon as he could, and immediately after she complied, they both heard someone else walking down the hall. Curtis was concerned because the hallways were rarely empty: West Hollywood was a very sociable neighborhood, and on the weekend, many people were attending parties in different apartments and visiting each other.

In 1979, two years after his divorce from Mary, Cecil made a spectacular second marriage. It emphasized his immersion in the music business, where serial or unusual marriages are as common as they are in Hollywood and the difficulties celebrities encounter when they try to find loving partners outside their inner circle.

First, a little history. More than a dozen years earlier, singer Sam Cooke, the Valentinos' mentor, had been shot to death in Los Angeles. According to the official account, the gun was fired by a motel manager after Sam raced downstairs and into her office naked but for a sports jacket, in pursuit of a woman who had stolen his money and the rest of his clothes.

In 1965, three months after Sam's death, Bobby Womack, the third-oldest Womack brother, married Barbara Cooke, Sam's widow. The couple divorced in 1970. In his 2006 autobiography, Bobby Womack attributed the split to Barbara's discovery that he had begun having sex with one of Barbara and Sam's daughters. The woman whom Cecil married in 1979 was that former stepdaughter of Bobby's—his own former step-niece—Linda Cooke, who was twenty-six.

Many people would find Cecil's marriage to Linda as shocking as they found Curtis's relationship with Mary. Curtis put forward a charitable theory about both relationships, however. "It was go-with-who-you-really-like time."

Friendly Jr.'s analysis is probably the most accurate, as far as it went. "Cecil was devastated by Mary and Curtis. Mary was the first and the only girl that I knew Cecil to be serious about. He'd never had experience with any women. When the door was open—when Mary left—Cecil was looking for someone to fill the void, and Linda was it."

Cecil and Linda remain married. Calling themselves Womack & Womack, they became hugely successful as songwriters and performers. They specialized in songs about couples battling, straying, accusing, and reconciling. Among their recordings are the US R&B hits "Baby, I'm Scared of You," "Strange & Funny," and "T.K.O.," and the British pop hits "Teardrops," "Love Wars," and "Celebrate the World." "Womack & Womack wrote beautiful songs together," Maye James-Holler said. Millions of fans agreed.

In a 1994 interview, Cecil and Linda talked about their marriage as the major relationship in both of their lives. Linda recalled that she had first met Cecil when she was eight and he was fourteen. Her father, Sam Cooke, had invited the Womack brothers to their home. Cecil, she said, "fixed me with this serious stare. I found him very intriguing. . . . It was kind of instant. I liked him immediately." Cecil proposed to her soon after her father died in 1964. "Here he was talking about marriage and I hadn't even kissed a boy yet, and I certainly wasn't looking for another father figure." So she said no.

Nevertheless, the two kept in touch for more than a dozen years. Shortly after the dissolution of his marriage to Wells, Cecil again proposed to Linda, Linda said, and this time she accepted. They were married in Las Vegas in 1979.

Cecil, noting that his marriage to Mary Wells had lasted eleven years, called that marriage "a success as far as I was concerned." He noted that he was "a very faithful person, but it's tough to keep a relationship going in the entertainment business." He didn't mention Mary's liaison with his brother Curtis.

He added, though, that "underneath I suppose I was always thinking of Linda. I always knew in my mind that it was going to happen. When I finally separated with Mary I knew something positive would come out of it."

Within a few years after Mary moved from Cecil to Curtis, all three parties had reconciled. Curtis remembered that he and Cecil "would talk and then he would get with her and he would talk to her, and then he and I would talk about everything else, him and I, spirit to spirit, just like brothers."

Both Mary and Curtis were credited as background singers when Womack & Womack scored a number 14 British pop chart hit with their single "Love Wars" in 1984. Mary and Curtis also both participated as background singers in a subsequent Womack & Womack concert in London. When Mary came on stage for the finale, she made a spectacular entrance: wearing a blonde wig, pink blouse, black pants, and stiletto shoes—and carrying her and Curtis's baby, Sugar—she tripped as she came on stage and fell to her knees. Someone helped her and the baby up after a few seconds and the show continued. The couple also backed up for Cecil and Linda on the 1985 Womack & Womack album *Radio M.U.S.C. Man*. On this album, Curtis and Mary are listed as members of the "Womack Congregation," the name given the background group.

"There's not just an episode here, there's a whole miniseries," Will Porter said recently, summing up the events that included Sam Cooke's death, Bobby's marriage to Barbara Cooke, Bobby's alleged sexual relationship with Linda Cooke, Bobby's divorce from Barbara, Mary's divorce from Cecil, Mary moving in with Curtis, Cecil's marriage to Linda, and the reconciliation among Cecil, Curtis, Linda, and Mary.

In 1978, after Mary had recovered from her second suicide attempt, she and Curtis moved to the Mediterranean Village Apartments on La Brea and Santa Monica in Hollywood. They remained together as common-law spouses. The decision not to marry was mostly Mary's. After two marriages and two divorces, "I was scared to marry again," she said. "And for some strange, stupid reason, I felt that if I didn't get married, then mentally I wasn't totally bonded to Curtis. But it happened anyway. When you fall in love with a person, you basically are married to him anyway. . . . It becomes that deep."

Later in her life, Mary called her long-term relationship with Curtis "normal, with some good moments," and enthused about the couple's physical chemistry. "Our lovemaking at times was fantastic," she said. "Some people make love and don't feel hardly anything, so they don't make love anymore. But we had a great sex life."

Mary also was pleased, she said, that she was able to exercise more control over her performing life when she was with Curtis. While Cecil had managed Mary's performing career himself, Curtis turned it back to her. "He didn't want to be in control of it because he had seen what Cecil had done when he had control."

On the negative side, Wells said that she was the only one bringing in money. Her relentless performing, week after week, year after year, at one club after another and at one concert after another, had provided much of the income for her and Cecil. Now it supported Mary and Curtis.

Nevertheless, Curtis said, Wells was so happy about how things had turned out that she began to write a song about her move from one brother to another and about Mary and Cecil remaining friends, just like she and Cecil had cowritten "Two Lovers History" about their marriage. Although this second song was never completed, Curtis sang the beginning of it for me. It includes lines such as "A friend is what you wanted of me / but we had to grow up at the age of thirty-three" (Mary's age when she got involved with Curtis) and "Now let's face it / boy let's erase it / time will heal it / if friendship don't kill it." Its jazz-like melody is haunting.

21

MARY ON DRUGS AND BOOZE

I am so disgusted that I abused my voice with the cigarettes.

—MARY WELLS, 1991

AS A YOUNG MOTOWN PERFORMER, Mary had largely abstained from excessive drinking and illegal drugs. As she grew older, however, and her responsibilities and problems increased, she became a heavy user of both. She'd sometimes stop when the effects became debilitating, when she was frightened about what her habits might do to her, or when her friends forced her to quit or put her in rehab. After a short time, however, she would always return to substance abuse when her life seemed to be going downhill, she needed solace for disappointments, or she simply missed the feelings the alcohol and drugs produced.

Drinking was a prominent feature of Mary's relationships with both Cecil and Curtis. Her uncle, the minister from whom she received spiritual guidance as a young girl, had preached energetically against alcohol and drugs when Mary was a young girl, but her mother's example may have pushed Mary in the other direction in the long run. Maye James-Holler had noticed that Mary's mother "liked her drinks a lot."

Curtis said that Mrs. Wells's drinking made her aggressive. When she started drinking, he said, she looked around for someone to fight. Friendly Womack Jr. agreed. "Geneva was a real giving kind of person and likeable," he said, "but when she started to drink, she was a different person."

Sometimes Mrs. Wells took this to extremes. On one occasion, Curtis said, she was living at Cecil and Mary's house in Los Angeles while the couple was on tour, Mary's older brother Fletcher was visiting from Detroit, and Curtis had just brought over some groceries. Curtis said Mrs. Wells had a few drinks and then started disciplining Mary's kids by banging their heads against the wall. This was too rough for his taste. He stopped her, which made her mad. She picked up a police sap, a leather-wrapped lead club that unaccountably was kept in the house, put it behind her back, and approached Curtis. "Oh, honey, Mama's sorry, come here and give me a hug," Mrs. Wells said.

Fletcher saved the day by "grabbing that thing from behind her. She was going to whack me across my face with it," Curtis said.

As her age and responsibilities increased, Mary drank more and more. She rarely if ever acted intoxicated in public, but she often did at home. "We'd go to lots of parties," Curtis said, "and Mary would be just as cordial as you can be, and then when me and her got together it was like, 'Hey, why don't you go down there and get a fifth of that . . . ' and then, after she'd been drinking for about three days, she'd chase me around the house." Curtis said that Cecil had warned him not to give Mary anything to drink, but "I'd be sitting there drinking with her and I wouldn't think."

When Mary was drinking, Curtis said, she, like her mother, was "like the littlest guy in the bar who gets drunk and then wants to fight the biggest guy." Curtis and Mary would start arguing and then she'd say, "C'mon, I'm going to beat your ass," grab a frying pan, and chase him around the house with it.

When shed do this, he said, he was forced to protect himself by holding her down and sitting on top of her. Shed try to sweet-talk him into getting up by telling him shed be peaceful for the rest of the evening. "C'mon, baby, let me up. I ain't gonna do nothin'," shed say, but he knew she was lying so hed sit on her until he started falling asleep. As Curtis would slump into sleep, he said, hed feel her pushing at him, trying to get out from under him, and threatening him with how shed beat him when he finally did let her up. This would wake him up.

According to Curtis, Mary then would tell him, "I'm going to call the cops and tell them you're beating me, and they'll put you in jail." And hed say, "Well, I haven't touched you; you have no bruises on you, and I have nothing on me. I've just got to hold you down." And shed say, "'Well, you're going to get sleepy,' and it would be like twelve oclock, one oclock, two oclock. I'd sit on her till she got sober, me and her both, and then wed just fall over on the floor."

While splitting with Cecil and taking up with Curtis around 1978, Mary also started using hard drugs. "I was very upset," Mary said. "My whole life was changing. . . . Because of the confusion between the brothers and me being in the middle, I could not endure the pain . . . so I used drugs for relief, like so many other people do but never talk about it."

Mary's favorite drug was heroin. The first time she took it, she said, she found it "fantastic." It began when a woman across the hall in her apartment building asked her to come along one morning on a visit to the woman's cousin. Mary's children were in school by then, so she could go. When she arrived at the cousin's house, she saw he had "this powdery stuff, this brown powdery stuff." Mary said she never had seen heroin before, which she called "brown boy" or "boy." (Cocaine was "girl.") She exclaimed, "That's dope," and the neighbor lady told her, "Yeah, but you could do some of this. A little of it will relieve the pain." Mary said, "Yeah, and you get hooked." The lady replied, "Not if you do it a few times and don't keep doing it." Mary claimed this to be true.

Many drug users, some of whom call themselves "chippers," insist that if heroin is snorted rather than injected and if it is not used continually, it's not necessary to take it every day. Many chippers have boasted about how they use heroin on the weekend and are still able to go to work during the week.

Mary said she avoided becoming a heroin addict by snorting the drug rather than shooting it into her veins, taking breaks from using it, and never using more than a certain amount at any one time. From then on, off and on until her death, she would snort heroin "for one or two days and then lay off it for about a week." At other times, she said, "I would do it every day for a few weeks but then I would leave it alone."

Curtis said he sometimes attempted to take the drugs away from Mary, but she'd rebuff such attempts by trying to knock him down. Later in their relationship, when he'd make a more serious effort to prevent her from using drugs, she would leave him for weeks or even months.

Wells said the side effects of heroin were similar to those of a tranquilizer. "It's like a Valium, maybe a little stronger. But it didn't make you feel like you're falling on down. . . . You won't be falling over and going to sleep."

Because she limited her heroin use and did not get high every day, Wells said, "I kept the best furniture, the house stayed nice, and the kids would get nice clothes. They were all-American, and you would never know we were using drugs, just like it was in so many other homes." Wells also said that "most of the time," she wasn't on drugs when she was performing.

Like thousands of others in the entertainment industry, Mary also snorted cocaine, although it's not clear when she started. "In the 1970s, record people were saying that cocaine was the rich man's high, and you didn't get addicted to it," Maye James-Holler explained. "I'm sorry she got caught up in that world. She couldn't have had her senses about her."

Cocaine "relieved me of every bit of pain I ever felt," Mary told Steve Bergsman. "It made me relax. It's too bad that drugs are bad for you, because they can be good for you too."

Drugs affected Mary in other ways as well. They made her secretive, Brenda Holloway said, and often caused her to be confused. Often Mary "was not thinking properly because something else [a drug] was thinking for her. . . . She fought for her kids, she fought for her men, but because of the drugs she was her own worst enemy."

Wells also smoked crack, a form of cocaine, for what she said was a period of about nine months, ending in 1985. That was when she realized she was pregnant with Sugar, her only child with Curtis. Mary insisted that she decided on her own to stop using drugs during the pregnancy. "Quite naturally," she said, "if you've got any civilization about yourself, you're not going to want to bring a baby into this world with drugs in your system. . . . I just quit cold turkey. Without going to any doctor or anything, I just eliminated it. . . . So Sugar was born completely clean." She underwent natural childbirth with Sugar. "I had no drugs in me when she was born."

It's not clear, however, that Mary's abstention from drugs was totally voluntary. "She was pregnant with Sugar and she was smoking that stuff [crack]," Curtis said. "I was so scared for my baby. I got those drug dealers—I told them, 'Don't sell her nothing. Don't let her have nothing' . . . but they would come and get Mary, and you couldn't tell her nothing when she wanted to do something." When his efforts started to fail, Cecil and some other friends of Mary intervened.

The interveners, reasoning that they had to get Mary out of her drug-soaked environment, packed up Mary's and Curtis's clothes and belongings without Mary's knowledge and moved everything to her mother's house in Inglewood, a Los Angeles suburb. They then invited Mary and Curtis out for a drive, headed to her mother's house, and told Wells she would need to live there while breaking off crack. The intervention apparently worked. Mary told Bergsman she never went back to using crack.

She did continue using other hard drugs, however. She told Bergsman somewhat defensively that she was being honest with him about her own drug use because "everybody in this country really is on drugs. . . . Some of the richest people in the world take drugs, and some of the most educated people in the world take drugs, I guess because it relieves pressure. But they don't talk about it. But I'm discussing this. I'd as soon lay it on the line as not, because I'm so tired of the hypocrites. You know, so much stuff is put underneath the carpet instead of being just said straight out."

Mary certainly wasn't this open when she appeared on television shows and at antidrug events as an antidrug crusader in her later years. Curtis said he used to look at her out of the corner of his eye when she gave antidrug speeches on TV or at public meetings. "She'd go on there and talk about drug prevention and 'kids need to do this and kids need to do that' and give a good hurrah speech. You would think she was the purest thing going on, and then we'd leave and she'd say, 'C'mon, let's go get one [take drugs].'"

In addition to continuing to take heroin and snorting cocaine, Mary also made extensive use of methadone. She didn't bother to tell Bergsman about it, probably because much of its widespread use is legal, as a way to wean addicts off heroin. "Methadone doesn't make you drunk or anything like that. It's not like liquor," Curtis said. "It just makes you feel euphoric, and it lasts all day long."

Joyce Moore, a close friend of Mary's during the last half of Mary's life, described Mary to author Susan Whitall as "a heroin addict who intermittently used methadone and did other drugs."

A young Mary Wells at Motown. AL ABRAMS.

Mary as a brunette. AL ABRAMS.

Mary as a blonde. AL ABRAMS.

Herman Griffin, Mary's first husband, in 1962. IAN LEVINE.

Mary celebrates her twenty-first birthday with, from left to right, Maye (Hampton) James-Holler and Gene Chandler. MAYE JAMES-HOLLER.

In 1964, at the height of her Motown career, Mary performs at the Regal Theater in Chicago. RAY FLERLAGE/CACHE AGENCY.

Berry Gordy outside Motown headquarters. AL ABRAMS.

Cecil Womack in 1984. RANDY RUSSI.

Mary in 1972 with Tony Russi, prior to a performance in Orlando. RANDY RUSSI.

A pregnant Mary in 1974 seated at left, her son Cecil Womack Jr. seated at right, and standing left to right, Randy Russi, Tony Russi, Cecil Womack, and Rick Russi. RANDY RUSSI.

Curtis Womack holding his and Mary's daughter Sugar, 1988. RANDY RUSSI.

A blonde mid-career Mary performing at the Sheraton airport hotel in Los Angeles, 1984, with Gladys Horton of the Marvelettes. RANDY RUSSI.

Backstage at the same show: Martha Reeves, Randy Russi, and Mary Wells (Leslie Clark seated in front). RANDY RUSSI.

Mary Wells with Will Porter at Bill Graham's Old Waldorf Club, 1981. WILL PORTER.

Mary on stage in Orlando, Florida, in 1988. RANDY RUSSI.

San Quentin News
THE PULSE OF SAN QUENTIN
Vol. LI, No. 8 TAMAL, CALIFORNIA 94964 Friday, Feb. 20, 1981

Holiday Show Features Mary Wells, Will Porter

POPULATION COUNT
2,932
Friday, February 20

By B. Washington

For a while it seemed doubtful as to whether or not the holiday show would go off as planned. Friday the general population was rushed back to their cells for a body check after two bloody coats were found on the upper yard. After a short lockdown, during which staff investigated the incident, we were released to go about a semi-regular routine. Apprehension filled the air all the way up to showtime.

Minutes before the show was due to start an alarm went off in the west block.

WILL PORTER singing theme song "If You Want to Act Like a Fool, Go Right Ahead."

☆☆☆☆☆☆☆☆☆☆

The next outside guest was Will Porter, and he too had a hard job following the mood that Buena Vista had set. But as they did with the Brothers of Soul, Will Porter proved to be a capable performer. Will Porter calls his style of music "sweat music," and that's exactly what he had the house doing. He did a funky rendition of "You Don't Miss Your Water," which got the audience in the mood for his theme song "If You Want To Act Like a Fool Go Right Ahead." Next he featured his sax player Kieth Crossan on "When Something's Wrong With My Baby," and the house flew apart again.

Assault Slams East Block

More Buckshot For C Section

Max B Con Assaulted

When the curtain opened Mary Wells was standing stage center shining like the star she is. Ms. Wells started her set with "The One Who Really Loves You" which brought the house to its feet.

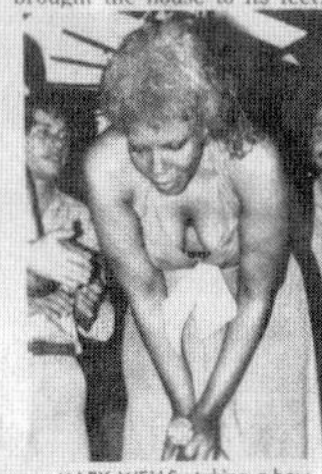

MARY WELLS, taking a bow after a performance par excellence.

Before they could sit back down she had them dancing in the aisles off of "You Beat Me to the Punch," "Let's Go for a Walk in the Park," "Two Lovers," "My Guy," and "Bye Bye Baby." Throughout her whole set there were people dancing all over the north dining hall, police and convicts alike.

MARY WELLS, a star who's never stopped shining.

Ms. Wells just finished an engagement at San Francisco's Old Waldorf where she packed the house nightly. She also has a new record that's due to hit the charts soon on the Epic label. And she's going to Los Angeles for some club engagements that she has in that area.

CAPTIVATING the audience as only she can do.

☆☆☆☆☆☆☆☆☆☆

Warning Shot Fired, Movie Interrupted

Lockdown Called

Mary charms the audience at San Quentin, 1981. WILL PORTER.

Mary as a recording star at CBS-Epic Records. This photo was displayed at her funeral. SONY MU

While Mary was using heroin in California, Curtis said, she saw a methadone clinic near her apartment and wanted to visit it. Curtis told her she didn't need to go on methadone, because her heroin habit wasn't that bad, but Mary said she wanted to try it.

At the time, in Curtis's words, "Mary had no shame" about her drug use. She wanted Curtis to come with her, but he protested. "I'm not going anywhere near there," he said. "I mean, everybody knows you." Mary replied, "Curt, I know who I am. I'm not stuck up or anything." So, he said, "She went in there talking to the people and laughing and dealing with them, and I was thinking, 'OK, this will jar her back into reality. There's all kind of people in there.'"

But Mary enjoyed the experience. She went to the clinic again the next day and started telling Curtis, "This stuff is good!" He was waiting for her outside on the third day, and she came out with methadone in her mouth and her lips pursed. Curtis said Wells "got right up in my face," indicated to him he should open his mouth, "and spit it in my mouth. And I ain't going to lie to you, I enjoyed doing it with her." Mary told Curtis, "You can come in and get this stuff every day, and you'll be feeling good all day long." Mary visited the clinic for about eight years, Curtis said. Every time she stopped going there during that period, she would say, "I miss those people. I miss going down there. Those are our friends."

While Mary was taking methadone, she also continued taking heroin. She kept telling Curtis she'd stop going over to the dealers for her twenty-five- or fifty-dollar heroin hit, but she never did. When Curtis pointed this out, she'd say she didn't have to do as much heroin while using methadone but nevertheless had to use some. "That's not how it's supposed to work," Curtis noted.

Mary liked methadone so much that an L.A. methadone clinic gave her a case of the drug to take with her on the road on at least one occasion, so she wouldn't have to stop and search for it along her route. On other tours, observers noted that Mary made appointments at methadone clinics along the way or stopped at one in each town she came to.

It's a wonder Mary needed the heroin. The methadone they gave her was so pure, Curtis said, that you didn't have to drink it, you only had to stick your tongue in it to get the full effect. Mary learned how to mix it in a blender with some non-narcotic material and some raw heroin (called "tar"), and liked the mixture so much she'd wake Curtis up in the middle of the night and ask him to make some more for her. "C'mon, baby, mix it up," she'd say. Irritated at being forced out of bed and into the kitchen, Curtis would ask Mary, "Why do you keep asking me for some? You already had some." But eventually he would comply. "Mary was just a person that if you had something, she was going to get it from you, not make you, not rough you up or anything like that, although she could get like that too, but she would always sweet talk me into making it."

Mary's heroin use lasted until nearly the end of her life. In 1990, Joyce Moore put Mary in drug rehab at St. Joseph's Hospital in Burbank, California. Mary stayed there for five weeks, attending twelve-step meetings and otherwise fully participating in the program. It worked, but she had only a short time left to live.

Wells's long-term drug use may have eased what she described as her emotional pain, but it also affected her personality and hurt her chances for favorable publicity and for work.

Norma Fairhurst, a member of the Velvelettes and an acquaintance and admirer of Mary's, was working for the Flint, Michigan, convention and visitor's bureau in the mid-1980s when a representative of the local impresario who had hired Mary to perform that evening called her on the phone. "She's here," the woman told Fairhurst, "but she doesn't have anything to wear for her performance." Mary had arrived with only the dress she was wearing. "I went over to the hotel, and she was sitting on the edge of the bed in her one dress," Fairhurst said. She "had a lot of suspicion then" that Mary was using drugs.

Mary's lack of replacement clothing may have been at least partly due to the cost of her habit. Holloway said that on one concert tour, Wells made $19,000, but very soon thereafter "she was fussing because she didn't have any money." Holloway immediately thought, "Mary spent all that money on drugs."

Mary's friend Joyce Moore said she noticed that when Wells arrived for a performance, "She often looked like a bag lady, like she had had a tough night and was not kempt." Moore would then marvel at Mary's transformation when she appeared on stage. "She had put on her stage look. It was like somebody waved a magic wand and provided her with lipstick, a gown, and a wig. And she always had great grace and poise. She knew who she was."

Moore added, however, that "if you looked closely, you could see that the gown was really in shambles, the wig didn't fit right and needed some cleaning, and that as good as she looked, it really was an illusion."

At about this time author Gary Kyriazi said his antennae went up about Mary and drugs when he listened to Wells screaming at her agent over the phone. Kyriazi had proposed to Gladys Horton of the Marvelettes that he write a book that would be partly about her and Mary. Horton liked the proposal and told Mary's agent she thought it was a good idea. But Kyriazi hadn't yet spoken with Mary. While he was in the agent's office, the representative called Mary on the phone and described the proposal. After a few seconds, he motioned to Kyriazi to pick up the extension. Kyriazi said he heard Mary scream, "How dare Gladys offer me a project I know nothing about! I was the biggest star at Motown! They used to call me the female Jackie Wilson!'" She kept repeating this.

"It reminded me of Gloria Swanson playing Norma Desmond," Kyriazi said. The agent tried to calm Mary down by reading her a favorable passage about Mary from a biography of Smokey Robinson in the hopes that praise would calm her down, but Kyriazi said the whole conversation "sounded like he was talking to her through a haze. She said, 'Oh yeah, I forgot about that' but then jumped right back to 'I was Motown's biggest star! They called me the female Jackie Wilson!'" Wells's performance on the call disturbed Kyriazi intensely. "It put me against the wall," he said. "I didn't like the star thing, the affectation thing. 'What am I doing here?' I thought." He left Hollywood for good soon after.

Also in the mid-1980s, after Mary had agreed to record the song "Yes" for the soundtrack to the movie *Dirty Dancing*, she failed to appear for the recording session. Another vocalist, Merry Clayton, was hurriedly drafted to fill in for her, costing Mary a much-needed opportunity at what was certainly a low point in her career. Clayton's rendition of the song rose to number 79 on the *Billboard* R&B chart and number 45 on the *Billboard* pop chart in 1988.

Although drugs hurt Mary's career, her own natural generosity had made her sympathetic to other drug users. When she was performing at the Apollo Theater in the 1960s and vocalist Frankie Lymon was asking everyone for money, Mary was the only one who gave it to him. Everyone else said Lymon was just going to use the money to buy drugs, but her only reply was "He's going to get it somewhere." Lymon died of a drug overdose in 1968 at age twenty-five. Years later, an Apollo employee complained to Martha Reeves about how often Mary had asked him to go out and purchase drugs for her while she was performing there later in her career.

Joyce Moore, who never knew this younger version of Mary, described her friend as "aloof and not particularly social. She held herself away from people. She wasn't great at bonding. She'd just space out and not be involved." Mary was "very sweet, but you could never get a read on her. She was just in her own space. Sam and I didn't realize for a long time that part of the reason Mary was like that was because she was high and she was using."

22

STILL ON THE ROAD, STILL ON HER OWN

As her drinking and drug problems escalated and her age increased, Mary continued to find it necessary to make constant and energetic stage appearances to pay her bills.

But money problems and the lack of her formerly extensive Motown resources forced her to call on brothers, husbands, lovers, and pickup bands to fill gaps in her retinue. The results were extremely varied.

Among Mary's early recruits was her older brother Thomas Wells, who was perhaps a little too loyal. On one occasion, Mary told Randy Russi, when she was performing in Detroit and some admiring male fans wanted to kiss her hand, Tommy "went crazy" and attacked the boys with his fists. Police had to be called to calm the situation, Mary said.

In May 1972, somewhere in Alabama, things got a lot worse. Tommy was driving Mary, Cecil, and one of their backup musicians from one gig to another and fell asleep at the wheel. According to the account that Mary and Cecil gave Randy Russi, their gold Cadillac had been moving so fast that when it went out of control, it flipped nose over nose four times. Mary said she could hear Tommy "screaming for the Lord." Although no one was seriously injured in the accident, glass fragments buried themselves in Wells's face, and the car's hood and trunk were destroyed. Wells, a determined trouper, showed emotion only when a nurse at the local emergency room told her that her face was a "mess," according to this account. Her greatest fear seemed to be that disfigurement might end her touring career, and she was very relieved when she realized that no lasting damage had occurred.

During that same year, Mary performed at the Wattstax Music Festival in Los Angeles, an event attended by one hundred thousand fans and often called the Black Woodstock.

Her audience, many of whom had aged along with her, almost always supported her. But as her recording career diminished and her disposable income grew smaller, the incompetence of the backup bands she could afford and the competence of her audiences sometimes clashed weirdly. The *Washington Post* wrote that during one of her performances at the Warner Theatre in Washington, DC, in 1980, "each of her hits was buttressed by a mighty chorus from the audience, which, at times, seemed more familiar with her songs than her backup band."

That was because while running already low-cost tours, Wells was often trying to save additional money by scrimping on her bands. Sometimes, for instance, she'd eliminate the horn section, saving three to four hundred dollars but undoubtedly hurting the quality of the sound.

The man who came to the rescue of her act was singer, songwriter, and bandleader Will Porter, who joined the Wells team after watching one of her less successful concerts in 1981. Although he was a big fan of Mary's, Porter said, "Everything about her show that night was terrible except Mary's singing." In an attempt to demonstrate his skill as a bandmaster and organizer, Porter asked Mary to be his guest on a show he was putting on at a San Francisco nightclub, the Old Waldorf. Porter said he secured Mary as his guest artist for only a few hundred dollars although she had to drive the four hundred miles from Los Angeles to San Francisco to make the gig.

Porter's ploy worked: Mary asked him to become her musical director after participating in his concert. He held that post from 1981 through 1992, often doubling as the opening act at her concerts, and he even ran the music at her funeral.

Porter improved Mary's show, but he has few fond memories of the pickup bands that Mary's sometimes precarious financial situation forced them to put together for some performances. "I would yell at the band, 'Here it comes, the bridge!'" Porter said, referring to the part of a song during which the band keeps playing but the vocalist keeps silent. His warning, he said, was aimed at allowing the band to brace itself for the demanding labor of playing an unfamiliar tune without Mary covering up its mistakes.

Sometimes her onstage entourage had all it could do to keep Wells's show going. When Mary performed at New York City's Palladium in 1981, the *New York Times* reviewer criticized "the occasional meanderings of an apparently unrehearsed and unprepared backing band." The *Times* conceded, however, that the band "did kick the music along" and that Mary's backup singers "managed to keep it on track."

On other occasions, the pickup groups were somewhat better than expected. "I hit the stage and was shocked that the band knew the song," Wells said of one underfunded concert.

Nevertheless, Mary seemed to be popular everywhere. She sang at San Quentin prison in February 1981, and the next issue of the prison newspaper featured the following routine stories: "Assault Slams East Block," "Bloody Lockdown in D Block," and an unusual good-news piece, "Holiday Show Features Mary Wells." According to the prison newspaper, "Throughout [Mary's] whole set there were people dancing all over the north dining hall, police and convicts alike." Four photos illustrated the story, one of Will Porter and three of Mary, including an extremely revealing shot of Mary bowing dramatically forward in her low-cut dress. In all-male San Quentin, this made the newspaper a major keeper.

Wells's continued fame was one of the reasons she and Martha Reeves were invited to perform in 1984 as the premier act at a preview opening of Canada's largest nightclub, a former Kitchener, Ontario, K-Mart transformed into Lulu's Roadhouse. The club's owner insisted they could serve four thousand patrons simultaneously and boasted of the world's longest bar. Porter remembered that it was "freezing cold" at that opening, and that the cold may have affected the behavior of Mary and Martha. "First they'd be all lovey-dovey, hugging each other and saying things like 'Sister Woman, we created all this!'" he said, "and thirty minutes later, it would be 'If that bitch says one more thing, I'll snatch that ugly wig off her ugly head!'"

Luckily, Mary remained a marvelous onstage performer. But much of her success on the road was due not to her new songs but to her Motown classics. In her early days as a post-Motown performer, the songs were almost contemporary. Then, as the years flew by, the excellence of those songs, as well as the strength of Mary's continuing renditions of them, gave her an unexpected new status—as uncontested Queen of the Oldies.

History was on her side. As baby boomers who were teenagers in the 1960s became middle-aged in the '80s, that generation's favorite music made a big comeback. Oldies stations were established, and their audiences grew rapidly. Classic pop and rock 'n' roll songs, including a large percentage of Motown hits, were featured on these stations and on the soundtracks of new films, including *The Big Chill*, a 1983 film about the end of the 1960s that uses five Motown tunes. Many 1960s Motown songs were combined into albums that were widely produced and successfully marketed. Motown even rereleased eight of Mary's hit tunes from the '60s in 1982 and 1983 on four *Motown Yesteryear* 45 rpm records. As Mary's career as a Top 10 recording artist faded into history, nostalgia kept her performing career alive.

In 1984, twenty years after her greatest hits, Wells and her now-oldies were a big success at the Wax Museum Night Club in Washington, DC. Although the Dynettes and the Shirelles were also on the bill, the *Washington Post* noted that only Wells, by singing "Two Lovers" and "My Guy," had any success in luring people onto the dance floor.

During that one concert, Wells also performed "You Beat Me to the Punch," "The One Who Really Loves You," "What's Easy for Two Is So Hard for One," and "Bye Bye Baby." The reviewer wrote that Wells vocalized "her 'whoa-whoa-whoa's' like punch lines, and the audience responded with applause like she was punching a buzzer." Apparently tireless, Mary proceeded, with help from Curtis, to perform a medley of 1950s R&B hits before segueing into the very appropriate "Yesterday," of Beatles fame.

"I couldn't get on stage without performing my Motown hits," Wells said. "They're part of me now." In an interview with Gerri Hirshey, she noted that the term Motown now meant "oldie but *goodie*." At other times, she displayed some ambiguity about her situation. "I don't like the whole oldies scene," she told another interviewer. "It makes me feel like I will never have another hit record."

Nevertheless, when she was the featured performer at DC's Great Oldies Concert, held at the Coliseum, the *Washington Post* reported that "the crowd shouted her name throughout the night."

Taking advantage of her continued popularity, Motown put out four albums in the 1980s and in 1990 of Mary's Motown oldies: *Bye Bye Baby / The One Who Really Loves You* in 1987, *Two Lovers / My Guy* in 1987, *Original Motown Classics Mary Wells* in 1990, and *Compact Command Performances: 22 Greatest Hits* in 1991.

When appearing on television in 1988 as one of the *Legendary Ladies of Rock 'n' Roll*, she wore a gold lamé robe over white slacks and snapped her fingers while moving back and forth as she sang each song. At the end of her performance of "My Guy" on this program, she sang the words "My Guy" five times while banging a tambourine between each repetition. While singing "You Beat Me to the Punch," she clenched her fist when delivering the "punch" line, and turned her back on the audience and sashayed toward the back of the stage when delivering a line about "walking away."

Despite Wells's incredible endurance on the road, where she earned fees varying from $200 to $10,000 per concert, with the higher figures occurring after Porter joined her team, "Mary was always broke," Porter said.

Sometimes, Wells could be her own worst enemy as far as money was concerned. George Scheck, who had become her manager soon after she left Motown and signed her with Twentieth Century, certainly got many bookings for her and tried to get others. In the early 1970s, he told Wells he was trying to land a beer commercial for her that would require her only to record a jingle for radio play and would pay her $20,000. She told him she didn't want to do it because people knew she didn't drink, and she didn't want to be hypocritical. (It's not clear if Mary really was on the wagon in 1970 or not.)

The more she thought about the commercial, though, the better it seemed. Finally, she told Randy Russi, "For twenty thousand dollars what do I care what people think?" and told Scheck to land the commercial for her if he could. But it was too late.

A friend who wanted to remain anonymous remembered Wells buying a van in 1984 that required a $350 installment payment every month, a large amount at the time. It was soon trashed while it sat behind a service station awaiting repair. "She probably bought it for whatever it said on the sticker rather than bargaining," said the friend, who knew Mary's habits very well, and she also most likely failed to make sure the van was under warranty.

On a more upbeat note, Tony Russi, who traveled with Mary for a while, noted that on every stop Wells would buy a toy car or a toy gun to take home to her kids, whom her mother was usually babysitting.

23

COMING IN FROM THE APPLAUSE

Mary's continued on-the-road performing benefited her in 1981 in a very big way: a record company exec who had grown up on a steady diet of Motown hits offered her a chance to reenter the recording industry.

He was Larkin Arnold, senior vice president for black music for CBS, which owned Epic Records and Columbia Records. According to Curtis, Arnold saw and admired one of Wells's performances and invited her to visit his office. Wells was excited but worried. She told Curtis that because she hadn't made any records in years, "We don't have any material to take up there."

Womack told her, "Just bring your greatest albums. I want this man to just see you and [remember your glory days in] rock 'n' roll."

Wells took Curtis's advice, and the result, Curtis said, exceeded their expectations. Mary showed Arnold the records, and he looked at them, got up from his desk, and walked over to the window. He looked out of the window for a while. When he turned around he had tears on his face. "It's a deal," he said.

Interviewed in 2010, Arnold didn't remember seeing Mary perform or the specific details of the scene in his office. Whether or not he initiated the contact, he was the perfect choice for Wells. Shortly before their meeting, he had successfully recorded other former

Motown acts, including Michael Jackson, the Jacksons, and Gladys Knight and the Pips.

Arnold also was a major Mary admirer. "She was one of my favorite artists growing up," he said. "I had the utmost admiration for her and empathy for her plight. Her songs had brought so much joy to so many people, and I wanted to help her as much as I could. I wanted to give her one last shot."

Noting that Wells had been employed by other record firms since leaving Motown and hadn't had much success at those companies, he said, "It was obvious she had fallen on hard times. She told me that things were kind of rough and that her career hadn't progressed the way she had hoped it would." He sympathized, knowing that artists find it hard to work successfully as performers without a current record of their own on sale. Moreover, "the music business, unfortunately, is a youth-oriented business." And Mary, at thirty-eight, was no longer young.

When Wells told Arnold she was "recommitted to her [recording] career," he said that "seeing as how I had sentimental feelings for what she had done in the past, I gave her another chance. I owed her that." He was "hoping something could happen" with her career.

Arnold's plan was to put Wells together with a producer and songwriter who would give her material that "was happening" in the early 1980s, as opposed to the 1960s tunes she was relying on for her performances. Mary felt even more welcome at Epic when it turned out that the associate producer of her records was to be Robert Bateman, whose group she had tried to join before she joined Motown, and that the top producer would be Bateman's nephew, Greg Perry.

Arnold signed Mary to CBS for one album, with an option for another, a standard deal at the time. He then made her day by offering her a $25,000 advance, which she accepted. What he was most pleased about, however, was the picture he soon had taken of her, both for publicity purposes and for her album cover. "I'm very happy that we got her dressed up and got her great makeup and a great hairstylist," he said. Mary was so glamoured up for the picture that she looked like a superstar all over again.

She looked so different, in fact, that Will Porter could barely recognize her. "That lady had *never* looked like that," he said. He said she usually showed up for performances with what he called "raggedy-ass hair." (That was the Mary who appeared at San Quentin.) The Epic photo that Arnold commissioned was the photo displayed at her funeral, a fact he remains proud of.

During a subsequent meeting in Arnold's office, Arnold played for Mary, Curtis, and Porter the rhythm tracks for what Arnold thought was a promising composition, later to be titled "Gigolo." He hoped the song would be the breakout hit Mary needed. Arnold liked it partly because its rhythm track would appeal to the disco-dancing crowd. Several black artists at the time, including Gloria Gaynor, were in fact crossing over to the pop charts and pop radio by combining a disco hit with black radio play.

Mary loved the rhythm track. "As soon as she heard it, she laughed and said, 'Oh, that's funky. We can make something out of that,'" Porter said. Mary complimented the track's producers, the brothers Alphonso (Fonce) and Larry Mizell, for "getting in the groove and hanging with it like that." The Mizell brothers had actually played the rhythm track as well as produced and arranged it: Fonce, a former Motown songwriter, played the drums, Larry played the keyboards, and their brother Rodney played bass. Mainly record producers and arrangers, the Mizell brothers had been Arnold's friends at Howard University. Also, along with Berry Gordy, they had been members of the Motown team the Corporation, which had written and produced several Jackson 5 hits. (Fonce Mizell died in 2011.)

The Mizell brothers characterized Mary as "near the top as far as being easy to work with." They said they were surprised at this because, as Larry Mizell put it, "sometimes people who have had some success are harder to work with."

Neither the title nor the lyrics of "Gigolo" had been written yet. Its appeal was based on its groovy rhythm and instrumental track. Porter said he thought the tune would be a success unless the lyrics were "stupid." After the lyrics were written and recorded, "alluring," not "stupid" became the appropriate descriptive adjective. On the seven-inch version, as well as the dance club twelve-inch version, Mary hisses the words *sexy* and *gonna get ya* before the brass even starts playing, and goes on to boast melodically, "Tonight he is my guy" and "Even Cinderella had her gigolo." Female background singers accompany her with singing and applause. "Gigolo," which also was the name of a dance at the time, became a hit at dance clubs across the country in 1982.

The twelve-inch version of "Gigolo" includes an extended rock guitar solo and is backed with "Let's Mix It Up." "Let's" extends the sexy theme of "Gigolo," with lyrics such as "You're dancing close to me / don't know whaa-aaaa-aaaa-aaat's come over me," and "You're such a sexy sexy sexy thing / and how you groove me!" Mary had come a long way from her somewhat prim Motown days.

The 45 rpm version, backed with "I'm Changing My Ways," rose to number 69 on the *Billboard* R&B chart in 1982. It also hit number 13 on the *Billboard* hot dance club play chart and number 2 on the *Billboard* disco chart. (While Wells had been marrying, producing children, and performing on stage, record charts also had been multiplying.) But the single's success did not carry over to the *In and Out of Love* album on which it first appeared in 1981, which failed to chart.

Arnold's reaction was: "'Gigolo' wasn't a gigantic hit, but it was OK." Although he would have been happier if the song had done better, Arnold noted that it had put Mary's name out there again and put some money in her pocket. Both developments, he said, were very useful to her.

And, as Arnold had hoped, "Gigolo" did jump-start Wells's badly stalled recording career. CBS Records planned to do even better with a second single release from the *In and Out* album, the Motown soundalike "These Arms," backed with "Spend the Nights with Me," to be issued in 1982.

Porter liked "These Arms," but being very aware of Mary's constant need for money, probably for buying drugs, he was not surprised when she seemed uninspired at first during the recording of the tune. He said she told the crew, "Let's just finish this as best we can and split the remaining money [the money left after recording costs had been paid]," a perfectly legal move but not exactly a wholehearted one. However, as Wells kept working on "These Arms," which the production people all thought was a great song, the technicians heard her remark over an open mike, "This song is really something, isn't it?"

"These Arms" is upbeat and infectious. It is helped along by lyrics such as "These arms used to rock you, baby" and by a five-member background chorus that includes Curtis Womack and producer Greg Perry. But the tune failed to chart in either its disco version or its regular version. Arnold said a singer needed two or three successful records in a row to move her career forward, and "These Arms" just didn't do the job.

In addition to "Gigolo" and "These Arms," the *In and Out of Love* album contains the yearning, dreamlike songs "(Will You Still Love Me) Share My Love," "You Make Me Feel So Good Inside," "Spend the Nights with Me," "Indian Giver," "Let's Mix It Up," "I'm Changing My Ways," and the bouncy, aggressive "I'm Not the One (You're in Love With)." (Mary and Cecil had written "I'm Changing My Ways.")

Later on, Wells blamed the failure of the "These Arms" single, as well as the *In and Out of Love* album, on the company's refusal to follow her marketing plan. She had wanted to release "These Arms" before "Gigolo," in order to recapture her share of the black music market by reminding the world of her Motown greatness and then to release "Gigolo" as the next step in her comeback. But the company insisted on the reverse, she said.

Porter blamed Mary's problems at Epic on Arnold's refusal to take *his* marketing advice, which was to direct Mary's releases at what he believed was her large Latino audience. Porter said that when he told Arnold about the overwhelmingly enthusiastic Latino reactions to her concert performances, Arnold's response was, "There ain't no Mexicans in Kansas City."

Arnold said he couldn't remember the details of the meeting but disagreed with Porter about the nature of Latino enthusiasm for Wells. He agreed Latinos liked Mary but said the Mary they loved was the woman who sang "Two Lovers," "You Beat Me to the Punch," and her other Motown hits. Latinos were uninterested in any of her post-Motown recordings. At any rate, Epic's goal was to get Mary exposure to as many audiences as possible.

Arnold told *Unsung* that he partly blamed the company's failure with Mary on the great success Epic was having with other artists. (This was an updated version of what had happened to Mary at Atlantic Records, where she was told the company had to concentrate on Aretha Franklin rather than Mary and its other R&B women.) Arnold said DJs would tell him, "Larkin, I'm playing seven, eight of your records. I can't play any more. It'd look like things are going on," that is, that they were taking payola.

In 1982 Wells produced the second album called for in her contract, an adult contemporary collection titled *Easy Touch*. It includes Mary's versions of hits by Stevie Wonder, Melissa Manchester, the Carpenters, and Donna Summer, including "If You Love Me, Really Love Me," "Don't Cry Out Loud," "Touch Me When We're Dancing," and "Dim All the Lights."

Released on CBS records' 51 West subsidiary, the album failed to chart. Reviewers were so uninspired by it that they speculated it had been recorded merely to fulfill a contractual obligation. The album's sales were not helped by its cover, which displays an unflattering illustration of Wells wearing a garish head scarf and sundress.

Wells left CBS shortly thereafter. Arnold told *Unsung* that when a recording artist doesn't meet success after a couple of tries "there's a negative balance that accrues to the artist . . . and the record company." For a company to continue on in that situation, he said, "would be to throw another three hundred [thousand], half million dollars down the tube." Motown, by contrast, was renowned for keeping its artists going for years while trying to coax hits out of them. But at the time, unlike CBS, it desperately needed every possible hit it could get just to stay alive.

Mary's experience at CBS-Epic, of course, was a continuation of her post-Motown pattern: a couple of solid two-base hits followed by a foul out. And, as she remarked later, after she left Motown, even her initial hits for other companies tended to drop off the charts much more swiftly than they had before. At Motown, by contrast, her hits often had taken a long time to wend their way down the charts, making money for Motown and keeping Mary's voice on the radio during that elongated period.

For instance, Mary's number one Motown tune, "My Guy," stayed on the chart for seven weeks on its way down. Even her less successful Motown tunes, such as "Laughing Boy," which never rose above number 27 on the *Cash Box* pop chart, remained on that chart for four weeks after hitting its peak. But songs she sang for other companies crashed quickly. "Dear Lover," which she recorded for Atlantic, hit its peak at number 45 and was nowhere to be seen the following week. Her Twentieth Century song "Never, Never Leave Me" achieved the number 53 spot and was gone two weeks later. "Use Your Head," also a Twentieth Century tune, hit number 41 and then died.

The relative longevity of Motown's hits was partly due to that company's devotion to promoting each of its records throughout the product's cycle. When a Motown song had hit its chart peak and began to slide, Gordy's promo men would immediately begin a second offensive, visiting DJs and talking up the record. Sources say that some of them also may have provided inducements to some of the DJs, such as one hundred free copies of the record that the DJ could sell to a jukebox distributor. The DJ knew that to peddle these copies a record had to be still getting airplay, thus giving the DJ even more incentive to keep playing it.

An analogy with the stock market is unavoidable. A dying stock often revives at its last stages for what stock market gurus, totally bereft of political correctness, call the "dead cat bounce." What they mean is that a dying stock often clings to life longer than it logically should if investors think they can still make a profit, no matter how infinitesimal, on its barely living hulk. Records and stocks may be more similar than people think.

Discouraged but still fighting, Mary made several more attempts at restarting her recording career even after her somewhat disappointing experience at CBS. Later in 1982, she dipped her toe in the freezing waters of the record world once again, recording "Jingle Bell Rock" and "Silent Night" on an album called *Christmas Soul Special*. It was released by QAG Records in 1982 and went nowhere.

She then made another attempt, this one involving a greater number of songs, by recording musically updated versions of her Motown hits on an album produced by Allegiance Records in 1983 called *The Old, the New and the Best of Mary Wells*.

The album includes a disco version of "The One Who Really Loves You," although this time around Mary sings the title line as

"The One Who Really *Love* You." The album also contains a slowed-down, emotion-laden version of "Two Lovers."

Also on the album is a version of Wells's first recorded song, "Bye Bye Baby," accompanied by a syncopated drumbeat and sung by Mary without the strain in her voice that characterizes the original recording. Other featured tunes include reworkings of her earlier hits such as "My Guy" and "What Love Has Joined Together." Critics said the originals of every one of the hits had been better, and the album failed to chart.

These failures may have hurt her with the judges at the Rock and Roll Hall of Fame. Artists cannot be inducted into the Hall of Fame until twenty-five years have passed since the release of their first record, so Mary first became eligible in 1985, a year before the hall was to induct its first honorees. To nobody's surprise, she was nominated for the 1986 class by a committee consisting of about thirty music historians, journalists, and record company executives. Although it should have been her time to bask in the glow of the highly coveted honor of admission to the Hall, Wells didn't survive the final round of voting, in which five hundred music industry participants from around the world selected the inductees. She was nominated again, for the 1987 class, lost again, and has not been nominated since.

(Ten recording artists and groups were inducted in 1986: Chuck Berry, James Brown, Ray Charles, Sam Cooke, Fats Domino, the Everly Brothers, Buddy Holly, Jerry Lee Lewis, Little Richard, and Elvis Presley. Inducted in 1987 were fifteen: the Coasters, Eddie Cochran, Bo Diddley, Aretha Franklin, Marvin Gaye, Bill Haley, B. B. King, Clyde McPhatter, Ricky Nelson, Roy Orbison, Carl Perkins, Smokey Robinson, Big Joe Turner, Muddy Waters, and Jackie Wilson. Only one of the twenty-five inductees was a woman.)

It is not known how many votes Wells received in each of the years she was nominated for the Rock and Roll Hall of Fame, but her rejection was even more stinging because it meant that she was unable to join "My Guy" there, where it is permanently listed as one of the Hall's "Songs That Shaped Rock and Roll."

Also in 1987, Allegiance Records rereleased *The Old, the New and the Best of Mary Wells* as a CD as part of a two-album set. Its second section, titled *I'm a Lady*, consists of some songs Mary had not previously recorded, including tuneless, driving renditions of "I'm a Lady" and "Make Up, Break Up." It also features Mary's version of "I Feel for You," including the phrases "f—— it, f—— it" and "pop it, pop it." In the final song on the album, a heavily syncopated and musically complex "Money Talks," Mary breaks completely out of the semi-robotic trance in which she seems to be reciting the previous four songs. She enlivens her singing with what sounds like genuine pleasure and delivers with honeyed conviction lines such as "I'm never bored with this rich conversation" and "Money / Just the very *mention* / and you've got my undivided *attention*." Unfortunately for her actual monetary situation, this new dual album failed to chart.

Finally, in 1990, Pair Records tried to repeat part of Allegiance's effort by releasing an album of Mary's Motown classics, updated with her glamorous Epic photograph on the album cover. It sank like a stone.

Mary's disappointment at these failures was greatly offset by the result of another huge, and joyous, twist in her life that occurred at the same time. While she was being considered for the first Rock and Roll Hall of Fame award, she found out she was pregnant. At first, Wells, forty-three, didn't realize the significance of her weight gain. She thought she had a tumor. Curtis said her girlfriends kept asking her, "Say, Mary, you think you might be pregnant?" and she'd say, "No, I have a tumor, and I think it's growing." Finally, one of her friends started laughing and told her, "Your tumor's going to be walking and talking soon, girlfriend."

Wells thought they were joking, but her friends told her there was a new test out called ultrasound that was used for pregnancy detection. After some urging, Wells allowed herself to be tested and came out beaming. "Curtis," she said, "it's a baby girl! We're going to have this baby!" (In addition to the miscarriage of twins, the couple had previously had several abortions.)

When Wells was more than eight months pregnant, she performed at a Coconut Grove, Florida, club called Biscayne Baby, which specialized in female vocalists. "Mary wore a pretty gown that was made big enough to give her space," Curtis Womack said, adding admiringly that "she didn't miss a beat on stage. She carried very well and had absolutely no lack of energy when pregnant." Staffers joked about what an event it would be if Wells actually gave birth at the appropriately named club. As it turned out, she gave birth to Sugar, as the baby was named, on June 13, 1986, in Los Angeles, the day after concluding her Florida engagement.

As this incident indicates, Wells, an experienced mother of three, was not worried about pregnancy. When people asked her if she was nervous about labor, she'd tell them, "I go through labor like nothing."

That turned out to be untrue this time around. When Mary started labor, Curtis was in her hospital room, sitting at the foot of her bed. He made the mistake of sitting in a wheeled office chair within range of Wells's legs, which were muscular from years of stage performing.

When the first pains hit, Mary "kicked me clean out of the room," Curtis said. "The nurses were laughing because they saw me shoot out of there like a cannonball and roll across the hall." Womack claimed he didn't stop until he hit a desk in an adjacent room. Wells then ordered him out of the delivery room for good, blaming him for her labor pains. "Get him out of here!" she yelled. "Get him out of here!"

"I never saw two people doting more on a baby than on Sugar," Joyce Moore said. "She was the world. She was it." Brenda Holloway called Sugar "Mary's heartbeat."

Wells carried the baby around on her hip while touring and would only relinquish her just before going on stage. Sometimes, though, Sugar came out on stage with Wells, entrancing the audience. Occasionally Mary would set up a little chair in view of the audience, so Sugar could watch her as she performed and the audience could watch her watching Mary.

"Sweet little Sugar was always there in the dressing room with her crayons and coloring books," said David Bell, who saw Mary in concert several times in England. According to Bell, Mary once signed one of her albums for David backstage and Sugar was going to "sign" her name on it too, but Mary stopped her.

Martha Reeves, who often toured with Mary, was entranced by Sugar, whom she called "a beautiful baby with glorious eyes, an adorable, precious child." Martha became the baby's godmother and cared for her while Mary was performing and at other times "as often as she'd let me," Martha said. She said Mary "didn't trust anyone" except Curtis and Martha to watch Sugar.

Curtis was a doting daddy. When Sugar was an infant, a baby, and a toddler, "he'd clean her and he'd play with her," Moore said. Wells said Curtis also would "feed Sugar and rock her and put her to bed. He was a good father."

The joys of a new child aside, Mary's recording career had almost run its course. With no alternative in sight, she envisioned spending the rest of her life singing mostly oldies on tour. But in 1986 her career seemed to be rudely interrupted.

24

KIDNAPPED FOR A SONG?

In September 1986, less than three months after Sugar was born, Mary and Curtis were already back on the tour circuit, carrying Sugar with them. Mary was enjoying a series of concert dates in her old stomping ground, Michigan. These engagements attracted the usual adoring crowds. Some of them were there to hear Wilson Pickett, who was performing on the same bill, but many were there to see Mary, their favorite star.

This was an international tour as well. After performing two shows on the first Sunday in September at the Heritage Theatre in Saginaw, Michigan, Mary, Curtis, and Sugar were scheduled to fly to Toronto on Monday to perform for a week in the Imperial Room of the Royal York Hotel.

The Toronto portion of the tour never occurred. What follows is what Mary told newspaper reporters about what happened.

A limousine took Mary, Curtis, and Sugar to the Saginaw airport, ninety miles north of Detroit, on Monday, September 8. They were scheduled to catch an afternoon flight to Toronto for Wells's first performance at the Imperial Room that night.

After the limo dropped them off, they were walking toward the terminal when a well-dressed young couple waved Mary over to their Mercedes, where they asked her for an autograph. The couple then asked her to slip into the backseat of their car to listen to a tape of a song they had written. Curtis and Sugar joined Mary in the backseat.

After listening to the tape, Wells told them, "I like the tune, but I don't have a record deal," and therefore she was not interested in recording it. The couple "got upset" and said, "We'll convince you; we've come a long way."

The husband locked the car doors and windows via the electric switches on the inside front door. He then started the motor and pulled away from the curb. Mary and Curtis objected but the husband "insinuated" that he had a weapon.

The husband said they would drive to California, where, he insisted, Mary would record their song.

The car rolled into Indiana and continued west toward California as the husband's whining continued. "I begged these people for forty-eight hours to please let us go," Wells said.

At about 3 PM on Wednesday, September 10, the apparently irrational husband and wife "became nervous." As the car rolled into California, Mary finally convinced them that if they let her and her family go, "she wouldn't contact the police." The couple stopped and let Mary, Curtis, and Sugar out near the desert town of Mojave, California, about ninety-five miles north of Los Angeles.

Meanwhile, Mary had not arrived at the Toronto airport as scheduled at 5 PM Monday evening. Nor did she arrive on any subsequent flight. "This is really, really weird," her New York booking agent, John Regna, who was staying at the Royal York, told the *Toronto Star* on Tuesday, September 9.

Steve Cohen, Wells's manager from 1978 on, told the *Star* from Los Angeles on September 10 that the performer's disappearance was a matter of "grave concern" and would be reported to "high level authorities" in the United States. "I haven't heard anything,"

Cohen said, "but I intend to call in proper and high level authorities if it isn't cleared up by the end of the day. . . . No one seems to know where she is. She's not at her home in Los Angeles, and her friends and associates haven't heard a word from her."

Regna said he and Cohen had called Mary's relatives, the Saginaw airport police, and hospitals in the Saginaw area and had come up with nothing. He also said a relative of Mary's had registered her as a missing person with Michigan State Police on Tuesday.

Mary's Michigan promoter, Max Oates of Flint, Michigan, told the *Star* that in Saginaw she had given "two fine performances and seemed in good health and very happy. . . . This is a real shock to me."

When Mary, Curtis, and Sugar reached Mojave, they told their story to a reporter for the *Mojave Desert News*. Versions of the story appeared in the *Toronto Star*, the *Miami Herald*, the *Orlando Sentinel*, and other newspapers.

The Mojave journalist noted in his story that Mary and Curtis hadn't reported the kidnapping to the Mojave Police Department. As it turned out, this was not in reaction to any promise made to their alleged kidnappers. Lying to a reporter brings no jail time; filing a false police report might.

All concerned insisted at the time that a kidnapping had taken place. Cohen, noting that Mary had missed only two shows in the previous seven years and that those were due to airline delays, told reporters the story was true and not a publicity stunt. "We lost thousands of dollars in Toronto," he said, referring to Mary's engagement, which had been canceled due to her disappearance. "Why would she be sounding terrified? That's hard to put on." Mary was described as "dazed out" and recovering at her L.A. home.

Years later, in 2010, in an interview for this book, Curtis told the truth: the entire story was false. He and Mary had driven to the Saginaw airport and were scheduled to leave for Canada. They were all set to go when Curtis remembered he had mistakenly packed his ID into his checked baggage, which the airline had erroneously sent to another destination. Mary had her own ID with her and could easily have proceeded to the concert date that evening while Curtis waited in Saginaw for his ID to be shipped back to him.

Although the concert date was a major engagement centered on Mary, "Mary wouldn't cross the border without me," Curtis said in 2010. "She said, 'If he's checking into a hotel, then I'm checking into a hotel.' Something freaked her out." Curtis said he was never able to find out what it was.

And the kidnapping story? "Mary blurted it out," Curtis said, and, aided by her convincing repetition and elaboration of the story to various reporters, "it got legs." She wouldn't move without her "My Guy."

25

ON THE ROAD AGAIN

The "kidnapping" incident did nothing to diminish Mary's on-the-road popularity. In the summer and fall of 1987, twenty-three years after leaving Motown, Mary did seventy-five shows, all based mainly on her Motown hits. If some of those shows were two-day appearances, she was performing almost every other night, week after week.

That fall, however, a dramatic auto accident threatened to throw her off schedule. Wells had landed a performance date with Sam Moore, formerly of the singing duo Sam and Dave, at the Fort Hood military base in Texas. Joyce Moore, Sam's wife, agreed to drive Sam, Mary, Curtis, and Sugar the sixty-nine miles from the Austin, Texas, airport to the fort.

Joyce was at the wheel of the rented Ford Crown Victoria that was carrying the five of them when, on a dark road somewhere on the extensive military installation, "all of a sudden there's a huge steer in the middle of the highway," Moore remembered. "I honked and swerved to avoid him," she said, but he moved and she smashed right into him. "It was like hitting a building," she said.

When the car and its occupants came to a halt, Moore said, she found herself looking goggle-eyed at the steer's rear end, which had hit the windshield on the driver's side and shattered it. Luckily for Moore, it hadn't broken through. It hadn't broken off the steer, either, as everyone realized when the animal rolled off the hood and walked away. Moore, shaking and yelling "Oh my God!" over and over, saw that the steer had left a rather artistic, and very complete, rendition of his nether region in the now cracked and buckled windshield. Less an appreciator of animal art than a realist, Moore noted, "I couldn't see out of the f——ing windshield" and that they needed to drive forty to fifty miles per hour if they were to make their concert date. They managed to do this with no further incidents, although the steer's weight had crushed the car's hood into the engine block. Wells's only recorded reaction was trying to decide whether the incident had been a "cowtastrophe," a "cowlission," or a "cowlamity."

Although the concert was a success, the military authorities were not pleased with news of the steer's presence on the road. Soldiers quickly found the animal, slaughtered it, and offered the traveling musicians some of the steaks.

They refused the offer, but earlier in the trip Wells could have used some food—or at least the money to pay for it. On the way in, they had stopped at a Luby's Cafeteria in Killeen, Texas (later the scene of a mass murder), and were about to order when, Joyce Moore said, Wells took her aside and said, "I don't have any money, and won't have any until I get paid." She asked Joyce to pay for her and her family's food. Moore did so but was shocked that Wells and Curtis Womack, traveling on their own with their fifteen-month-old daughter, had no money between them.

The cash shortage at this stage of her career may have been partly caused by Wells's drug use. It also may have stemmed from the fact that Wells was often supporting, on her tour earnings alone, not only herself, but other members of her extensive family, while also paying fees to her managers, agents, and backup musicians.

Moreover, by this time, some nightclubs were paying Mary relatively low performance fees. Tony Russi said Mary's usual pay was

$500 a night for Friday night and Saturday night plus a percentage of the take at the door for Sunday night. Clubs in Los Angeles paid approximately half the rate of clubs elsewhere, Russi said. The clubs argued unconvincingly that the reduced fees were justified because the record industry was concentrated in L.A. Therefore, they said, every club in the area was really a "showcase" for vocalists or musicians because music industry execs might be in the audience and offer them a recording contract.

Mary told Steve Bergsman that in her biggest-earning years after she left Motown, from 1981 to 1991, when by far the largest part of her income came from touring, she earned no more than $65,000 annually. During that decade, she told friends she was struggling economically. When Bergsman asked her, on her death bed, how she had supported many family members, she replied, "I don't know. That's probably why I'm sick now."

Norma Fairhurst of the Velvelettes had known Wells at Motown and met her again years later in Michigan, where Wells was touring on her own. She said Wells looked like "she was accustomed to living a certain lifestyle years ago and missed it."

On the other hand, Wells's continued attempts to save money by economizing on her backup singers sometimes worked out to her advantage. Her band manager, Will Porter, had been working as background singer for Wells on some occasions, but at one Sacramento appearance Wells appealed for additional help, and Curtis joined Porter up on stage. "All at once he was perfect," Porter said. "Curtis could hear what I was singing. He would instantly make the harmony to it, instead of saying, 'I'm singing this and you'll have to go along.'"

While returning Porter's compliment about harmonizing, Womack said Porter was so good at organizing the background musicians that Wells sometimes got the same sound she had had on her best records. Womack also said he himself added value to the trio because Wells was "a lead vocalist and I knew when to give her her space." The reviewer for the *Toronto Globe & Mail*, writing about a concert in which Curtis backed up Mary, called Womack "a talent in his own right," and opined that "it's conceivable that Womack (the brother of noted R&B singer Bobby Womack) is the one with the real vocal talent in the family." Encouraged by such admiration, Womack sometimes sang lead while Wells sang backup.

(A commercially available DVD of Wells at a Los Angeles performance during 1987's "Dancing in the Street" tour, with Curtis Womack singing background, captures both Womack's somewhat inappropriate clothing—he is wearing a red undershirt while everyone else on stage is dressed elegantly—and his singing skill.)

Porter soon took the team-making process a step further by opening some of Wells's concerts with his own solo vocals. Building on his experience with Mary, Porter has built a substantial pop music career in recent years.

Audiences loved the trio, and Porter and Womack continued to perform as Wells's background singers for most of the rest of her life. They all performed at Toronto's Speakeasy Club in 1987, where the *Toronto Star* noted that Mary "seemed untouched by travel or travail in her rousing first set." She was at San Francisco's City Cabaret in 1988.

Also in 1988, Mary could be seen at the Sheraton Waikiki Hotel in Hawaii, appearing with the Drifters, Dennis Yost, and Sam Moore. At the other end of the spectrum and the country, she performed at Seminole Community College in Florida, where she was backed by a local rock band.

The differences between her venues impressed everyone who was with her. "Sometimes you show up somewhere and you're on the back of a flatbed truck out in the field for an oldies show or a fruit festival, and the next night you're in a luxury suite at a big hotel," Porter said.

Author Gerri Hirshey wrote that Mary's performing outfit at around this time was a cashmere sweater and purple wool slacks tucked into low white boots. Her hair was simply tied back, she had no wig, she wore only a trace of eye makeup, and she was otherwise adorned only with a heart-shaped pendant resting on her collarbone. She had come a long way from her early diva days, when long gowns, heavy makeup, and high-heeled shoes were her standard stage attire.

Her clothes may have been less decorative, but they were also much less restrictive. "Freed from the very real constraints of a sequined sheath skirt, Mary moves around the stage more than she used to," Hirshey wrote. "And her 'yeahs,' which came out of her mouth as 'oooh, hee-yeah,' could do strange things to your neck hairs." As Hirshey summed it up, "Mary's soulful shorthand does the work of six paragraphs of proper English."

Even at this late stage of her career, Mary's humble upbringing caused her to act occasionally in ways that surprised some people. "She'd act very elegant and had a high-toned personality due to her songs," Porter said. "But in a fancy restaurant when the wine steward came around she would ask if they had grape soda or strawberry Fanta." Porter remembered that when she was performing in one upscale San Francisco nightclub that catered to African Americans, Wells would wear "those big satin lounging pajamas with belts that were sold on late night TV. She would tell the audience, 'Aren't these lovely? They're so comfortable,' and the women in the audience, dressed to the nines to see her, would be thinking 'This bitch has her pajamas on!'"

Wells's varied onstage attire, which included wigs of different colors, elicited varying comments on other occasions. After one concert, the *San Francisco Chronicle* complimented her on her tailored black outfit. The *Toronto Globe & Mail* wrote favorably about a flowing gown, which it called "a symphony in tangerine," that she wore at a different appearance. But after one Washington, DC, concert in which Wells wore purple slacks and a hot pink sweater and "was crowned by a halo of golden curls," the *Washington Post* reviewer noted that although Wells sounded like a great Motown singer, "she didn't look like one."

As Mary's crowded schedule indicates, she remained popular as a touring artist even while producing no new recordings at all for years. She sang at Disneyland, at the Playboy Club at Anaheim, at Smokey Stover's in Newport Beach, and in Los Angeles, where she opened for the Four Tops. (She also opened for the Temptations, who had formerly opened for her, a comedown she took in stride.) In Reno, Nevada, where Mary performed at the Reno Classic Car show, she made her entrance between two lines of people throwing flowers at her feet. In Las Vegas, B. B. King attended her show every evening. In Detroit, she sang with the Contours.

Mary and her friend from their Motown days, Martha Reeves, appeared together at numerous venues, sometimes accompanied by additional former Motown artists. Reeves said they costarred nearly continuously during the last three years of Mary's life.

Mary also performed informally whenever and wherever she could at neighborhood clubs. According to Curtis Womack, "Mary could go into some club and sing a little bit or talk a little bit without a band and they'd give her some money like she was doing a gig." Wells never stopped trying, whatever the nature of the venue.

She even continued to receive celebrity-oriented publicity. On one radio program in California, the host discussed a proposal for a chain in California of Mary Wells Hot Dog Stands. The major product sold would be a large all-beef hot dog, naturally dubbed the "My Guy," which would be washed down by an ice-cold glass of "You Beat Me to the Punch" punch.

Wells's special popularity in California was due to her huge Latino following, which was partly a result of the conga beat

Smokey Robinson had written into her classic Motown hits. Porter said her appeal to Latinos also stemmed from the late introduction of Mary's pop classics to Latin America, which kept her profile high among young Latino immigrants during the next two decades. "She'd have twenty thousand people, many of them Latino low-riders, at one concert," Porter said. According to Porter, Mary "would pull up to the side of the stage and perform with a shitty four-piece band, but *Mary Wells Greatest Hits* was the soundtrack of every Latino neighborhood on the West Coast. She was queen of the whole thing. Every car that went by you could hear playing Mary Wells." Porter added that many Latino families named their children after Mary, and that as a result "there are lots of Mary Wells Garcias running around today."

At one low-rider concert, Porter said, the backup band was an uptight, unionized group that usually performed at relatively passive concerts at Disneyland. The band members had expected a staid oldies concert that would be attended by middle-aged suburbanites, and they were shocked when "thousands of screaming Latino teenagers rushed the stage like it was Madonna," Porter said. "The teenagers knew all the lyrics to every Mary Wells song and screamed them out throughout the concert."

Brenda Holloway has a theory about Mary's popularity among Latinos. "Latinos are lovers," she said. "And 'My Guy' and 'Two Lovers' are songs for lovers." Holloway insisted that even in 2011, with a Latino audience, "All you have to do is sing one of these songs and the crowd goes over the top with happiness." Mary said she didn't know what pulled her Latino audiences. "I give what I can," she said.

What she gave audiences at these later-in-life concerts was mostly her Motown classics, and whenever she tried to move away from those well-known tunes, some fans objected. A *San Francisco Chronicle* review of a 1988 concert at the City Cabaret called her non-Motown songs "gratuitous side trips," while praising her for "sculpting glistening renditions of her hits with all the polished certainty that marked the original records 25 years ago."

At that concert, she started with "You Beat Me to the Punch," "The One Who Really Loves You," and "Two Lovers," all from 1962, and added in her 1963 tune "What's Easy for Two Is So Hard for One." Then she segued sentimentally into her first Motown song, "Bye Bye Baby," finally capping her performance triumphantly with 1964's "My Guy." She occasionally referred to "My Guy" as "the cream of *my* crop, the song that has kept me working all these years."

Mary told interviewers that the disco popularity wave, which hurt many of her fellow performers, didn't injure her as badly. She said that was partly because she had recorded some disco songs, but also because the Motown oldies she sang had remained favorites.

After watching one Wells concert in Del Mar, California, the *San Diego Union Tribune* reviewer noted that Wells "earnestly worked through her earliest hits, 'You Beat Me to the Punch' and 'Two Lovers,' as well as others before she settled down for the song the crowd wanted to hear: 'My Guy.'" Describing the crowd's reaction, the reviewer said that "she might not have had them Dancing in the Streets, but she did have them Dancing in the Stands."

According to author Tony Turner, "Mary went out there to a sold-out house and she delivered. That is what made her a star. She delivered what you had paid your money to see. Even when her voice was showing a lot of strain, audiences went wild when she appeared and just adored her. She was a very sweet, polite lady, not a diva, not demanding, very happy-go-lucky, although she looked like she had fallen on hard times. . . . You just wanted to help her."

In the summer of 1987, Mary found herself busing back to the past as she and Curtis, one-year-old Sugar, and Mary and Cecil's son Harry climbed onto a tour bus along with performers Martha Reeves, Eddie Kendricks, and David Ruffin for the six-week, twenty-eight-night "Dancing in the Street" tour. Mary opened each performance, Reeves appeared second, and Kendricks and Ruffin came on third before they all joined together on stage to sing their grand finale, "The Way You Do the Things You Do."

Reeves recalled this tour, and the other two tours she did with Wells during these years, as a time of "great audiences and great performances. . . . Mary was loved everywhere no matter if she was at her best or not. Absolutely everyone in the audience sang 'My Guy' with her."

As usual, Mary distinguished herself by her perseverance and energy, carrying Sugar on her hip while directing Curtis and Harry in loading and unloading the numerous pieces of luggage the party carried with them.

The number of people who showed up to watch Mary perform didn't seem to affect her at all, Porter said. "She ran on her emotions," he remarked. When she was in a bad mood, even when her audience exceeded ten thousand, he said, she'd be anxious to get off the stage after fifteen minutes. She'd ask Porter, "Can we end the show?" and he'd say, "No, you've got twenty more minutes." But at a show when she was in a good mood, "Mary would want to sing for an hour and a half, make jokes and do all the dance steps," even "with three people in the audience and nine people on stage," Porter claimed.

Often, despite an exhausting show, afterward, "Mary would sit for three hours saying hello to every person who wanted to meet her," Porter said. "She would sit in some ratty auditorium somewhere and sign every piece of old vinyl, every thing, every body part." Porter insisted that Mary "would spend more time making sure her fans were OK" than making sure her background music was all right.

But Mary wanted something from her tours besides emotional connection: money. Not only because she was supporting herself and other family members but because to her, money was a way of measuring her true worth. It made her very angry when she believed she was being cheated out of cash she had earned and very sad when she couldn't earn more of it than she did. In many ways, this trait explains her departure from Motown at the top of her fame and her endless energy in pursuing fortune, not fame, for the rest of her life.

The very talented Diana Ross was almost completely the opposite, quite possibly because her family was well-off compared to Mary's. She sought fame from early youth and was never particularly worried about money. In one of the autobiographical books she wrote, she noted without bitterness that when she left the Motown Company after years as its reigning superstar, she walked away with no money to speak of. She seemed pleased to relate that instead of giving her earnings to her, the company had put those funds into developing her career and making her more famous. By contrast, whenever Ross was ignored or only a few people showed up for one of her concerts, she often erupted in fury.

Wells, however, appeared disinterested in celebrity per se. "She didn't care about seeing her face on a billboard. She didn't watch video performances of herself on TV. You couldn't get her to sit down and watch one," Tony Russi said. "She wouldn't go to rock clubs, like the Roxy in L.A., even though all those English rock guys were crazy about her" and would have made a tremendous fuss over her.

Because of this lack of interest in fame, and, according to Porter, "due to all of Mary's traumas, her changing relationships and changing apartments," she didn't hold on to anything, including the gold records she had been awarded, or, in fact, almost any records at all. When Randy Russi was visiting Wells at her home in California, he noticed that her warped album of *Mary Wells Greatest Hits* had been tossed aside and not replaced.

Indefatigable as usual, however, Mary tried again to revive her career once again in the late 1980s, this time under unique circumstances.

26

AN ENGLISH REVIVAL

When Wells toured the United Kingdom with the Beatles in 1964, she had provided hundreds of thousands of Britons with their first exposure to Motown's music. In recognition of this, the first Motown fan club in England was named the Mary Wells Fan Club until its name was changed later to the Tamla-Motown Appreciation Society. (Tamla-Motown was the name of the label on which many Motown tunes were distributed in Britain.) Motown flew the society's founder, Dave Godin, to Detroit to interview Mary in order to emphasize the company's international reach.

Because the British record-buying market was much smaller than the American one, its impact on Motown's economic fortunes was not as great. But Motown's impact on British music was tremendous. British artists started rerecording songs sung by black Americans, and British record buyers bought songs by both African Americans and the British artists who sounded like them.

The general reaction in England to many of Motown's artists leaving the company was disappointment. So it's no surprise that an English record producer, Ian Levine, made one last attempt to revive Wells's recording career, as well as those of many other Motown performers who had left Motown but had failed to prosper at other labels.

Levine, who grew up in the English resort town of Blackpool, was always listening to the radio. At eighteen, he became a DJ in one of the many British clubs that featured the Detroit sound. In 1987, he founded his own record label, Nightmare, which was named after the song "(Like A) Nightmare" recorded by the Andantes in 1964 before they became better known as a Motown backup group. Levine later founded Motorcity Records.

For Nightmare, he first recorded some songs by former Motown vocalist Kim Weston, who was best remembered for "It Takes Two," a 1966 duet with Marvin Gaye. Wells, who was the first of Gaye's duet partners, was the obvious next step. Levine first hired her to rerecord her classic hits. Then, when she was performing in London in the late 1980s, he took the opportunity to record her singing two tunes he cowrote for her, "Don't Burn Your Bridges" and "You're the Answer to My Dreams," both of which he released as singles on the Nightmare label. (Both songs were released again in 1990 on the Motorcity album *Keeping My Mind on Love*.)

Mary poured her usual energy into "Don't Burn Your Bridges," but her vocal range seems somewhat limited. The record is also marred by two cheesy exchanges between Mary and Curtis Womack at the beginning of the tune. Womack sings, "Oh, baby, I don't want to leave, but I think I gotta go now." Mary sings in reply, "If you must leave, make it the last time. Get your hat and get your coat." She then tells him, by singing the song, not to burn his bridges. Then, near the end of the record, Curtis tells Mary in a spoken-word voice, "Baby, I thought it over, and I don't think I want to go anywhere. I want to stay here right with you, baby." She responds by singing, "Ooooooh, come on, come on, baby, come on back to me, sweet friend."

Levine cowrote and Mary recorded four other new songs between 1988 and 1990: "Walk the City Streets," "Hold On a Little Longer," "Keeping My Mind on Love," and "Stop Before It's Too Late," all of which are on the Motorcity album.

"Walk the City Streets" starts with vocalist Liz Lands singing an impossibly high operatic musical phrase, followed by a couple of deep breaths from Mary, indicating how fast she's been walking, then by Mary's energetic rendition of the body of the song. The blatantly sexual "Stop Before It's Too Late" is highlighted by Mary's repeated deep rhythmic sighs and moans, and ends with the repeated words "Stop, stop, stop, stop, stop."

The *Keeping My Mind on Love* album also contains new recordings of Mary's classic hits, including jazzed-up versions of "What's Easy for Two Is So Hard for One," "Once Upon a Time," "You Beat Me to the Punch," and "My Guy." It was released in the United States by Quality Records. The first of these songs began with Mary's assurance to the listening audience that it's the "same song, but with love again."

The rerecording of "Once Upon a Time," which occurred in Los Angeles, took on special meaning, since it was one of the duets she had recorded with Marvin Gaye. Because Marvin Gaye had been shot to death by his father in 1984, this time around Wells performed the duet with his brother, Frankie. Frankie sounded so much like his brother that Mary started to call him Marvin during rehearsals (though during the recording of the tune itself, in 1989, she remembered to call him Frankie).

He starts off their recorded dialogue with the words "Oh, Mary" and she responds with "Oh, oh Frankie, my skies were never blue, we're gonna make it all right, we're gonna make it." He responds to each of her phrases in turn with the phrases, "I was so lonely," "Welcome in my life," and "So glad you're here" in a voice that sounds as least as charming as that of his much more famous brother. On this and the other songs on this album, though, Mary's voice sounds both limited and strained.

After Britain's army of Motown fans urged Levine to expand his recording effort, the developing record mogul, by then a thirty-four-year-old Motown fanatic, decided to live his dream by recording, in both America and England, every ex-Motown artist whose contract allowed them to cooperate, including Martha Reeves, Marv Johnson, the Contours, the Elgins, Rare Earth, and the Velvelettes. In all, Levine, in the 1980s and '90s, recorded more than 850 songs by more than one hundred former Motown artists (including Wells's ex-husband, Herman Griffin) on both Nightmare and Motorcity.

To his great delight—one reporter noted that Levine was the kind of guy who would walk into an old Motown studio and gasp, "This is a piece of history!"—he was able to complete much of the project at a Detroit studio owned by former Motown songwriter Sylvia Moy. He did additional work on the project in L.A.

Levine's project was great fun for everybody. It led to a much-publicized reunion of many ex-Motowners outside the former Motown studios at 2648 West Grand Boulevard in Detroit, complete with outlandish outfits, bear hugs, and numerous exchanges of old-timey memories. (Early Motowners often referred to themselves as a family, and Levine was big on reunions. In 1996, he reunited 660 members of his own family on his mother's side in what was called the biggest family reunion of all time.)

Mary, Curtis, Sugar, Porter, and Martha Reeves toured England to promote the album and the singles that Levine had recorded. Porter recalled that they "stopped and ate everything fried in the f——ing country." He said their chauffeured van "always smelled of grease and vinegar."

The fifteen-day tour in late October and early November hit towns such as Great Yarmouth, Stoke on Trent, Westcliff on Sea, Crawley, Isle of Sheppy, Bognor Regis, and Minehead, and night-spots such as the Barkers Pool in Sheffield, the Corn Exchange in Cambridge, the Pavilion in Bournemouth, the Buttermarket at Shrewsbury, the Football Club in Enfield, the Blazes in Windsor, and Madhouse Studio in London. According to Porter, Mary and

Martha would perform together in London and then split up and do solo concerts outside the city.

Although she was still very popular in England, Mary's attempts to relate to English audiences sometimes flew over their heads or perhaps clashed with their desire to be polite. Porter, who has darker skin and eyes than his blond, blue-eyed siblings, has said his father was a Creole man. Mary and Curtis loved playing on this theme with Porter, and Mary once introduced Porter to an English audience as "My musical director, Will Porter, who's passing." Curtis shot Porter a look and giggled, but the English audience had no reaction whatsoever.

Unfortunately, however, relatively few copies of the Motorcity and Nightmare singles or albums that resulted from Levine's exertions were sold during Wells's lifetime.

In fact, the only really successful single Levine's project produced for anyone was "Footsteps Following Me," sung by former Motown vocalist Frances Nero and cowritten by Ivy Jo Hunter, the man who had cowritten Martha Reeves's hit "Dancing in the Street." It rose to number 17 on the UK chart in 1991, was dubbed "the soul anthem of the Nineties," and became the biggest hit of Levine's career.

27

LAST CRUISE TO CATALINA

Forty kilometers in a leaky old boat
Any old thing that'll stay afloat
When we arrive we'll all promote romance
Romance, romance, romance

—"26 Miles (Santa Catalina)," sung by the Four Preps, written by Bruce Gelland and Glen Larson

As the 1980s became the '90s, Wells's voice, formerly her glory, became her burden.

As usual, she was performing everywhere. But her voice was cracking when she performed on the TV program *Live from the Rock 'n' Roll Palace* in 1987. She attributed her condition to swollen lymph nodes in her throat, a common singer's ailment for which she had been successfully treated during the 1960s.

Pop and rock 'n' roll singers, few of whom are operatically trained, often strain their voices in various ways. One vocal coach has compared the pop style of singing to driving a car with both the gas and the brake pedal pushed to the floor, and many singers eventually lose their voices as a result. Backstage on Motown tours, Smokey Robinson, Mary, and several other Motown vocalists would routinely wrap wet towels around their neck to ease the strain on their throats. Many developed swollen lymph nodes. But Mary's problem had progressed beyond the lymph node stage.

She refused to see a doctor, however. "Mary didn't like being detained," Curtis said. "She liked to do what she wanted to do. . . . She didn't believe anyone who told her that if you don't do this or that, you won't make it."

Womack offered various other reasons why Wells liked to make what he called "daring moves," such as ignoring a potentially serious medical condition. "Mary liked getting people upset," "it made her feel powerful," and "she liked getting attention," he said at various times while discussing the subject.

Wells herself put her reason for avoiding doctors more succinctly. Her condition "wasn't a possibility I wanted to admit," she said.

It didn't help, healthwise, that Mary clung stubbornly to her decades-long smoking habit. As she became "thinner and thinner and more and more ill" during the 1980s, "there was nothing I could say or do to help her or stop her from smoking cigarettes," Martha Reeves said.

"Each night when she sang, her voice became fainter and fainter," Reeves continued. "On song after song, she would ask the audience to 'sing it along with me' so that she didn't have to use up her voice. Offstage, I would watch helplessly as she smoked one cigarette after another, destroying what precious little voice she had left."

In February 1987, one year after Mary had missed her performance date in Toronto because she had been "kidnapped," she and Reeves appeared at that city's Imperial Room for a new engagement. "Wells's body was there, all right," the *Toronto Star* reviewer noted. "But her voice was a breathy, shapeless fog that drifted into the ether every time she opened her mouth."

Curtis, Wells's backup singer, had to sing most of "My Guy" himself. "Mary looked great, but she was hardly singing," Reeves said. She asked Curtis, "What's wrong with her?"

Wells apologized to the audience. She blamed her vocal problems on a combination of the flu and a cold and promised a better performance "later in the week." Her performance did not improve.

She did, briefly, go to Hollywood, however, singing "My Guy" on screen in the 1989 movie *My Boyfriend's Back*. She gamely played herself as a performing artist while wearing a silvery, fringed gown.

The film stars three white actresses—Sandy Duncan, Jill Eikenberry, and Judith Light—playing the fictionalized middle-aged versions of the three white women who, as the girl group the Angels, had made the song "My Boyfriend's Back" a number one pop hit in 1963. Although Mary was only peripherally involved in this movie, she certainly made an impression on at least one of her coworkers. Peggy March, an actress who worked with her, told an interviewer that Wells "was always friendly and warm to me and a joy to work with."

In 1989 and 1990, however, while Mary was recording the songs that became the album *Keeping My Mind on Love*, her voice began actually cutting off. Wells may have been able to fool an audience with her "cold and flu" story, but Curtis and Porter, her two handlers, knew something was seriously amiss. They began taking steps to hide her condition, which continued to worsen.

At a Hot August Nights performance in Reno, Porter said, Wells was "really really hoarse throughout the whole set" while performing for an audience of fifteen thousand. But at least she could make a sound above a whisper. "She would jack up her charm and her talking, and Curtis and I would really work the background vocals," he told *Unsung*.

At a subsequent performance by Wells, however, "We had to hide her and get paid before we went on," Porter said. "Mary smiled and whispered throughout the set while Curtis and I danced around and sang the background. When she did 'You Beat Me to the Punch,' she'd be whispering while Curtis and I would sing the melody." The cover-up worked because the audience knew the songs, and the efforts of Wells, Womack, and Porter succeeded in convincing the audience to sing along rather than listen carefully.

At a later date, Wells performed on a cruise ship shuttling back and forth to Santa Catalina, a resort island off the California coast. "Mary had no voice left," Porter said. He said the people who had hired Wells to perform were "very upset. . . . We escaped off the ship as soon as we could."

The situation reoccurred on another cruise vessel Wells performed on in May 1990.

"I was singing the songs," Womack said, "and Mary was lip-synching, like she was doing it for the deaf and dumb." He said that Wells, who could still talk in what he called "a little whisper," was valiantly communicating with the audience as best she could, aided by their daughter Sugar, who, still a little girl, was "running all around."

Wells's condition was severe, but whoever made this date had chosen well or chosen lucky. The audience was made up of wealthy people on a religious cruise.

"When Mary whispered to the audience that 'I'm really having some trouble,'" Curtis said, "they really seemed to catch on to it."

According to Curtis, while the cruise passengers dressed casually during the day, at night "they dressed up like *Love Boat*." Elegant bejeweled ladies with beautiful white hair would pray for Mary after the show and offer her places to go where she could get treatment. Some invited her to stay in their summer homes. They'd tell her, "You won't have to sing until we can find out how to get you well."

Unlike the Catalina cruise managers, the execs on this ship, pleased with the audience's response, displayed no anger. Anyway,

Womack said, "Mary was right there and they could see her. She was working the audience, and I kept the melody going."

Adding to the show was an elaborate ending for "My Guy" devised by Cecil Womack. "It was real dramatic," Curtis Womack said, "Not a man today—booma boom boom boom—can take me away—booma boom boom boom—from my boom guy boom my boom guy boom, drum roll myyyyyyyyyyyyyyy guyyyyyyyyyyyyyyyyyyyyyyyyyy."

The five-day cruise also allowed Wells to relax, since she was required to perform only once on the way out and once on the way back and was able to spend the rest of the time sunning herself in a deck chair.

That was the good news. The bad news was that in her cabin, Wells's throat would begin to spasm and her legs would kick out violently and involuntarily. "Something's choking me!" she'd whisper frantically. "Something's choking me! I can't breathe!" Womack called the onboard doctor and nurse, who treated Wells by administering oxygen from a tank. Eventually Mary's spasms would subside. This experience, combined with months of increasingly urgent pleas from her friends and her doctors, finally forced her to seek medical assistance when she got ashore. The doctors had some bad news for her: she had an advanced case of cancer of the larynx, or voice box. And it was a particularly aggressive form of this cancer.

Joyce Moore had been worried about Mary's health during this period but first heard definitively about Wells's condition when Wells called her collect in August 1990 from Los Angeles County-University of Southern California Medical Center. "I have cancer. I need help," Wells whispered to the stunned Moore. Moore said Wells chose to call her, in particular, not only because they were friends, but because Mary knew that Joyce was a trustee of the Rhythm & Blues Foundation. With help from that foundation, Joyce had taken care of Jackie Wilson after he suffered a massive heart attack in 1975 while performing on stage and spent the rest of his life in a hospital, dying in 1984.

Only one year before receiving Wells's call, in 1989, Moore had watched while the same foundation had given Mary one of the Pioneer Awards it awarded to pathbreaking vocalists. The award, presented at the Smithsonian Institution's National Museum of American History in Washington, DC, had been accompanied by a $15,000 check.

"She kissed the award and it got a big laugh, but she was serious," Porter said. "The award, and the check, meant a lot to her." Moore had noticed at the time that even while accepting the award, Wells had "looked just horrible. You held at your heart."

Now Moore was learning why Mary had looked so sick. She told Wells to ask somebody who could talk to call her back immediately. Curtis did so and explained the situation.

28

WELLS VS. CANCER

It was at this point that Steve Bergsman entered Mary's life. Although later in his career he became a real estate writer (his five books include *After the Fall: Opportunities and Strategies for Real Estate Investing in the Coming Decade* and *Growing Up in Levittown: In a Time of Conformity, Controversy, and Cultural Crisis*), in the 1980s he was the managing editor of a local business publication and freelancing for national magazines. He often wrote about 1950s and '60s era singers and had been talking to Joyce Moore, who like Bergsman was a Phoenix-area resident, about a biography of Jackie Wilson. After Mary called Joyce, Joyce put Mary and Steve in contact and suggested Steve talk to Mary for a prospective Wells biography. He soon began his extensive interviews.

Wells's treatment proceeded in stages. Before her doctors had given her the initial cancer diagnosis, they had removed polyps—abnormal growths of tissue—from her throat. To enable her to breathe, the doctors also had been forced to perform a tracheotomy, cutting a hole in her neck and inserting a breathing tube. Now they were recommending a laryngectomy, or removal of Wells's larynx, which includes the vocal cords, to prevent the malignancy from spreading.

While Mary was considering this, Moore took her to visit actor Joseph Cotten, who had had a laryngectomy and spoke through an artificial voice box that he pressed against his throat when he wished to talk. Wells was shocked. She thought Cotten's voice box made him sound like a robot.

She knew that a laryngectomy would cause her other problems, also. Removal of the voice box is devastating. People without a larynx usually lose their sense of smell or taste and have trouble showering because of the open breathing hole in their throat. They also have to learn to speak again, with an artificial voice box or a mechanical vibrating device that's inserted in their mouth.

But Wells's biggest problem with losing her larynx was that it would end her singing career. Emotionally and financially, her voice was her life. "She didn't want to live without hope of ever singing again," a friend said.

Wells's fear of permanently losing her voice may have occasionally pushed her over the edge into irrationality. Among the physicians who urged her to have a laryngectomy were a group recommended by vocalist Dionne Warwick. When they recommended removing her vocal chords, Wells told them, "You're going to take them out and give them to some white girl!" according to Curtis, who was present. Shocked, one doctor blurted out, "No white girl wants your cancer."

Wells went on to insist that the doctors should operate on Womack as well, although Womack didn't have cancer or any other illness. "I'm not going in the operating room unless he goes in," she told the astonished physicians. "He ought to have done to him whatever you do to me, because he does everything I do. You don't know him, he can do things, he thinks, he's smart, he probably gave me this stuff. He's got it but you just can't see it, because he does everything that I do."

"Ms. Wells," one doctor responded, "I don't care if he's a genius. He can't give you cancer, and besides, he wouldn't want to."

"Well, take him too," she said.

"We can't do that," they said.

Womack, interviewed about the situation years later, remarked, "Kids say the darndest things, but Mary, she would say some stuff." He later interpreted Mary's words as an attempt to make sure that he stayed with her in the hospital 24/7. Like most people, she did not look forward to lying alone in a large institution while her life slowly slipped away.

Mary decided to forgo the laryngectomy and began receiving six and a half weeks of intensive radiation at the USC Kenneth Norris Jr. Cancer Center. The physical effects were traumatic. Visitors noted that at one point Wells had to take the breathing tube out of her own throat twice a day, polish it with a toothbrush, and reinsert it. Her lungs also had to be drained several times daily.

Mary was terrified, before and during the radiation. "Can you imagine what it's like for a singer, to know they're getting ready to fry your vocal chords?" Joyce Moore told Susan Whitall. "When her neck started turning black, we went and got makeup to cover it."

Bergsman told *Unsung* that, according to Mary, one of the biggest recording stars of the time, whom she did not identify, "did the whole laying of his hand on her head thing and said, 'I'm healing you. I'm healing you. I'm healing you.' Mary actually believed for a while that he had healed her, but of course it didn't happen."

Perhaps because of her fright, Mary also became obsessively attached to one of her doctors, the resident physician who had been on duty when she first checked herself into L.A. County Hospital. A young, married man, he had performed the tracheotomy operation that allowed her to breathe. Wells had always fallen for men who helped and protected her, and this doctor certainly had.

Her crush was evident in comments she made to Bergsman when he was interviewing her in 1991. When Bergsman asked how she felt about Curtis coming to visit her in the hospital, she jokingly complained that he was "blocking my action," then giggled.

And when he inquired whether she would be resuming her liaison with Curtis or seeking a new relationship once she left the hospital, she remarked that "somebody would have to practically bring me back to life for me to go into a relationship. Like my doctor." She then laughed so hard and so continuously that she started gasping uncontrollably.

As Mary's condition became more intense, so did her obsession. One source said that while Wells was receiving radiation and chemotherapy on an outpatient basis and living at a hotel, she kept a radio without batteries with her at all times in the belief that the young resident had put monitoring devices in her body. She said he wanted her to have the radio so he would be able to check up on her continuously. Once, when she saw helicopters through the window of her room, she told friends she believed the resident had sent them.

After she completed her initial treatment, Wells would visit the young doctor's clinic in the hope of running into him, show up at his office for appointments she didn't have, or make up excuses to call him on the phone. When shortly thereafter he left L.A. for unrelated reasons and moved to another city, she flew to his new city to ask him to move in with her. "Mary had the absurd idea that she could capture the doctor, take him home with her, and start a whole other life," Curtis said. "His response was, 'I am a doctor. I don't run off with patients.'"

"It all made sense," Moore said of Mary's behavior, noting that "Mary was scared all to death. Her whole life revolved around communicating with her voice. It made her die, losing the single most prized asset she had except her kids. No money, four children, using drugs, couldn't work, couldn't sing, everything going sideways."

In spite of Mary's sometimes strange beliefs and behavior, she and Curtis stayed physically close while Wells was hospitalized. When her health took a brief turn for the worse and she had a code blue, Womack said, "She held my hand so tight I couldn't get it out."

Womack also said that at one point during her hospital stay he "moved right into the hospital room" with Mary "and slept in the bed with her and ate breakfast with her."

He also attempted an act that's probably somewhat rare in most hospitals. "Curtis tried to make love to me" in the hospital room, Mary said. Curtis said he hadn't really meant to try having sex, and it was just a misunderstanding. As he explained the incident, "The nurse said I could stay after hours, so I sat on the bed, and I'm talking and looking into Mary's eyes and kissing her." Wells, he said, "had all this medical stuff on, and I just wanted to lie next to her. I was lying in the bed with her, and the night nurses were out there playing music and stayed out there a long time."

Finally, Curtis said, the night nurses came in and noticed that the bed curtain was pulled and it was dark. "They got the wrong idea," he said, "and they said, 'Uh-uh, no, we can't have this. Not on this woman. No, no, no, no.' They didn't make me leave, but I was kind of embarrassed. You think you're not doing anything, but you're just creeping closer." Mary put her version of what had been happening more directly. "He wanted to take the catheter out," she said.

In addition to the pain, loneliness, and fear, Wells had another big problem. She couldn't pay for any of her medical care. An early conservative estimate of her initial medical expenses was $140,000, and her medical insurance had been canceled years before. Because her income depended on her performances, there was no money coming in. When her illness stopped her from singing, she had been evicted from the three-bedroom townhouse she had moved into in Van Nuys, California. Her phone was shut off, and her car repossessed.

Problems with medical insurance have afflicted many other performers besides Wells. Like most of her peers, at the beginning of her career Mary had arranged for coverage through her union, the American Federation of Television and Radio Artists (AFTRA). As part of a collective bargaining agreement with the recording industry known as the Phono Code, record companies were required to contribute to the AFTRA health fund, as well as to its retirement fund, in proportion to the royalties and other money they paid to artists.

AFTRA had failed to police that requirement, however. Companies underpaid the funds or didn't pay at all. One fund manager, hired in 1988, described the funds' office and files as a "shambles" in a *Billboard* interview. He also has said that Mary's policy was canceled by mistake.

Joyce Moore said that soon after she learned of Mary's illness and her medical insurance problems, she met with the director of AFTRA's pension and welfare fund. The union, she said, eventually paid for most of Mary's medical treatment.

Shocked by the situation that had been uncovered, however, Joyce and her husband Sam went on to initiate a class-action suit accusing eight major record companies, including Motown, of holding on to money that should have been contributed to the health and pension funds. It also accused AFTRA of neglecting its fiduciary duty to artists. Sam Moore was the lead plaintiff. As a result, in 2002, long after Wells's death, numerous recording artists, and Wells's estate, won an $8.4 million settlement against the union. In Mary's case, the suit resulted in a payout of about $30,000 to Mary's children. But that was later.

Although AFTRA would eventually pay for most of Mary's medical treatment, Mary needed money to live on and care for Sugar while being treated. Moore turned to the Rhythm & Blues Foundation.

Housed at the Smithsonian Institution in Washington, DC, the Rhythm & Blues Foundation had been created in 1988 by Atlantic Records president Ahmet Ertegun and others after they had learned that R&B singer Ruth Brown was working as a maid to make ends meet. The foundation's board of directors, chaired by musician

Ray Charles, also included politician Jesse Jackson, comedian John Belushi's widow Judy Belushi, singer Dionne Warwick, rock writer Dave Marsh, and a number of record industry executives. "Mary Wells is an institution, and we can't afford to see institutions fail," Warwick said when she heard about Wells's plight.

To help Wells, the foundation publicly solicited contributions for Mary. Its existing grant program, a low-profile effort, had offered ailing artists $3,000 to $5,000 each, but Bruce Springsteen, a member of the organization's advisory board, immediately upped the ante. He gave the foundation's Mary Wells Fund a badly needed boost by donating $10,000 to it. Springsteen, usually discreet in such matters, announced his donation to the press, saying he wanted it publicized to encourage others to help Wells. Another member of the board, Anita Baker, a Detroiter like Mary, held a benefit concert on Wells's behalf that raised another $10,000 for the ailing star.

Springsteen had learned of Wells's problems when he invited her to sing duets with him for what would be his next album, *Human Touch*. Because Mary was unable to accept, Sam Moore performed on the album instead, as did several other vocalists.

Other musicians also helped Wells. Her old intro group, the Temptations, gave $5,000. Rod Stewart gave $10,000, Diana Ross and Aretha Franklin each gave $15,000, Berry Gordy $25,000, and Bonnie Raitt, Martha Reeves, Phil Collins, Robert De Niro, and Frank Sinatra gave undisclosed amounts. Various radio stations urged their listeners to send contributions to the foundation to support Wells. By September 1990, her friends and fans had raised more than $55,000. A year later, they had raised a total of $150,000. Meanwhile, on Motown's thirtieth anniversary television special, Smokey Robinson, Stevie Wonder, and Gladys Knight performed a tribute to Wells.

(Wells was also the beneficiary at this time of a subtle tribute from the film industry: in *The Commitments*, a film about rock music, the white actresses Angeline Ball, Maria Doyle Kennedy, and Bronagh Gallagher, who play members of a fictional white Irish soul group, sing Mary's song "Bye Bye Baby" during a group rehearsal.)

Joyce Moore praised Gordy's donation. "He's doing it from the heart," she told an interviewer, "and I hope he serves as an example." She added, however, that in her view, Gordy had "served as a negative example [of generosity to performers] for a lot of years."

Wells mentioned Gordy's donation on the TV show *Entertainment Tonight* in September 1990. The program noted that Wells had smoked two packs of cigarettes a day for thirty years. On the same show, Wells urged everyone to fight cigarettes and air pollution and whispered to the audience, "I'm fighting for my life."

Mary was grateful for the funds provided her. "I'm so overwhelmed and so relieved . . . and very grateful," she rasped to one interviewer. "It's also been embarrassing to me," she added, "because I've always been self-sufficient and independent." The situation aggravated her feeling that she had never been paid the amount she deserved for her hit-making career.

"It just shouldn't be where I have to hold my hand out and say I need help. I had hit records. I made a lot of money for people," Wells said. "I don't think anybody gets what they want or deserve, because life isn't like that," she said. "But they shouldn't be thrown on the street."

Very appropriately, the president of Quality Records, which distributed Mary's recordings for the UK's Nightmare and Motorcity labels in the United States, donated to the fund a portion of the proceeds from Quality's five-album *Motorcity Dance Party*, a compilation of Motown hits, as well as some of the proceeds from Mary's 1990 album *Keeping My Mind on Love*. Although the foundation encouraged other record companies to make similar allocations or donations, it's not clear how many did. The *Record* (Bergen, New Jersey) reported in 1991 that the level of recording-industry participation in fundraising efforts for Wells "has not expanded as much as the Rhythm & Blues Foundation would like."

Mary Wilson of the Supremes said she would organize a benefit concert for Wells. Dionne Warwick, Stevie Wonder, Sam Moore, Billy Preston, the Temptations, Merry Clayton, and other stars offered to perform, but the concert, tentatively scheduled for November 1990, never took place.

Mary's fans were very supportive. One of them, Susan Watson, a *Detroit Free Press* columnist, urged all her fans to send Mary comforting notes and letters. "Do it for all the times 25 years ago and yesterday that she understood how your heart felt," Watson wrote.

After her initial medical treatment, Wells's first need had been a place to live while she underwent her prescribed weeks of chemotherapy and radiation treatment as an outpatient. Moore had found a room for Wells and her five-year-old daughter, Sugar, in a Grand Hyatt Hotel only ten minutes from the hospital. Finding the room was not a prolonged process, but easing Sugar's fears took a bit longer.

"Sugar had nightmares," Wells told a reporter who interviewed her in this room. "She told me, 'Mom, don't do this to me. Please don't do this.' But she's now running the show. She got in the elevator yesterday and announced, 'My mother's going to the hospital to get treatment!'"

Harry, the fifteen-year-old son of Cecil and Mary, had been living with Curtis, Mary, and Sugar before Wells went to the hospital. But after his mother became ill he was sent to live with his older siblings.

The fact that the foundation paid for Wells's room and medical treatment and gave her taxi passes to help her get around helped Mary financially. Shortly after her radiation therapy was completed, though, she was offered a chance to do a lot better than that.

29

GOING FOR BROKE

Never give in, never give in, never, never, never, never . . .

—Winston Churchill

When Wells found herself seriously ill and nearly penniless, she began thinking a lot more than she usually did about the money her Motown songs had been making over the years.

Gordy had contributed $25,000 to Wells's medical fund, but Wells believed the hit tunes she sang had made millions of dollars for Motown and its executives—including Berry Gordy, the chairman of the board of Motown Industries, and Smokey Robinson, the former Motown vice president. The songs had remained popular much longer than anyone had expected. After just a short time, they had paid off all the costs involved in recording them, and for many years since then had been pouring money into the pockets of Motown execs.

"It's no exaggeration that I helped build Motown," Wells often said, usually adding that she hadn't been sufficiently paid for her achievement. In truth, no one foresaw how popular Motown music would be years later or that Mary would sign away all her rights to future royalties. She was mentioning this to Curtis one day after she became ill, and, Curtis said, he realized he had just recently seen something in the newspaper about Steven Ames Brown, a San Francisco entertainment attorney.

What caught Curtis's eye was a story reporting that singer Martha Wash had sued for credit and royalties for the vocals she had performed on several hit records, including C+C Music Factory's "Gonna Make You Sweat (Everybody Dance Now)." Brown, an attorney who had represented many entertainers, was representing Wash.

Womack suggested that because Wells could only whisper, he would call Brown and ask Brown to represent Wells in a suit against Motown for back royalties. Womack did so, and very soon afterward, Womack said, Wells made a deal in which Brown would demand $100,000 in back royalties from Motown and keep $40,000 as his percentage. According to Womack, Brown was aware that Wells had signed a legal document giving up all her future royalties on her Motown hits but planned to embarrass Motown into paying by setting up numerous TV interviews. In those interviews, Wells would reveal to the world her pitiful present state compared with how much money her Motown tunes had made for the company.

Brown told a different story about how he came to be Mary's lawyer. He said he grew up in Detroit as a son of Dr. Albert R. Brown, a Detroit podiatrist whose office was a few blocks from Motown headquarters and who treated several members of the Gordy family and other Motown notables, including Marvin Gaye. After graduating from the University of Michigan and the University of Southern California Film School, the younger Brown got a law degree from the University of California's Hastings College of the Law in San Francisco. Shortly thereafter, as a result of a case he handled, Brown came to own a bar in that city and opened it as a performance venue called the Oasis in 1981.

Brown had been a boyhood fan of Mary's and remembered seeing her perform at the Michigan State Fairgrounds in Detroit with Martha Reeves and the Vandellas and other Motown groups when he was ten years old. He soon started trying to persuade Wells to appear at the Oasis. When she performed there for two days in 1982, the starstruck Brown said, he spent at least ten hours with her, driving her from airport to hotel, from hotel to club, from club to hotel, and many other places.

All Wells talked about at that time, he said, was how unfairly Motown had treated her financially. When Brown suggested she sue Gordy and Motown, Wells said she had tried but that Gordy offered each of her lawyers employment with Motown. Those lawyers, she said, found the offers too much to resist and never collected what she believed was due her. (There is no written evidence of such suits or offers.)

Brown said that based on what Wells told him then, he had suggested she sue Motown again on a contingency fee basis, meaning Brown would sue Motown and his only compensation would be a percentage of what she collected. "She was famous but impecunious," he said, and a contingency arrangement would enable her "to go toe-to-toe against a company that had major resources."

Wells said she would think about it, but she didn't ask Brown to file such a suit until 1991. He noted that by then "she was desperate for money for her kids," and "the handwriting was on the wall" in terms of her mortality.

Brown said he then called Gordy. After the two of them reminisced about the old days, Brown brought up Wells's complaints, being careful to call Gordy "Mr. Chairman," the title Brown said Gordy preferred. After they talked for a few moments, according to Brown, "Gordy said to me, right on cue, 'You know, Mr. Golden Tongue, you should be working for me.'" Brown said he responded, "I know what you pay your lawyers, and I don't want to subsidize your company."

Brown filed a lawsuit on Wells's behalf in Los Angeles Superior Court in March 1991. The suit accused Motown, in part, of not paying Wells the royalties due her. For this alleged dereliction, the suit demanded "in excess of $100,000."

Brown knew that former Motown Records president Ewart Abner, still on the Motown payroll as a consultant, had argued truthfully in media interviews that Wells had agreed under her 1964 court settlement to waive her future Motown royalties.

So, Brown said, he spent three days alone in his law office going over and over the documentation from the settlement attempting to find a loophole. Finally, he realized that although Motown owned the right to her voice, the company had never demanded or received from Mary her written permission to use her photograph or her name on any recordings to be sold by Motown after she left the company. He added this to the suit, demanding another $100,000 plus for this offense.

Brown said he then called up Gordy and said, "Feel free to continue selling Mary Wells records, but from now on, unless we come to an agreement, you'll have to sell them without her picture or name on them." This, he said, led to a quick monetary settlement. The amount was not disclosed.

Curtis Womack said Gordy also was feeling pressure from televised interviews with Wells that had begun to hit the airways on such venues as CNN, *Entertainment Tonight*, and *Inside Edition*. In those interviews, the singer whispered pitifully about her present situation and the millions she had made for Motown.

Soon after the interviews began to be televised, Womack said, Womack and Wells were sitting together when the phone rang. Womack picked up the receiver and was startled to hear Gordy and Abner tell him that Gordy had an offer for Wells.

According to Womack, Abner said, "I've got Berry here with me, and we're prepared to give Mary one million dollars and let her go out and have some fun and do all the things she's been wanting to do. You don't even have to tell your lawyer. If you want to, just give him the forty grand you promised to give him." (Abner died in 1997.)

As Womack listened openmouthed, Gordy came on and said, "I'll send a cashier's check over there right this minute. I've been going to golf outings and different events and people are looking at me and saying, 'You stole that girl's money!' It's embarrassing, and it hurts me." (Gordy turned down a written request for an interview for this book.)

Womack relayed the offer to Wells and then stood there dumbstruck. Wells snatched the phone out of his hand and whispered to Gordy, "You can't buy me. I'm worth ten million dollars." (Brown said there was no legal basis for demanding this amount.)

Womack heard the shocked Gordy laugh, respond negatively, and add, "Honey, you'll die before me." Womack yelled "Mary!" and she said, "Look at Curt, you want that money so bad."

Womack responded, "God, Mary, I don't care what you do with the money, just take it! This man is really trying to make it right with you out of the generosity of his heart. He doesn't have to give you a million dollars, but he's telling you he'll send it right over."

But, Womack said, "Mary just kept stonewalling, stonewalling, stonewalling. . . . She was just woofin' and the more it seemed like I wanted her to take it, the more she didn't want to take it."

"Oh boy, look at Curt," she whispered again to Gordy and Abner on the telephone. "He's salivating."

"I was looking that way, of course," Womack said. "I had never heard anybody make an offer like that. But Mary got a kick out of torturing us."

According to Womack, while Wells kept refusing, he could hear Abner and Gordy telling her, "We'll just messenger over a cashier's check," and "Right now, Mary," and "Put Womack back on."

Years later, Gordy indicated the depth of his annoyance with Wells's heavily publicized claims. "Let me tell you about Mary

Wells," he told the *Cleveland Plain Dealer* sarcastically in 1994. "She was sick in 1992. She was with Motown from 1960 to 1964. We got her many hits. She left in 1964 with a No. 1 hit, 'My Guy.' Twentieth Century Fox paid us a royalty to get her out of her contract with us. She went to five other companies. Then after 27 years she didn't have any money. So it's Berry Gordy's fault."

If it is true that Mary refused $1 million from Gordy, it was because she truly believed she was due $10 million. She had previously told *Blues & Soul*, an English rock magazine, that "Motown is gonna have to settle up the past, which is gonna cost a lot . . . It should be around $10 million, it certainly shouldn't be any less than that. They owe me more than that, really when you count up all the top ten records I had with them, and all the top ten albums."

Part of Mary's motivation for allegedly insisting on $10 million may also have been the bitterness, hurt, and anger she felt toward Gordy. "She was very disappointed and hurt with Berry, much more than he ever would have thought," Joyce Moore said. "She carried this with her all the time."

According to Curtis, Abner and Gordy finally gave up, and Gordy paid Wells $100,000, which Womack says was the size of the settlement arranged by Brown.

Brown denied that this call from Gordy and Abner to Mary ever occurred. "There's not a grain of truth in that story," he said. "Why would my own client not tell me? She had an obligation to tell me about a conversation with the defendant in the case that was admissible in court. If she had turned down the one million dollars, I could have used it as evidence."

The *San Francisco Chronicle* quoted an anonymous source describing Brown's settlement for Mary as "embarrassingly low," and noted that Wells "shared even that pittance" with her attorney. Brown was quoted at the time as calling it a "large" sum and said in 2010 that the amount paid was "way more than" $100,000. Aside from saying, "I got her a nice big fat check," however, he would not reveal the exact amount, because doing so, he said, would violate lawyer-client privelage.

Brown also said that although he was contractually entitled to 40 percent of the settlement, he discounted his fee because Mary was dying and that he took "way less" than that.

According to Curtis, Wells took her part of the sum, which he said was $60,000, and "blew it all, gave it to the kids," her friends, and others. Among the others was Curtis, to whom she gave $700. Sally Womack said that Mary also sent some of the money to the doctor she had a crush on.

Mary then issued a statement in which she thanked Gordy, "who has shown his compassion in helping me during these difficult times."

30

MY HEART IS STEADFAST

My heart is steadfast, O God, my heart is steadfast!
I will sing and make melody!

—From Psalms 108, "A Song of Confidence in God"

Wells was hopeful throughout her ordeal. In September 1990, while unable to speak at all and receiving daily intensive radiation therapy, she mouthed the words, "The doctors say I will be all right," to a *USA Today* reporter. She then added, in writing, "I'm going to beat this."

As Claudette Robinson told *Unsung*, "Mary truly hoped that there would be something they could do that would get her back to being the same Mary Wells . . . with the same voice."

Joyce Moore told *USA Today* that although Wells was "very, very scared, she's confident she's going to be fine." The *USA Today* reporter described Wells as looking fine, despite the tracheotomy tube protruding from her throat. "Her full pageboy is frosted gold, and her makeup is flawless," the reporter wrote. "She's chic in a silky orange jumpsuit."

She also remained the generous person she had always been. "We'd be on the way to chemo and radiation therapy when she was really not well, but if she saw a vagrant on the street, the neighborhood didn't matter," Moore said. "It didn't matter if he looked like an axe murderer. She would insist I stop the car so she herself could get out and give him a couple of dollars." She also made a special point of showing up at a rally for homeless people although she could barely speak.

But Mary's situation was wearing on her. She mouthed optimistic statements to many reporters but confessed to one scribe, "I can't get used to this. You can't imagine how hard this is for me." During this time, she told Bergsman, "I would rather die natural or commit suicide than die of a disease like this."

An apparently accidental snub lowered her spirits. When rap star MC Hammer gave a weekend concert in Los Angeles, he invited singer Janet Jackson, basketball star Magic Johnson, talk-show host Arsenio Hall, and Mary to visit him before the show. Jackson, Johnson, and Hall were admitted, but after Wells had waited twenty minutes, a security guard told her that "no one else was welcome to have an audience with Hammer," according to news accounts.

Wells said she was "embarrassed and humiliated" by the incident, which Hammer said he had been unaware of. He apologized and called the situation unfortunate, saying he "highly respected" Wells. Hammer said the offending guard was not his, since his personnel "don't handle anybody that way," and offered to fly Wells to one of his upcoming concerts as his special guest. But her daily treatments prevented her from taking him up on his offer.

In February 1991, Wells got good news. Her doctors told her that the radiation therapy had eliminated the cancer. The development cheered her immensely and her appearance soon improved. Steve Bergsman said she once again became "lustrous, pretty, and sexy."

As her energy returned, Wells immediately told Joyce Moore that she would resume her career by lip-synching to her songs while her voice recovered. This wasn't as humorous as it may sound, since lip-synching was very common at the time and Wells was very good at it. "There's no question in my mind that no one would have realized she was lip-synching," Moore said. She added, "Mary was the kind of person who, if someone handed her a lemon, would make lemonade and sell it and use the money to support herself."

Mary also began taking long trips, including one to New York where she appeared on the *Joan Rivers Show*. While on the show, she received a warm phone call from Little Richard and watched a video performance from Stevie Wonder. In her honor, Wonder sang "My Guy," substituting the words "my girl" for the words "my guy."

She also flew to Washington, DC, with Curtis to crusade against cancer. According to Curtis, he and Mary were chauffeured around in a limousine with Vice President Dan Quayle, Quayle's wife, Marilyn, and actor Jack Klugman as they spoke out against cuts in the federal cancer research budget.

After appearing at dinners, caucuses, and breakfast meetings, Wells capped her tour spectacularly with whispered testimony to a committee of the US Congress. "I'm here today to urge you to keep the faith," she said. "I can't cheer you on with all my voice, but I can encourage, and I pray to motivate you with all my heart and soul and whispers."

Although Mary was hard to hear, she was hoping for her voice's return. "I miss my voice, but hopefully it'll come back," she told a TV interviewer in 1991. "I'm praying that it does, because I put a lot of time in my career. I've been singing all my life. I don't know any other trade. I miss it terribly."

Wells sometimes would fly to Joyce and Sam's house near Phoenix and spend the evening sitting with Sam Moore in the backyard. There the two of them would gossip incessantly about everyone in showbiz and politics. After Sam went inside, Mary would stay in the yard and gaze at the stars for some time, just as she had as a little girl. "To this day," Joyce Moore said, "if I go outside and the sky is filled with stars, I call them Mary's stars."

While looking at the stars, Mary was also reflecting on her life. As Brenda Holloway told author Bill Dahl, "Mary always had problems. She always was a part of her problems. But then in those latter days, she began to reflect and she began to see and she knew."

During a long talk with Holloway two months before Mary died, Mary told Holloway, "I made a lot of wrong decisions in my life and I have a lot of regrets," Holloway said. In response, Holloway took off her wedding ring and gave it to Mary.

Holloway, who met Mary in the 1960s and spent time with her near the end of Mary's life, talked about what she called "the cry in Mary's voice" and insisted that "there was a sadness about her from the first day I met her to the last day I saw her. She never seemed to be really, really happy. She was just a shell, an unhappy shell. The only time she blossomed was through her voice."

Mary and Curtis Womack had argued and split up at one point during her treatment, and he had returned to West Virginia to attend his uncle's funeral and to take care of his aging mother. While Mary was in remission, however, she visited him and his extended family in West Virginia, then invited him back to stay with her in L.A. "I was lonely," she told Bergsman. "I wanted some kind of companionship. I had nobody."

When Curtis had visited Wells in L.A. earlier, she had come to the airport with everybody else to meet him. This time when he flew in, she wasn't there. "Where's Mary?" he asked the others. "When I went into her bedroom, I felt like a bull in a china shop." Wells had grown so small and quiet that Womack didn't even realize she was in the bed. When he snuggled up with her, however, her "spirit was still bubbling" as it had all her life, he said.

With Curtis back, Mary was happy for a while. Womack, pleased to be reunited with Mary, was also glad to see that she, while obviously under the weather, could still display a lot of spunk. One morning Curtis was astounded when Mary told him, "I've got to get up and get dressed. I'm going to the bank. I want to go arrange some things for Sugar's birthday." Trailed by the astonished Womack, Wells rushed over to see the vice president of the nearby Bank of America branch, who knew her. When the bank executive told her, gulping, "Oh, you didn't really have to come down here," she said, "Oh, I really wanted to."

Some of Mary's energy may have returned because she had lost weight as a result of her illness and had finally stopped using illegal drugs. "She got her hair done and looked fabulous," Moore told Susan Whitall. "After all the things she had given up when she was doing drugs, she would not go out if her makeup wasn't perfect and her hair wasn't together, if her life depended on it."

On one particular day with Womack, an event occurred that seems to happen often in the lives of the dying: she briefly recovered all her powers.

"I had just fixed her some food," Womack said, "and she said, 'Hey baby!' in her normal voice."

"My voice has come back!" she said.

"It *has*!" Womack said.

Mary then immediately *sang* the words *my* and *guy*.

"God, that's a *miracle*!" Womack shouted.

"She was like that for the whole day," he said. "It was like music from heaven to hear Mary talking without whispering that raspy whisper. Her voice had been raspy like that so long I had gotten used to it, and when I heard her voice I was looking to see where it was coming from." It was as though a dead person had returned.

Gospel singer the Rev. Dr. James Cleveland, who died in February 1991, had also experienced a return of his voice for one day shortly before he died. Rev. Cleveland had interpreted this event religiously: "I've been singing all morning," he told people, "and I've been talking, and I know now, I'm not worried about it, I'm ready to go." He felt this was God's way of telling him that he was going to heaven and that his powers would be fully restored there.

A more mundane interpretation holds that before the end, the body uses all its reserves in one last effort to return to normal before succumbing to the inevitable.

After her voice had departed once again, Mary moved into an apartment with her older daughter, Stacy, and Stacy's children. Wells loved the kids, but it was so loud in the apartment from all the children's activities that she asked Bergsman to take her out in his car to escape the noise. As they drove around the area near the L.A. airport, Bergsman would ask Wells if she wanted to go for coffee or anything and she'd say no, she just needed to sit and be quiet. "Her speech was measured," Bergsman said. "She had no appetite. She didn't want to eat anything. She didn't want to go anywhere. What she wanted to do was sit in a quiet place, my car, while I drove around."

Bergsman said that around this time Mary told him "a very strange story about how she had been in the park and she didn't see any birds in the park and she felt that Los Angeles was losing its bird population." He said he didn't think anything of the story at the time, but later realized Mary was using it as a metaphor for her own death. "It wasn't the birds who were going away, it was Mary," he said.

Bergsman described Wells even at this late and difficult point in her life as "a very sweet woman . . . unimaginably sweet." Mary's friend Joyce Moore said that Wells "had a lot of hurt bones but no mean ones" even in her final days.

In the spring of 1991, Mary experienced a sudden weight loss, was examined by her doctors, and got the bad news. Her throat cancer had reoccurred; cancerous lesions had been found in her lungs and her now-revitalized disease was advanced and inoperable. She allowed herself a brief spurt of hope in early July, when she was given weekly doses of edatrexate, a trial anticancer drug, to try to halt the growth and spread of her cancer. It failed.

After that, Wells was provided with around-the-clock nurses. Soon she could be fed only intravenously. Nevertheless, she still wanted something out of life.

According to Curtis, one morning she said to the nurses, "You know what would help me? If this is OK with you all, it would be good for me, can I have sex?" They laughed, but said if her husband would cooperate, she could do what she wanted. When Curtis arrived, he cooperated. He said the nurses told him Mary was always happy when he was there with her.

Her general attitude was that "now I really want to live," Mary told Bergsman. "Each day I gain back, each day I realize the importance of life. I realize when I wake up and see the sun shining, or some birds flying outside, or see life, I say, 'It's not that bad . . . nothing is that bad.'"

As her time wound down, Wells sounded even more accepting and philosophical. "I just look at the best things that happened in my life. I put those things behind me and let the Lord get in front of me," Wells told an interviewer. On another occasion, she said, "When it's over, we'll see what God's plan is. I know He has one."

31

YOU BEAT ME TO THE PUNCH

THIS ATTITUDE MAY HAVE HELPED her in July 1992, when, weakened from her extensive treatment, she was stricken with pneumonia. She was rushed to USC's Kenneth Norris Jr. Cancer Center in Los Angeles, where life-support systems kept her alive for another couple of weeks. At one point her heart stopped, but doctors were able to resuscitate her.

Still, Wells was not about to suppress her lifelong drive to succeed and to fight on regardless. While on her deathbed, she told one of her doctors what she would be singing on her next tour. And when she was asked if she wanted to keep on living, even though the machines that surrounded her were all that were keeping her alive, Wells mouthed the word yes.

"She really tried to fight the battle against cancer, but the cancer took over," Claudette Robinson said. "It beat her rather than her beating it."

Near the end, Steve Bergsman visited her in the hospital. "She was on a morphine drip to keep her comfortable, but she was so comatose and so shrunken and so riddled with cancer as to be almost unrecognizable," Bergsman said. "She was almost fetal at that point. It was one of the most awful sights I'd ever seen."

Wells died on July 26, 1992. She was 49. She was survived by her four children: Cecil Womack Jr., 24; Stacy Womack, 22; Harry Womack, 16; and Sugar Womack, 6; and one of her brothers, Fletcher Wells. (Stacy and Cecil Jr. became guardians for Sugar; Fletcher has since died.) Mary was identified on the funeral program and on her death certificate as Mary Esther Wells-Womack.

About four hundred people, including numerous celebrities, attended Wells's funeral and memorial service, which was called a "celebration of her life." It was held at Forest Lawn Memorial Park in Glendale, California, on July 30, 1992. Among the attendees were Cecil Womack and his family, all wearing African garb, Motown songwriter Janie Bradford, Sam and Joyce Moore, Maye James-Holler, Will Porter, and Bergsman. "The funeral was almost like a show, a tribute to Mary," Bergsman said.

Bergsman sat right behind Berry Gordy at the funeral. Mabel John, the first female soloist ever signed to Motown, whose career had tanked as Mary's rose, sat next to Gordy.

Many of the mourners and performers were non-Motown entertainers, such as the comedian Sinbad, Little Richard, and Quincy Jones.

Smokey Robinson, the musician and songwriter who had shared Wells's greatest days, delivered one of the eulogies. He added to his spoken words by singing portions of the hits that he had written for Wells, including, of course, "My Guy," a capella.

"Mary would have enjoyed the service," Claudette Robinson said.

Following Robinson was Stevie Wonder, who played a version of "These Three Words" on the piano. Little Richard told the audience, "I thank God for Mary Wells. She was the first lady of song to me." Claudette Robinson told the assemblage that she "always felt a kinship with Mary that never diminished. She could have been a cousin. She was family. I remember her as a good and decent woman who loved God and honored the talent that he gave her."

Eulogies also were delivered by two of Mary's doctors, one of them Oscar Streeter, chief of radiation oncology at the Norris Cancer Center. Joyce Moore remembered that Dr. Streeter "talked about Mary's poise, grace, dignity, and bravery and what a sad and great treat it was to have known her." Both doctors also talked about how heartbroken they were when she died and how they really had believed they had defeated Wells's cancer before it made its final reappearance.

Little Richard noted that many of the other stories about Wells ended about 1965 or 1966. He felt unique for not having met Wells until 1981, when she had to perform night after night to survive economically. During his remarks, in full preacher mode, Little Richard also asked loudly and somewhat rhetorically, "Who's going to take care of Mary's children?" Porter noted that the room "got very silent" in response.

In this same spirit of gritty realism, Porter, who performed "Will the Circle Be Unbroken?" at the service, provided an unvarnished portrait of the dead Wells in a recent interview. "She looked terrible," he said. "The casket was open and she was unprotected. People got in there with cameras. And she had this growth on her neck from cancer."

Among the nine pallbearers were Mary's children Cecil Womack Jr. and Harry Womack, as well as Berry Gordy and Smokey Robinson. Curtis Womack and others walked with the coffin.

Mary was the first Motown star to be laid to rest in Forest Lawn, joining the many Hollywood immortals there. She was cremated and her remains entombed in the cemetery's Freedom Mausoleum, where her tomb reads simply, MARY E. WELLS, 1943–1992, "OUR LOVING MOTHER."

Six other musical, movie, and TV stars are also Freedom Mausoleum occupants: Nat King Cole, Alan Ladd, Jeanette MacDonald, George Burns, and Gracie Allen, along with the 1920s "it girl" Clara

Bow. Michael Jackson is buried nearby in the Great Mausoleum, where numerous Hollywood stars, such as Clark Gable and Carole Lombard, also are buried.

Psalms 108, "A Song of Confidence in God," was read at Mary Wells's funeral. The funeral program rendered it as:

> My heart is steadfast, O God, my heart is steadfast!
> I will sing and make melody!
> Awake, my soul!
> Awake, harp and lyre!
> I will awake the dawn!
> I will give thanks to thee, O Lord,
> Among the people!
> I will sing praises to thee among the nations.
> For thy steadfast love is great above the heavens,
> Thy faithfulness reaches to the clouds.

Bergsman called the funeral "the last big Motown gathering for the death of an original Motown star." Even by 1992 the company "family feeling" that Mary had valued was slipping away before her death briefly revived it. Few Motowners ever gathered again for any other major Motown figure's funeral.

Berry Gordy has been widely credited for paying for Mary's funeral. Former Motown songwriter Janie Bradford told *Unsung* that she was the Motown employee assigned to process the entire cost of the event.

Wells's financial embarrassments, or, more accurately, those of her family, were hinted at immediately after she died. One source said the cemetery wouldn't allow Mary to be entombed until the bill for her mother's funeral was paid. The same source said Gordy paid her mother's funeral bill as well.

A sympathetic obituary writer opined that if Wells had been "meaner or luckier she might have died on some desert ranch like Michael Jackson's got." But in fact Wells had a lot to feel good about. With her terrific voice and her great skill as a singer, she had risen swiftly to the top in a blaze of glory and had then managed to help support two families for almost thirty years by vocally repeating her musical journey again and again on countless stages.

Also, as Wells herself said during the 1980s when looking back at her career, "I set out to be a big artist and to do something great. . . . I helped build a major company . . . and I made people happy for a while. I have no regrets."

Mary was certainly right about helping to build a major company. She also was a major force in helping it to become a record firm that appealed to white as well as black listeners. She was there at the beginning when Motown needed her and, in retrospect, there's no doubt that she'd helped the company establish itself solidly before she left for what she thought would be greener pastures.

Then, of course, she took the wrong turn and was never able to find her way back to her past glory. But she never stopped trying. As she did so, she showed the rest of us how to face decline, downfall, and disaster in life: by struggling and achieving until the very end.

A *Boston Globe* reporter saw a warning for everyone in Wells's decline and fall. "Faces fell and voices grew weak," the reporter wrote. "Motown had lied to us. The walls around us were real, and a catchy pop tune, even crooned in romantic delirium, wasn't enough to break through."

But as a person, Wells had been a success. Curtis Womack described her in 2010 as "vivacious, sultry, energized, gorgeous, and a good spirit." And that's the way hundreds of thousands of people remember her today.

Martha Reeves, a prominent figure in Detroit music and politics, said in late 2010 that when she walks around that city, people still come up to her and say "Mary? Mary?" and she tells them, "No. Martha." A lot of people "don't want to acknowledge that Mary is no longer with us," Reeves said.

EPILOGUE

SOME FURTHER DOINGS

Mary Wells is played on the radio every day that we live, 365 days a year. . . . She has a voice that lovers like. And love is universal and everlasting.

—Brenda Holloway to *Unsung*

Mary Wells will never die.

—Author David Ritz

In 1999, "My Guy" was admitted into the Grammy Hall of Fame, and in 2006 Mary was admitted posthumously into the Michigan Rock and Roll Legends Hall of Fame.

As of 2012, she had not yet been admitted to the national Rock and Roll Hall of Fame. In 2009, however, the Womack brothers, including Cecil and Curtis, celebrated together when their brother Bobby Womack was admitted to the hall.

Due to a loophole in American law, Mary's family has not been benefitting from the continued popularity of her hit songs to the extent that they should be. In Europe, any time a vocalist's song is played on the radio, she receives a payment. In the United States, only record producers and songwriters receive such payments, which are called airplay royalties. Throughout Mary's life, the most popular songs she sang, which were mostly songs she neither wrote nor participated in writing, were played millions of times on radio stations all over the planet, and she was paid nothing. These songs are still played on the radio worldwide and her family receives nothing. The US Congress has been considering legislation that would end this inequity for Mary and many other recording artists. Some inroads have been made toward compensating artists for radio play through private deals between large broadcasting corporations and major labels.

During the 1990s, Cecil Womack and Linda Cooke Womack traveled to Nigeria, where they discovered ancestral ties to the Zekkariyas ethnic group and adopted the tribal names Zekkariyas (Cecil) and Zeriiya (Linda). Calling themselves and the band they formed with their seven children the House of Zekkariyas, they moved to Thailand and lived and recorded in Bangkok. They also maintained residences in other countries, including Nigeria, where Cecil died in January 2013.

The oldest son of Cecil Womack and Mary Wells, Cecil D. Womack Jr., known as Meech Wells, first wanted to be an entertainment lawyer, but he became a hip-hop and rap producer instead. He has written and produced for George Clinton and Clinton's son, Tracey Lewis. He also has produced or coproduced for MC Brains, Mista Grimm, Queen Latifah, Mark Morrison, Shaquille O'Neal, Snoop Dogg, Supernatural, and Brigette McWilliams.

In 1993, Meech and his brother Harry Womack, known as Shorty Wells, a rap artist, joined with their sister Stacy, now known as Noel Wells, and their half-sister Nicole (Cecil and Linda's daughter), known as Neko, to form a singing group. They named the quartet Wells.

In 1995, Wells was preparing to release its debut album, *Life, Love, and Struggle*. According to the MCA record company, which was scheduled to release the album, Mary Wells had provided seed money for the early demos and speaks in snippets between cuts on the album. The album is said to mix contemporary R&B and hip-hop. Among the tracks allegedly planned for the album are "Tell Me," written by Meech and Noel.

It might have been a great album, but music industry politics intervened. The executive producer of the album was Andre Fischer, senior vice president of A&R for MCA. Before the album was released, Fischer left the company and the project was abandoned.

Maye James-Holler has described Mary and Cecil's daughter Noel (Stacy) as strongly resembling Mary and as a "beautiful singer," and said in 2010 that she had wondered for years why Noel didn't produce an album of some of Mary's songs. In 1998, Noel married Jeff Henderson, a convicted crack dealer. Henderson had spent ten years in federal prison, where he developed his culinary skills. He had met Noel shortly before his release in 1996. After they married, he worked his way up in the cooking trade, eventually becoming executive chef at Las Vegas's Bellagio Hotel. Besides his autobiography, *Cooked: From the Streets to the Stove, from Cocaine to Foie Gras,* he has published two cookbooks, the first one titled *Chef Jeff Cooks: In the Kitchen with America's Inspirational New Culinary Star,* and had his own TV show, *The Chef Jeff Project*, on the Food Network. The couple have three children, whom Noel homeschools. In honor of one of Mary Wells's favorite foods, one of the recipes in *Chef Jeff Cooks* is for Mary Wells Banana Pudding. Noel told Chef Jeff that the secret of preparing the pudding so Mary would like it was using condensed milk, not regular milk. Chef Jeff also adds extra vanilla wafers.

Mary's child with Curtis Womack, Sugar Wells, is a vocalist and the mother of a young child.

After stepping down as Mary's personal assistant, Maye (Hampton) James-Holler, her longtime friend, became national promotion director (radio) at Scepter Records. She was the first black woman to hold that title. At Scepter, which was owned by Florence Greenberg, James-Holler promoted Dionne Warwick, BT Express, and other artists. At Roadshow Records, which featured Tina Turner, Construction, Enchantment and other artists, James-Holler was vice president of promotion. She was also the first black woman to hold this title. She later became assistant program director and music director of New York's radio station WBLS, where she managed the programming staff. Maye then returned to the music business as general manager of black music at SBK Records, where she worked with platinum-selling artists Technotronic and Vanilla Ice. She now works on independent projects for major labels.

Will Porter, Mary's musical director, lives in San Francisco. After years as a critically acclaimed singer, songwriter, bandleader, and musical director he released his debut CD, *Happy*, to rave reviews in 2004. The CD was produced and arranged by Wardell Quezergue and features keyboardist Billy Preston, guitarist Leo Nocentelli (the Meters), and Atlantic/Stax soul singer Barbara Lewis.

ACKNOWLEDGMENTS

MY FIRST THANKS MUST GO to author and journalist Steve Bergsman for providing the interview tapes that served as a significant primary resource for this book. I'd also like to thank the brothers Randy and Tony Russi for urging me to write about Mary Wells and providing me with many insights into Mary and her career; David Bell, who supplied me with mountains of information on Mary and helped me ensure that the Mary Wells discography that appears as appendix 1 is as accurate as possible; Andrew Ballard, who supplied me with numerous English music magazines; William Staiger, for insisting that I could actually finish the book and providing me with material allowing me to do so; Al Abrams, for helping me tremendously with all three books I've written about the Motown Record Company and its fascinating artists; Frances Baugh, for providing information and contacts whenever I've needed them; Stephanie Campbell, a blogosphere radio star who's trying to make me one as well; John Smyntek, a former colleague of mine at the *Detroit Free Press*, for finding a crucial court suit that had been missing for decades; my other very helpful former or present *Free Press* associates Judy Diebolt, Peter Gavrilovich, Bill McGraw, Brian McCullom, Ruth Miles, and Marcin Szczepanski; and computer genius Ian Clarke.

I'd like to thank all my interviewees, who gave freely of their time to supply me with their detailed knowledge about Mary Wells, whether the interviews took place in person, over the telephone, or via e-mail: Al Abrams, Larkin Arnold, Rosalind Ashford, Robert Bateman, Rick Bueche, David Bell, Steve Bergsman, Sharon Wells Boyer, Lynne Bronstein, Steven Ames Brown, David Cole, Carl Davis, Norma Fairhurst, Mickey Gentile, Cornelius Grant, Michael Hathaway, Annette Helton, Brian Holland, Edward Holland, Brenda Holloway, Maye Hampton James-Holler, Elaine Jesmer, Gary Kyriazi, Weldon A. McDougal III (before his death in October 2010), Joyce Moore, Pete Moore, Will Porter, Martha Reeves, Brenda Reid, Jerome Richardson, David Ritz, Claudette Robinson, Randy Russi, Tony Russi, Katherine Anderson Schaffner, Barry Scheck, Carolyn Gill-Street, Tony Turner, Harry Weinger, Mary Wilson, Curtis Womack, Desiree Womack, Friendly Womack Jr., Sally Womack, and Curtis Woodson. Some additional interviewees asked to remain anonymous.

Also, for the moral and other support they provided to my research and writing efforts, I must thank Tom Adcock, Michelle Ballard, Annie Benjaminson, Eric Benjaminson, Wendy Benjaminson, Lynne Bronstein, Wendell Burke, David Cole, DJ Tennessee, Glenn S.O.N. Faide, Barbara Hagerty, Williamson Henderson, Richard Holbrook, Len Hollie, Steve Holsey, the staff of The Inn on Ferry Street in Detroit, Michigan, Andre Jardine, Brandon Kennedy, Athena Kokoronis, Marie Leighton, Leo Lewkowitz, Jim Lopes, Greil Marcus, the Marcus Book Club of Oakland, California, Sheryl McCarthy, Rodd McNamara, Deborah Miles, Wayne Miller, Romie Minor, Michael Musto, Nancy Oey, John Oppedahl, Sade Oyinade, Christopher Petkanas, Julie Reed, Clem Richardson, Ryan Richardson, Mark Rowland, Richard Sedlisky, David Seifman, Andy Skurow, Karen Spencer, Kim Sykes, and Wedigo Walter Watson.

Thanks also to my supportive colleagues at my day job, including Barbara Bonhomme, Sue Chan-Leung, Maxima Colon, Lety Escobar, Favio Escudero, Maria-Elena Fazzio, Pam Friedman, Yvonne Greene, Vincent Hammond, John Hopkins, Dawn Hughes, Lydia Irizarry, Paul Kalka, Cordie McCann, Shaela Montes De Oca, Pat Fitzgerald, Reta Murray, Emily Nieves, Cloty Ortiz, Magali Ramos, Julio Rodriguez, Tom Rose, Wei Sha, Betty Spencer, Carlos Suarez, Grace Tai, Carla Valencia, Milton Vera, and Maria Zalewska.

A tremendous shout-out to my publisher, Cynthia Sherry; my editors, Yuval Taylor and Michelle Schoob, two of the most thorough, persistent, professional, and indefatigable editors I have ever encountered; and Mary Kravenas and Meg Miller, Chicago Review Press's marketing and public relations gurus.

And a massive eternal shout-out to my wife, Susan Harrigan, who edited several drafts of this book and also has been my informal editor in all areas of life; to our greatest-ever joint production, Annie Benjaminson; to her husband, Greg Naarden, who has promised to be the full-time unpaid lead researcher on my next book until the job is done; and to my rockin' grandson, Leo Alexander Naarden, born October 2011.

APPENDIX 1

US AND UK DISCOGRAPHY

Compiled with the assistance of David Bell

This discography includes only singles, albums, and CDs released in the United States and United Kingdom during Mary Wells's lifetime that have songs performed by Mary Wells and no songs by other artists. The name of the A side of each record is always listed first. If no chart position is listed for a song or album, it did not chart. The number given is always the highest chart number reached.

Any discography is error-prone due to the freedom with which music-issuing firms produce and release songs and the lack of any central database of such releases. We have done the best we can in compiling this discography but please e-mail notice of any perceived errors to the author through the Contact the Author page on this book's website, www.marywellsbook.com. Thank you.

BB = *Billboard* chart (U.S.); CB = *Cash Box* chart (U.S.)

MOTOWN SINGLES

Title	Release Date	Top Chart Position
"Bye Bye Baby"/ "Please Forgive Me"	12/1960	A Side: BB R&B No. 8; CB Pop No. 41
"I Don't Want to Take a Chance"/ "I'm So Sorry"	07/1961	A Side: BB R&B No. 9; BB Pop No. 33

"Strange Love"/ "Come to Me"	09/1961	—
"The One Who Really Loves You"/ "I'm Gonna Stay"	02/1962	A Side: BB R&B No. 2; BB Pop No. 8; CB Pop No. 4
"You Beat Me to the Punch"/ "Old Love (Let's Try It Again)"	08/1962	A Side: BB R&B No. 1; BB Pop No. 9; CB Pop No. 9
"Two Lovers"/ "Operator"	10/1962	A Side: BB R&B No. 1; BB Pop No. 7
"Laughing Boy"/ "Two Wrongs Don't Make a Right"	02/1963	A Side: BB R&B No. 6; BB Pop No. 15. B Side: BB Pop No. 100
"Your Old Stand By"/ "What Love Has Joined Together"	05/1963	A Side: BB R&B No. 8; BB Pop No. 40
"You Lost the Sweetest Boy"/ "What's Easy for Two Is So Hard for One"	08/1963	A Side: BB R&B No. 10; BB Pop No. 22. B Side: BB R&B No. 8; BB Pop No. 29
"My Guy"/ "Oh Little Boy (What Did You Do To Me?)"	03/1964	A Side: BB Pop No. 1; UK Pop No. 5
"What's the Matter with You Baby" (with Marvin Gaye) / "Once Upon a Time"	04/1964	A Side: BB Pop No. 17; CB Pop 25; B Side: BB Pop No. 19; CB Pop 27; UK Pop No. 50.
"Two Lovers" / "You Beat Me to the Punch" (Motown Yesteryear Series)	1982	—
"My Guy" / "What's Easy for Two Is So Hard for One" (Motown Yesteryear Series)	1982	—
"The One Who Really Loves You" / "Bye Bye Baby" (Motown Yesteryear Series)	1983	—
"Once Upon a Time" / "What's the Matter with You Baby" (with Marvin Gaye) (Motown Yesteryear Series)	1983	—

MOTOWN ALBUMS

Title	Release Date	Top Chart Position
Bye Bye Baby / I Don't Want to Take a Chance	11/1961	—

"Come to Me," "I Don't Want to Take a Chance," "Bye Bye Baby," "Shop Around," "I Love the Way You Love," "I'm Gonna Stay," "Let Your Conscience Be Your Guide," "Bad Boy," "I'm So Sorry," "Please Forgive Me"

Background Vocals: The Andantes, the Supremes, the Lovetones, and the Rayber Voices

The One Who Really Loves You	09/1962	—

"The One Who Really Loves You," "Two Wrongs Don't Make a Right," "You Beat Me to the Punch," "I've Got a Notion," "The Day Will Come," "Strange Love," "You're My Desire," "I'll Still Be Around," "She Don't Love You," "Drifting Love"

Two Lovers and Other Great Hits	02/1963	BB Album No. 49

"Two Lovers," "Guess Who," "My 2 Arms – You = Tears," "Goody, Goody," "Stop Right Here," "Laughing Boy," "Looking Back" "(I Guess There's) No Love," "Was It Worth It," "Operator"

Recorded Live on Stage	09/1963	—

"Two Lovers" (recorded at the Regal Theater, Chicago), "Laughing Boy" (recorded at the Regal Theater, Chicago), "I Don't Want to Take a Chance" (recorded at the Greystone Ballroom, Detroit, 08/63), "Bye Bye Baby" (recorded at the Apollo Theater, New York City, 12/31/62), "The One Who Really Loves You" (recorded at the Regal Theater, Chicago, with accompaniment by the Lovetones), "Old Love (Let's Try It Again)" (recorded at the Greystone Ballroom, Detroit 08/63), "Operator," (recorded at the Greystone Ballroom, Detroit, 08/63 with accompaniment by the Lovetones), "You Beat Me to the Punch" (Recorded at the Apollo Theater, New York City, 12/31/62 with accompaniment by the Lovetones)

***Together* (with Marvin Gaye)**	04/1964 (CD reissue 1991)	BB Album No. 42

"Once Upon a Time," "Deed I Do," "Until I Met You," "Together," "(I Love You) For Sentimental Reasons," "The Late, Late Show," "After the Lights Go Down Low," "Squeeze Me," "What's the Matter With You Baby," "You Come a Long Way from St. Louis"

Background Vocals: The Lovetones and the Andantes

Greatest Hits	04/1964	BB Album No. 18

"The One Who Really Loves You," "You Beat Me to the Punch," "Two Lovers," "Your Old Stand By," "What's Easy for Two Is So Hard for One," "My Guy," "Laughing Boy," "What Love Has Joined Together," "Oh Little Boy (What Did You Do to Me)," "Old Love (Let's Try It Again)," "You Lost the Sweetest Boy," "Bye Bye Baby"

Background Vocals: The Rayber Voices, the Lovetones, the Andantes, the Supremes, and the Temptations

Mary Wells Sings My Guy	05/1964	BB Album No. 111

"He's the One I Love," "Whisper You Love Me Boy," "My Guy," "Does He Love Me," "How (When My Heart Belongs to You)," "He Holds His Own," "My Baby Just Cares for Me," "I Only Have Eyes for You," "You Do Something to Me," "It Had To Be You," "If You Love Me, Really Love Me," "At Last"

Background Vocals: The Lovetones and the Andantes

Vintage Stock	11/1966	—

"The One Who Really Loves You," "When I'm Gone," "He's the One I Love," "Two Lovers," "Guarantee (for a Lifetime)," "Honey Boy," "My Guy," "Everybody Needs Love," "You Beat Me to the Punch," "I'll Be Available," "One Block from Heaven," "Good Bye and Good Luck"

Background Vocals: The Rayber Voices, the Lovetones, the Temptations, the Supremes, and the Andantes

My Guy	1974 (Pickwick Records in association with Motown Records)	—

"The One Who Really Loves You," "Two Lovers," "Honey Boy," "My Guy," "One Block from Heaven," "You Beat Me to the Punch," "Everybody Needs Love," "He's the One I Love," "When I'm Gone"

Bye Bye Baby / The One Who Really Loves You	1987	—

"Come to Me," "I Don't Want to Take a Chance," "Bye Bye Baby," "Shop Around," "I Love the Way You Love," "I'm Gonna Stay," "Let Your Conscience Be Your Guide," "Bad Boy," "I'm So Sorry," "Please Forgive Me," "The One Who Really Loves You," "Two Wrongs Don't Make a Right," "You Beat Me to the Punch," "I've Got a Notion," "The Day Will Come," "Strange Love," "You're My Desire," "I'll Still Be Around," "She Don't Love You," "Drifting Love"

Two Lovers / My Guy	1987	—

"Two Lovers," "Guess Who," "My 2 Arms – You = Tears," "Goody, Goody," "Stop Right Here," "Laughing Boy," "Looking Back," "(I Guess There's) No Love," "Was It Worth It," "Operator," "He's the One I Love," "Whisper You Love Me Boy," "My Guy," "Does He Love Me," "How (When My Heart Belongs to You)," "He Holds His Own," "My Baby Just Cares for Me," "I Only Have Eyes for You," "You Do Something to Me," "It Had to Be You," "If You Love Me, Really Love Me," "At Last"

Original Motown Classics	1990	—

"My Guy," "Bye Bye Baby," "You Beat Me to the Punch," "You Lost the Sweetest Boy," "What Love Has Joined Together," "Shop Around," "He's the One I Love," "Bad Boy," "Operator," "Laughing Boy," "I'll Still Be Around," "If You Love Me, Really Love Me," "The Day Will Come," "I've Got a Notion," "I Only Have Eyes for You," "My Baby Just Cares for Me"

Compact Command Performances: 22 Greatest Hits	1991	—

"Bye Bye Baby," "I Don't Want to Take a Chance," "The One Who Really Loves You," "You Beat Me to the Punch," "Two Lovers," "Laughing Boy," "Your Old Stand By," "Old Love (Let's Try It Again)," "Oh Little Boy (What Did You Do to Me?)," "What Love Has Joined Together," "You Lost the Sweetest Boy," "What's Easy for Two Is So Hard for One," "My Guy," "Two Wrongs Don't Make a Right," "Everybody Needs Love," "I'll Be Available," "One Block from Heaven," "When I'm Gone," "He's the One I Love," "Whisper You Love Me Boy," "Does He Love Me," "Was It Worth It?"

TWENTIETH CENTURY FOX SINGLES

Title	Release Date	Top Chart Position
"Ain't It the Truth"/ "Stop Takin' Me for Granted"	1964	A Side: BB Pop No. 45; B Side: BB Pop No. 88
"Use Your Head"/ "Everlovin' Boy"	1965	A Side: BB R&B No. 13; BB Pop No. 34
"Never, Never Leave Me"/ "Why Don't You Let Yourself Go"	1965	A Side: BB R&B No. 15; BB Pop No. 54
"He's a Lover"/ "I'm Learnin'"	1965	A Side: BB Pop No. 74
"Me Without You"/ "I'm Sorry"	1965	A Side: CB Pop No. 95
"I Should Have Known Better"/ "Please Please Me"	1965	—

TWENTIETH CENTURY FOX ALBUMS

Title	Release Date	Top Chart Position
Mary Wells (Later rereleased by Twentieth on the Movietone label with the title *Ooh.*)	**1965**	BB Album No. 145

"Time After Time," "Why Don't You Let Yourself Go," "Everlovin' Boy," "He's a Lover," "Stop Takin' Me for Granted," "Use Your Head," "We're Just Two of a Kind," "My Mind's Made Up," "Never, Never Leave Me," "Ain't It the Truth," "He's Good Enough for Me," "How Can I Forget Him?" ("Time After Time" was omitted when the album was rereleased as *Ooh.*)

Love Songs to the Beatles	1965	—

"He Loves You," "All My Lovin'," "Please Please Me," "Do You Want to Know a Secret," "Can't Buy Me Love," "I Should Have Known Better," "Help!" "Eight Days a Week," "And I Love Him," "Ticket to Ride," "Yesterday," "I Saw Him Standing There"

ATCO SINGLES

Title	Release Date	Top Chart Position
"Dear Lover"/ "Can't You See (You're Losing Me)"	1966	A Side: BB R&B No. 6; BB Pop No. 51. B Side: CB Pop No. 91
"Such a Sweet Thing"/ "Keep Me in Suspense"	1966	A Side: CB Pop No. 93
"Fancy Free"/ "Me and My Baby"	1966	—
"Coming Home"/ "(Hey You) Set My Soul on Fire"	1967	—

ATCO ALBUMS

Title	Release Date	Top Chart Position
The Two Sides of Mary Wells	1966	—

"(I Can't Get No) Satisfaction," "Love Makes the World Go Round," "In the Midnight Hour," "My World Is Empty Without You," "Good Lovin'," "Dear Lover," "Where Am I Going?" "Shangri-La," "On a Clear Day (You Can See Forever)," "The Shadow of Your Smile," "The Boy from Ipanema," "Sunrise, Sunset"

JUBILEE SINGLES

Title	Release Date	Top Chart Position
"The Doctor"/ "Two Lovers History"	1968	A Side: BB R&B No. 22; BB Pop No. 65
"Woman in Love"/ "Can't Get Away from Your Love"	1968	—
"Don't Look Back"/ "500 Miles"	1968	—
"Never Give a Man the World" / "Mind Reader"	1969	A Side: BB R&B No. 38
"Dig the Way I Feel"/ "Love Shooting Bandit"	1969	A Side: BB R&B No. 35; BB Pop No. 115
"Sweet Love"/ "It Must Be"	1970	—
"Mr. Tough"/ "Never Give a Man the World"	1971	—

JUBILEE ALBUMS

Title	Release Date	Top Chart Position
Servin' Up Some Soul	1968	—

"Soul Train," "Apples Peaches Pumpkin Pie," "Stag-O-Lee," "Make Me Yours," "Two Lovers History," "Can't Get Away from Your Love," "The Doctor," "Don't Look Back," "Sunny," "Woman in Love," "500 Miles," "Bye Bye Baby," "Love Shooting Bandit," "Mind Reader"

Background Vocals: The Valentinos (Bobby Womack, Cecil Womack, Curtis Womack, Friendly Womack Jr., and Harry Womack) and Mary Wells.

STARLINE AND EMI ALBUMS

Title	Release Date	Top Chart Position
My Guy	1970	—

"Laughing Boy," "You Beat Me to the Punch," "Your Old Stand By," "What Love Has Joined Together," "Two Lovers," "The One Who Really Loves You," "My Guy," "What's Easy for Two Is So Hard for One," "Ain't It the Truth?" "You Lost the Sweetest Boy," "Old Love," "Operator"

REPRISE SINGLES

Title	Release Date	Top Chart Position
"I See a Future in You"/ "I Found What I Wanted"	1971	—
"If You Can't Give Her Love (Give Her Up)"/ "Cancel My Subscription"	1974	A Side: BB R&B No. 95
"If You Can't Give Her Love (Give Her Up)"/ "Don't Keep Me Hangin' On"	1974	—

KOALA ALBUM

Title	Release Date	Top Chart Position
My Guy	1980	—

"Laughing Boy," "You Beat Me to the Punch," "Your Old Stand By," "What Love Has Joined Together," "Two Lovers," "The One Who Really Loves You," "My Guy," "What's Easy for Two Is So Hard for One," "Ain't It the Truth?" "You Lost the Sweetest Boy," "Old Love," "Operator"

EPIC SINGLES

Title	Release Date	Top Chart Position
"Gigolo"/ "Let's Mix It Up"	1981	—
"Gigolo"/ "I'm Changing My Ways"	1981	A Side: BB R&B No. 69, BB Disco No. 2, BB Hot Dance Club Play No. 13.

"These Arms" / "Spend the Nights with Me"	1982	—
"These Arms" (disco version) / "Spend the Nights with Me"	1982	—

EPIC ALBUMS

Title	Release Date	Top Chart Position
In and Out of Love	1981	—

"These Arms," "(Will You Still Love Me) Share My Love," "You Make Me Feel So Good Inside," "Spend the Nights with Me," "Let's Mix It Up," "I'm Changing My Ways," "I'm Not the One (You're in Love With)," "Indian Giver," "Gigolo"

Easy Touch	1982 (Released on the 51 West label)	—

"I've Never Been to Me," "Dim All the Lights," "Touch Me When We're Dancing," "Don't Cry Out Loud," "Fame," "If You Love Me, Really Love Me," "Reunited," "Why Do Fools Fall in Love," "Slow Hand," "The Boy from New York City"

ALLEGIANCE SINGLES

Title	Release Date	Top Chart Position
"My Guy"/ "My Guy" (Instrumental)	1983	—
"My Guy"/ "My Guy" (Instrumental) (12-inch record)	1983	—
"You Beat Me to the Punch/ "Oh Little Boy (What Did You Do to Me)"	1983	—

ALLEGIANCE ALBUMS

Title	Release Date	Top Chart Position
The Old, the New, and the Best of Mary Wells	1983	—

"My Guy," "The One Who Really Loves You," "Two Lovers," "You Beat Me to the Punch," "Oh Little Boy (What Did You Do to Me?)," "Bye Bye Baby," "What's Easy for Two Is So Hard for One," "What Love Has Joined Together," "You Lost the Sweetest Boy," "Old Love, Let's Try It Again"

Title	Release Date	Top Chart Position
The Old, the New and the Best of Mary Wells / I'm a Lady	1987	—

"My Guy," "The One Who Really Loves You," "Two Lovers," "You Beat Me to the Punch," "Oh Little Boy (What Did You Do To Me)," "Bye Bye Baby," "What's Easy for Two Is So Hard for One," "What Love Has Joined Together," "You Lost the Sweetest Boy," "Old Love, Let's Try It Again," "I'm a Lady," "Make Up, Break Up," "I Feel for You," "To Feel Your Love," "Money Talks"

NIGHTMARE SINGLES

Title	Release Date	Top Chart Position
"Don't Burn Your Bridges"/ "Don't Burn Your Bridges" (Instrumental)	1987	—
"Don't Burn Your Bridges"/ "Don't Burn Your Bridges" (Instrumental) (Additional vocal by Curtis Womack)	1987	

MOTORCITY SINGLES

Title	Release Date	Top Chart Position
"You're the Answer to My Dreams"/ "You're the Answer to My Dreams" (Instrumental)	1989	—

MOTORCITY ALBUMS

Title	Release Date	Top Chart Position
Keeping My Mind on Love	1990	—

"Keeping My Mind on Love," "Hold on a Little Longer," "Stop Before It's Too Late," "What's Easy for Two Is So Hard for One," "Walk the City Streets," "My Guy," "You Beat Me to the Punch," "You're the Answer to My Dreams," "Don't Burn Your Bridges," "Once Upon a Time" (with Frankie Gaye)

QUALITY RECORDS ALBUM

Title	Release Date	Top Chart Position
Keeping My Mind on Love (Originally released in UK by Motorcity Records)	1990	—

"My Guy," "Hold on a Little Longer," "Walk the City Streets," "Don't BurnYour Bridges," "What's Easy for Two Is So Hard for One," "Keeping My Mind on Love," "Stop Before It's Too Late," "You're the Answer to My Dreams," "You Beat Me to the Punch," "Once Upon a Time" (with Frankie Gaye)

PAIR RECORDS ALBUMS

Title	Release Date	Top Chart Position
Original Motown Classics: Mary Wells	1990	—

"My Guy," "Bye Bye Baby," "You Beat Me to the Punch," "You Lost the Sweetest Boy," "What Love Has Joined Together," "Shop Around," "He's the One I Love," "Bad Boy," "Operator," "Laughing Boy," "I'll Still Be Around," "If You Love Me, Really Love Me," "The Day Will Come," "I've Got a Notion," "I Only Have Eyes for You," "My Baby Just Cares for Me"

APPENDIX 2

TV, VIDEO, AND FILM APPEARANCES

Mary sings on the soundtrack or performs on screen, or others perform her songs, in the following television shows, videos, and movies. (Unless otherwise noted, songs are sung by Mary Wells.)

New American Bandstand, TV series, five TV episodes, 1961–62
The Eamonn Andrews Show, TV series, one episode, 1964
Thank Your Lucky Stars, TV series, one episode, 1964
Shindig! TV series, two episodes, 1964–66
Nothing But a Man, movie soundtrack, "You Beat Me to the Punch" and "Bye Bye Baby," 1964
Where the Action Is, TV series, one episode, 1965
Hullabaloo, TV series, 1965
It's What's Happening, Baby, TV special, June 28, 1965
Ready Steady Go! UK TV series, one episode, 1966
Catalina Caper, movie soundtrack, "Never Steal Anything Wet," 1967
Rabbit's Moon, movie soundtrack, "Bye Bye Baby," 1972
Cooley High, movie, "You Beat Me to the Punch" plays on a car radio, 1975
More American Grafitti, movie soundtrack, "My Guy," 1979
Motown 25: Yesterday, Today, Forever, TV documentary, Mary performs portion of "My Guy" on stage, May 16, 1983
Today, "Red, White and Rock: Motown Girls," TV segment, November 20, 1984
ABC Rocks, TV special, December 7, 1984
Motown Returns to the Apollo, TV special, 1985

Motown Revue, 1985
Hand in Hand, movie soundtrack, "My Guy," 1985
Best of Cinemax Sessions, TV special, 1987
Live from the Rock 'n' Roll Palace, TV special, 1987
Dancin' in the Street, video documentary, 1987
Legendary Ladies of Rock 'n' Roll, TV special, 1988
Whose Baby?, TV movie, 1988
My Boyfriend's Back, movie soundtrack, 1989
Let's Rock Tonight Concert, TV special, 1989
Entertainment Tonight, TV series, 1990
Smokey Robinson, The Quiet Legend, TV documentary, 1990
The Joan Rivers Show, TV series, 1991
Golden Age of Rock 'n' Roll, TV documentary series, 1991
The Commitments, movie, Angeline Ball, Maria Doyle Kennedy, and Bronagh Gallagher perform much of "Bye Bye Baby" on screen, 1991
Nightline, "Reliving the Glory Days of the Apollo Theater" TV episode, 1992
Jennifer Eight, movie soundtrack, "Two Lovers," 1992
Sister Act, movie, Whoopi Goldberg sings a version of "My Guy" titled "My God," 1992
Friends, TV series, "The One with Mrs. Bing" episode, "My Guy," 1995
Dead Presidents, movie soundtrack, "Once Upon a Time" with Marvin Gaye, 1995
Live from Greenwich Village video, "Two Lovers History," 1996
The Wire, TV series, "Stray Rounds" episode, "You Beat Me to the Punch," 2003
Glory Road, movie soundtrack, "My Guy," 2006
R & B Jukebox, DVD, Mary Wells performs "Bye Bye Baby" and "My Guy" on stage, 2007
Don't Forget the Motorcity, video, performer, 2008
Worried About the Boy, TV movie soundtrack, "My Guy," 2010
Unsung, TV documentary series, one episode, 2011

APPENDIX 3

1991 SUIT AGAINST MOTOWN RECORDS

STEVEN AMES BROWN
Attorney
69 Grand View Avenue
San Francisco, California 94114-2741
415/647-7700
Attorney for plaintiff

SUPERIOR COURT OF CALIFORNIA
COUNTY OF LOS ANGELES

MARY WELLS,	
Plaintiff	Civil No. BC022930
vs.	
MOTOWN RECORD COMPANY, L.P.,	COMPLAINT FOR
MOTOWN MANAGEMENT CORPORATON,	MONEY DAMAGES
MCA RECORD VENTURES, INC.,	
DOES I-XXX, inclusive	
Defendants	

Plaintiff alleges as follows:

1. Plaintiff is a resident of Los Angeles County.

2. Defendants Motown Management Corporation and MCA Record Ventures, Inc. are foreign corporations, whose principal places of business within California are located in Los Angeles County. Motown Record Company, L.P. is a foreign limited partnership doing business within Los Angeles County whose general partners are Motown Management Corporation and MCA Record Ventures, Inc.

3. Plaintiff is ignorant of the true names and capacities of defendants sued herein as DOES I-XXX, inclusive, and therefor sues these defendants by such fictitious names. Plaintiff will amend this complaint to allege their true names and capacities when ascertained. Each of the fictitiously named defendants is responsible in some manner for the occurrences herein alleged, and plaintiff's damages.
4. Each of the defendants was the agent of the other and at all times herein acted within the course and scope of such agency. Each of the defendants conspired with the others to perform the acts herein alleged, acting in union, for common profit.

FIRST CAUSE OF ACTION
[Breach Of Contract]
[all defendants]

5. Plaintiff incorporates paragraphs 1 through 4, inclusive.
6. Plaintiff and defendants are all parties to written agreements under which plaintiff agreed to perform as a recording artist and defendants in turned agreed to pay royalties to plaintiff and to account to her for their manufacturing & sales activities in respect of plaintiff's recordings.
7. Plaintiff has performed all conditions required of her under said written agreements.
8. Within four years last past defendants materially breached the agreements by failing to pay and by continuing to refuse to pay to plaintiff royalties owing to her.
9. As a direct and proximate result of defendants' actions, as aforesaid, plaintiff has been damaged in a sum in excess of $100,000.00.

[SECOND CAUSE OF ACTION]
COMMERCIAL APPRORPRIATION
[All Defendants]

10. Plaintiffs incorporate paragraphs 1 through 4, herein.
11. Within three years last past, the defendants have utilized the natural voice and physical image of plaintiff on goods which were available for sale and consumption by the general public within and outside California, without plaintiff's permission. Such acts also constitute unfair business practices.
12. It was necessary for plaintiff to hire an attorney to prosecute this action.
13. As a direct and proximate result of defendants' action, plaintiff has been damaged by each defendant in a sum in excess of $100,000.00.

14. The actions of defendants were in conscious disregard of the rights of plaintiff and for the purpose of injuring her. The utilization of a person's natural voice or physical image on items for mass consumption without her permission is inherently oppressive and likely to inflict injury, thereby entitling plaintiff to an award of exemplary damages to punish defendants and to make examples of them to others.

WHEREFORE, plaintiff prays judgment as follows:

1. For damages in excess of $100,000.00;
2. For exemplary damages according to proof;
3. For reasonable attorney's fees;
4. For costs of suit;
5. For such other relief as the Court may deem just.

Dated: March 6, 1991

Respectfully submitted,
Steven Ames Brown
STEVEN AMES BROWN
Attorney for plaintiff

SOURCES

NEWSPAPERS

Atlanta Journal-Constitution, 09/06/82, 08/15/87
Austin American Statesman, 08/09/90, 09/01/90
The (Bergen, NJ) Record, 08/29/90, 10/19/91
Black Echoes, 11/79
Bluefield (WVA) Daily Telegraph, 02/19/09
Boston Globe, 04/10/91, 11/14/91, 10/07/92
Chicago Sun-Times, 08/26/90, 07/31/92, 08/02/92, 08/30/92
Cleveland Plain Dealer, 09/28/90, 11/25/94
Daily (Torrance, CA) Breeze, 09/13/86, 07/31/87
Daily News of Los Angeles, 03/24/89
Dallas Morning News, 08/26/90
Denver Post, 06/09/89, 09/05/90, 10/17/90, 05/18/03
Detroit Free Press, 05/23/63, 05/17/65, 10/15/65, 06/19/91, 07/27/92
Detroit Metro Times, 04/21/04
Detroit News, 10/03/62, 05/14/64, 07/27/92, 09/29/92, 02/11/99, 08/05/02, 06/28/03
Detroit Times, 02/25/60
Houston Chronicle, 09/14/86, 08/05/90
Independent (London), 01/30/94
Indiana Post-Tribune, 05/21/69
Los Angeles Times, 03/16/90, 09/05/90, 10/09/91
Miami Herald, 09/13/86, 09/04/90, 09/07/90
Michigan Chronicle, 09/10/66, 02/14/95, 12/25/07
Morning (Allentown, PA) Call, 12/13/66

New Musical Express, 08/1972
New York Daily News, 07/24/64, 07/25/64, 08/22/93, 11/19/98
New York Times, 06/23/65, 12/14/81, 06/30/82, 06/25/88, 07/27/92, 06/11/12
Oakland (CA) Press, 07/27/92
Philadelphia Daily News, 07/28/92
Philadelphia Inquirer, 10/31/93, 12/12/02
Pittsburgh Post-Gazette, 10/09/91
Saginaw (MI) News, 09/12/86
San Diego Union Tribune, 07/02/87
San Francisco Chronicle, 09/13/86, 05/22/88, 06/12/88, 06/16/88, 08/18/90, 05/09/92
Seattle Times, 7/27/92, 09/07/09
Toronto Globe & Mail, 04/13/83, 09/10/86, 09/11/86, 02/10/87, 09/15/90
Toronto Star, 09/05/86, 09/10/86, 02/11/87, 06/04/87, 08/01/92, 09/28/06
Tulsa World, 09/16/90
USA Today, 08/27/90, 09/12/90, 09/19/90, 02/18/91, 06/18/91, 01/20/06
Washington Post, 06/02/79, 06/30/80, 09/06/82, 09/25/84, 10/09/91, 05/11/03
Washington Times, 07/29/92, 11/20/94

MAGAZINES

Billboard, 07/18/64, 10/17/64, 11/7/64, 11/14/64, 10/16/65, 04/24/71, 07/23/92, 08/08/92, 11/05/94, 03/18/95, 12/16/95, 08/30/97, 03/27/99, 10/09/99, 06/01/02, 11/02/02, 03/13/04
Blues & Soul, 08/72, 09/91, 08/92
Chartbusters, Issue 21
Discoveries, 01/94
Entertainment Weekly, 08/07/92
Forbes, 01/08/10
Goldmine, 10/80
History of Rock, Volume 3, Issue 36, 1982
Hollywood Reporter, 02/17/94, 04/14/94
In the Basement, Summer 2009, February 2012
Jet Magazine, 01/26/61, 03/07/63, 04/16/65, 05/13/65, 05/20/65, 07/22/65, 08/18/66, 02/29/68, 03/28/68, 04/11/68, 12/25/80, 09/17/90, 10/01/90, 07/15/91, 07/29/91, 11/11/91
Melody Maker, 06/10/69

Mersey Beat, 10/22/64
Motown Chartbusters, Issue 6
People magazine, 08/10/92
Rock's Back Pages, 1992
Rolling Stone, 10/18/90, 07/92, 09/03/92
Soulstar Chartbusters, Issue 33, June 2006
Vanity Fair, December 2008

INTERVIEW TRANSCRIPTS

Interview transcripts from *Unsung* TV Show on Mary Wells broadcast in 2011: Larkin Arnold, Steven Bergsman, Janie Bradford, Micky Gentile, Nelson George, Brian Holland, Edward Holland, Brenda Holloway, Maye James-Holler, Fonce Mizell, Larry Mizell, Will Porter, Claudette Robinson, Mary Wilson, Curtis Womack.

COURT PAPERS

Mary Griffin v. Herman Griffin, Case No. D-1192, Wayne County Circuit Court, State of Michigan, 1963.

The People of the State of New York against Herman Griffin, Record of Cases 52-66, #4422, District Attorney – New York County Records, 11/03/64.

Mary Wells vs. Motown Record Corporation, a Michigan Corporation, International Talent Management, Inc., a Michigan Corporation, Berry Gordy, Jr., and Barney Ales. Civil Action No. 32563, Wayne County Circuit Court, State of Michigan, 1964.

Mary Wells vs. Motown Record Co., Case No. BC022930, Superior Court of California, County of Los Angeles, 03/06/91.

OTHER OFFICIAL DOCUMENTS

Mary Esther Wells, Certificate of Birth, Michigan Department of Health, certified copy 09/01/64.

Mary Esther Wells-Womack, Certificate of Death, Local Registration District and Certificate Number 39219032297, County of Los Angeles, Registrar-Recorder/County Clerk, State of California.

LINER NOTES

Baumgart, Malcolm. *Mary Wells Complete Jubilee Collection*, 1993.

Bronson, Fred. *Ain't It the Truth: The Best of Mary Wells 1964–1982.* Varèse Sarabande Records, Inc., 1994.

Cole, David. *Mary Wells, In & Out of Love.* New York: Sony Music Entertainment, 2010.

Cole, David. *Mary Wells, Never Never Leave Me, The Twentieth Century Sides.* New York: Polygram Records, Inc. and Ichiban/Soul Classics, 1996.

Levine, Ian and Paul Klein. *Mary Wells, The Very Best.* Miami: Hot Productions, Inc.

Nathan, David. *Mary Wells, Dear Lover, the Atco Sessions.* New York: Soul Classics, 1995.

Ritz, David. *Mary Wells Looking Back 1961–1964.* Los Angeles: Motown Record Co., 1993.

Ritz, David. *Mary's Magic* (from *Mary Wells The Ultimate Collection*). New York: Motown Record Company, 1998.

Rolontz, Bob, *The Two Sides of Mary Wells*, New York: Atco Records, 1966.

Romanus, Tina Bohlman. *Will Porter: Happy.* San Francisco: All Star Sound, 2003.

Sheppard, Doug and Bob Rolontz, *The Two Sides of Mary Wells.* San Francisco: Runt LLC and Elektra Entertainment, 2005.

PRESS RELEASES

Abrams, Al, *The Girl Who Beat the Beatles.* Detroit: Hitsville, U.S.A., May 11, 1964.

BOOKS

Abbott, Kingsley ed. *Calling Out Around the World: A Motown Reader*. London: Helter Skelter Publishing, 2001.

Abrams, Al. *Hype & Soul: Behind the Scenes at Motown*. Lilleshall, Shropshire, U.K.: Temple Street Publishing, 2011.

Benjaminson, Peter. *The Lost Supreme: The Life of Dreamgirl Florence Ballard.* Chicago: Lawrence Hill Books, 2008.

Benjaminson, Peter. *The Story of Motown.* New York: Grove Press, 1979.

Betrock, Alan. *Girl Groups: The Story of a Sound.* New York: Delilah Books, 1982.

Bianco, David. *Heat Wave: The Motown Fact Book.* Ann Arbor, MI: Pierian Press, 1988.

Bogdanov, Vladimir. *All Music Guide to Soul: The Definitive Guide to R&B and Soul.* Milwaukee: Backbeat Books, 2003.

Bowles, Dennis. *Dr. Beans Bowles "Fingertips": The Untold Story.* Ferndale, MI: Sho-nuff Productions, 2005.

Bronson, Fred. *The Billboard Book of Number One Hits,* 4th ed. New York: Billboard Books, 1997.

Bronson, Fred. *Billboard's Hottest Hot 100 Hits,* 3rd ed. New York: Billboard Productions, 2003.

Broven, John. *Record Makers and Breakers: Voices of the Independent Rock 'n' Roll Pioneers.* Champaign, IL: University of Illinois Press, 2010.

Brown, Mick. *Tearing Down the Wall of Sound: The Rise and Fall of Phil Spector.* New York: Vintage Books, 2007.

Burton, T. *Home in Detroit.* Detroit: Shaking the Tree Publishing LLC, 2008.

Carson, Mina, Tisa Lewis, and Susan M. Shaw. *Girls Rock! Fifty Years of Women Making Music.* Lexington, KY: University Press of Kentucky, 2004.

Cashmore, Ellis. *The Black Culture Industry.* New York: Routledge, 1997.

Churchill, Winston S. *Never Give In!: The Best of Winston Churchill's Speeches.* New York: Hyperion, 2004.

Clemente, John. *Girl Groups: Fabulous Females that Rocked the Word.* Iola, WI: Krause Publications, 2000.

Creasy, Martin. *Beatlemania! The Real Story of The Beatles UK Tours, 1963–65.* London: Omnibus Press, 2010.

Dabydeen, David, John Gilmore, and Cecily Jones, eds. *The Oxford Companion to Black British History.* Oxford University Press, 2007.

Dahl, Bill. *Motown: The Golden Years.* Photos by Weldon A. McDougal III. Iola, WI: Krause Publications, 2001.

Dannen, Fredric. *Hit Men.* New York: Random House, 1990.

Davis, Carl H. Sr. *The Man Behind the Music: The Legendary Carl Davis.* Matteson, IL: Life to Legacy, LLC, 2009.

Davis, Sharon. *Motown: The History.* Enfield, Middlesex, UK: Guinness Books, 1988.

Davis, Sharon. *Chinwaggin': The Blues & Soul Interviews.* West Sussex, UK: Bankhouse Books, 2006.

Douglas, Tony. *Jackie Wilson: The Man, the Music, the Mob.* Edinburgh: Mainstream Publishing, 2001.

Eliot, Marc. *Rockonomics: The Money Behind the Music.* New York: Citadel Press, 1993.

Evanier, David. *Roman Candle: The Life of Bobby Darin.* Emmaus, PA: Rodale Books, 2004.

Fong-Torres, Ben. *The Motown Album.* New York: St. Martin's Press, 1990.

Francis, Connie. *Who's Sorry Now?* New York: St. Martin's Press, 1984.

Gavrilovich, Peter and Bill McGraw, eds. *The Detroit Almanac: 300 Years of Life in the Motor City.* Detroit: Detroit Free Press, 2000.

George, Nelson. *Where Did Our Love Go? The Rise and Fall of the Motown Sound.* New York: St. Martin's Press, 1985.

Gordy, Berry. *To Be Loved: The Music, The Magic, The Memories of Motown.* New York: Warner Books, 1994.

Greenfield, Robert. *The Last Sultan: The Life and Times of Ahmet Ertegun.* New York: Simon & Schuster, 2011.

Henderson, Jeff. *Cooked: From the Streets to the Stove, From Cocaine to Foie Gras.* New York: William Morrow, 2007.

Henderson, Jeff. *Chef Jeff Cooks: In the Kitchen with America's Inspirational New Culinary Star.* New York: Scribner, 2008.

Hirshey, Gerri. *We Gotta Get Out of This Place: The True, Tough Story of Women in Rock.* New York: Grove Press, 2001.

Hoffman, Frank. *The Cash Box Singles Charts, 1950–1981.* Metuchen, NJ: Scarecrow Press, 1983.

James, Etta and David Ritz. *The Etta James Story: Rage to Survive.* New York: Villard Books, 1995.

Kempton, Arthur. *Boogaloo: The Quintessence of American Popular Music.* New York: Pantheon Books, 2003.

Licks, Dr. [Allan Slutsky]. *Standing in the Shadows of Motown: The Life and Music of Legendary Bassist James Jamerson.* Milwaukee: Hal Leonard Corporation, 1989.

Love, Dennis and Stacy Brown. *Blind Faith: The Miraculous Journey of Linda Hardaway, Stevie Wonder's Mother.* New York: Simon & Schuster, 2007.

McNutt, Randy. *Guitar Towns: A Journey to the Crossroads of Rock 'n' Roll.* Bloomington: Indiana University Press, 2002.

O'Neil, Thomas. *The Grammys: For the Record.* New York: Penguin Books, 1993.

Posner, Gerald. *Motown: Music, Sex, Money and Power.* New York: Random House, 2002.

Reeves, Martha and Mark Bego. *Dancing in the Street: Confessions of a Motown Diva*. New York: Hyperion, 1994.

Ribowsky, Mark. *The Supremes: A Saga of Motown Dreams, Success, and Betrayal*. New York: Da Capo Press, 2009.

Ribowsky, Mark. *Ain't Too Proud to Beg: The Troubled Lives and Enduring Soul of The Temptations*. Hoboken, NJ: John Wiley & Sons, 2010.

Ritz, David. *Divided Soul: The Life of Marvin Gaye*. New York: McGraw-Hill Book Company, 1985.

Robinson, Smokey and David Ritz. *Smokey: Inside My Life*. New York: McGraw-Hill, 1989.

Ross, Diana. *Secrets of a Sparrow: Memoirs*. New York: Villard Books, 1993.

Schmidt, Randy L. *Little Girl Blue: The Life of Karen Carpenter*. Chicago: Chicago Review Press, 2010.

Schultheiss, Tom. *The Beatles: A Day in the Life*. New York: Perigee Books, 1981.

Singleton, Raynoma Gordy. *Berry, Me, and Motown: The Untold Story*. Chicago: Contemporary Books, 1990.

Talevski, Nick. *The Unofficial Encyclopedia of the Rock and Roll Hall of Fame*. Westport, CT: Greenwood Press, 1998.

Taraborrelli, J. Randy. *Call Her Miss Ross*. New York: Ballantine Books, 1991.

Waller, Don. *The Motown Story*. New York: Charles Scribner's Sons, 1985.

Warwick, Neil, Jon Kutner, and Tony Brown. *The Complete Book of the British Charts, Singles and Albums*. Omnibus Press, 2004.

Wexler, Jerry and David Ritz. *Rhythm and the Blues: A Life in American Music*. New York: Alfred A. Knopf, 1993.

Whitall, Susan. *Women of Motown: An Oral History*. New York: Avon Books, 1998.

Whitall, Susan. *Fever: Little Willie John, a Fast Life, Mysterious Death and the Birth of Soul*. With Kevin John. London: Titan Books, 2011.

Whitburn, Joel. *Joel Whitburn's Top Pop Albums, 1955–1985*. Menomonee Falls, WI: Record Research Inc., 1985.

Whitburn, Joel. *Joel Whitburn's Top R&B Singles, 1942–1988*. Menomonee Falls, WI: Record Research Inc., 1988.

Whitburn, Joel. *The Billboard Book of Top 40 Hits, Revised and Enlarged 6th Edition*. New York: Billboard Books, 1996.

Whitburn, Joel. *Billboard Top 1000 Singles, 1955–1996*. Milwaukee: Hal Leonard Corporation, 1997.

Whitburn, Joel. *Joel Whitburn's Top Pop Singles, 1955–2006.* Menomonee Falls, WI: Record Research Inc., 2007.

Whitburn, Joel. *The Billboard Book of Top 40 Hits, 9th Edition.* New York: Billboard Books, 2010.

Williams, Otis and Patricia Romanowski. *Temptations: Updated Edition.* New York: Cooper Square Press, 2002.

Wilson, Mary. *Dreamgirl: My Life as a Supreme.* New York: St. Martin's Press, 1986.

Womack, Bobby and Robert Ashton. *My Autobiography: Bobby Womack, Midnight Mover: The True Story of the Greatest Soul Singer in the World.* London: John Blake Publishing Ltd., 2006.

RADIO SHOWS

Clark, Dick. Interview with Mary Wells. *Rock, Roll & Remember*. Undated.

TELEVISION SHOWS

(For shows on which Mary Wells appeared in person, on film, on a soundtrack, or on tape, please see appendix 3: "TV, Video, and Film Appearances.")

Henderson, Jeff. *Chef Jeff Cooks*. Food Network.

King, Larry. *Larry King Live*. Interview with Connie Francis. CNN, 3/11/02.

INDEX